she's a bad
MOTORCYCLE

she's a *BAD*

edited by **GENO ZANETTI**

writers on riding

MOTORCYCLE

thunder's mouth press ▪ new york

SHE'S A BAD MOTORCYCLE: WRITERS ON RIDING

Published by
Thunder's Mouth Press
An Imprint of Avalon Publishing Group Incorporated
161 William St., 16th Floor
New York, NY 10038

Library of Congress Cataloging-in-Publication Data

She's a bad motocycle : writers on riding / edited by Geno Zanetti.
p.cm.
ISBN 1-56025-317-7
1. Motorcycles—Literary collections. 2. Motorcycling— Literary collections.
3. Motorcyclists—Literary collections. 4. American literature—20th century.
5. Motorcyclists. 6. Motorcycling. 7. Motorcycles. I. Title: She is a bad
motorcycle. II. Zanetti, Geno.

PS509.M67 S48 2001
810.8'0355—dc21   2001027052

9 8 7 6 5 4 3 2 1

Designed by Pauline Neuwirth, Neuwirth & Associates, Inc.

Printed in the United States of America
Distributed by Publishers Group West

Thanks to Carlos Bromulus; to Tav Falco and Panther
Burns for the title and to Harry for the subtitle; and
humble thanks to Fred Courtright for his permission. DO'C

contents

editor's note

"Why do people ride motorcycles?"

The answer goes beyond simple questions of utility. Thomas Krens, the curator of "The Art of the Motorcycle," the most popular exhibition ever mounted at the Guggenheim Museum, notes: "For much of society, the motorcycle remains a forbidden indulgence, an object of fantasy, and danger." And envy. No other machine is thought of as the vehicle—"the perfect vehicle" Melissa Holbrook Pierson calls it—of rebellion, lawlessness, and freedom. There is a downside, a bad edge that Joan Didion underlined when she wrote of the bike movie craze of the late sixties, "Bike movies have constituted a kind of underground folk literature for adolescents, have located an audience and fabricated a myth to exactly express that audience's every inchoate resentment, every yearning for the extreme exhilaration of death. To die violently is "righteous," a flash. To keep on living, as Peter Fonda points out in *The Wild Angels*, is to keep on paying the rent."

Marx was on to something when he wrote about seizing a "realm of freedom" from the "realm of necessity" (somewhere in Volume Three of *Das Kapital*), and even though he was talking about proletarian revolution and never lived to sample the pleasures of bikeriding, seizing a realm of freedom is what this collection is all about. Muchas gracias to Dan, Neil and Ghadah at Thunder's Mouth; to Stephen Hyde for ideas and Paul Long for the expletives; to SA at the end of the Rainbow

Geno Zanetti
Solentsea, England
November 14, 2001

When my mood gets too hot and I find myself wandering beyond control I pull out my motor-bike and hurl it top-speed through these unfit roads for hour after hour. My nerves are jadod and gone near dead, so that nothing less than hours of voluntary danger will prick them into life. . . .

—T. E. Lawrence

from

THE PERFECT VEHICLE

melissa holbrook pierson

I love to sail forbidden seas,
and land on barbarous coasts.
—Melville, *Moby-Dick*

when you ride, you travel light. As you would see, this is one of biking's great virtues. You take along what is in your stomach, and on your back, and whatever fits into the tankbag between the tools and the rain gear, all of which you will need sooner or later, especially the electrical tape.

At some point, you will throw your gloves to the ground in exasperation. Something's broke. But that is also the source of a strange relief: You've got to fix it. So you discover that you brought your wits along too, those rusty mechanisms that work on old-fashioned principles, wherein you can see the crankshaft turn and the chain progress and the up, down, up, down of levers and legs. For this brief time, you get to forget the maddening prevalence of electronic impulses you cannot feel and shiny boxes you cannot get inside of, and you become the scavenger the gods of old intended you to be. Sink your teeth into this one, the silent motorcycle says; go ahead, see if that bottle cap by your feet will be of use. Of course, it is a relief only in retrospect, after you've had a night or two in the bed that seems so far away now from the darkening road-side it could almost make you weep. Yes, the relief comes much later, and even then you may not know it is relief, because it has been applied directly to your soul. And later this whole sweaty, lonely frustration will be further transformed by the requirements of the campfire-story form into laughs and empathetic nods and you too will laugh as if it happened to someone else long ago, to a character out of a book.

When the sun is at the correct angle, your shadow races next to you as you fly along. The dark shape is your own hair streaming out, a mobile portrait in the medium of light on asphalt. It's a peculiar sight, but the start it gives is not like when you catch yourself in a mirror. This one is almost someone else, mysterious, featureless, perhaps even fearless.

When everything is going just fine, you can raise your weight off the saddle by standing on the pegs and the air itself seems to carry you; the smells of countryside or suburb or industrial fief are immediately upon you, then gone. There are uncanny presences all around. Rotting pumpkins, manure, road salt, Spanish moss in humid wind, a scent like a million burning tires in the yellow sky over Newark, pine, oyster shells. Some will never get a name. Not half of them would reach you in a car, even with all the windows down. This weekend, for four miles, I had the odor of cigarette in my nostrils, from the lit end hanging out from the pickup truck ahead. Then again, some smells just tell you you are riding much too close behind.

The temperature, too, and permeable quality of the air is astonishingly variable, as if you were riding in a slo-mo dream in and out of rooms as numerous and surprising as those at Versailles. As you're riding along in the warm envelope of a summer night, the country ether a pillow of moist hay and fecund dirt, suddenly there will be a blast of cold from a pocket held in the hollow of some land beyond you in the dark; you shiver, then you're out of it again, back in a caress of warmth. The coming rainstorm announces itself first in the quick change of the air, carrying you into the mounting thickness that only later comes out and shows itself.

Riding is something that hovers between you and the road. Or rather, it is about removing as much as possible between you and the road, about extending yourself past the very vehicle that enables you to feel the road in the first place. So in one sense it's about the way a road moves past you.

It is possible to feel more alone on a motorcycle than anywhere at rest. When you're sealed in your apartment, or even standing in a secret field halfway up a mountain, there is always the chance that someone could find you; someone could call, could spot you from a plane, could come walking up at any moment. Knowing where I can hide if necessary is always on my mind, and where else but on a bike is there somewhere truly safe to be? On a bike, there are people all around, in a car in the next lane not five feet away, but they can't get you. You may communicate with the friends who ride along by using signals, but you can't talk. You are spared the burden of words. There is so little privacy anywhere these days that this knowledge feels like the last available comfort, in the absence of knowing there is someplace left on earth not infected with Colonial brick houses or cut through by a new Wal-Mart's access road.

Your thoughts are pinned close to your head by the helmet, where they may exit only a fraction of an inch from your scalp but then stay to buzz around, thousands of little trapped sand flies.

At no time, though, are you more joyfully alone than when it is raining. Often it's lovely to sit indoors and hear the soft whiteness of rain hitting glass or roof; with the lights on, in your dry castle, you smugly note how close and yet how far the bad weather is. The safe protection of the walls seems to belong to you, a projection of your skin. On a bike, the house's walls shrink to become the rainsuit's thin rind. The water hits it, but you are cozy enough inside. The fact that you can feel it landing on you without touching you brings the impression of haven into high relief—which is pretty damn ironic, since there can be no greater danger than riding in the rain.

Sensing the tires slip a bit under you in a car is not usually cause for celebration, but you can generally regain control easily if you're a decent driver. Recovery is not so simple when there are only two wheels in question. Riding on the back of a friend's bike through southern Germany's excessive picturesqueness, I took in the passing sights secure in the knowledge that he was as able a rider as they make. We took the turns at a good lean, overcoming an instinctual fear to emerge into the pleasure of having done so. Then a light drizzle started washing the streets to a gleam, and everything changed. My seat noticed it first, a slight side-to-side motion that I almost thought was in my head. When we stopped, I asked if I had in fact felt something, and my friend just looked pale in response. So I mounted up behind another member of the party, whose experience was equal but whose rear tire was less bald. Confidence returned, even though the rain now fell in hard sheets. The beer at lunch I allowed myself as consolation for being a mere passenger was having its effect under the canopy of trees. The next thing I knew my hands thrust themselves into the air. Every sinew pulled itself tight. In a flash the seat had gone out from under me, shimmied curtly side to side to side. Then in a second it was over, and we were going on as before. Who knows? It could have been a bit of patched paving, slippery tar, some chameleon oil behind the sheen of wet.

But no matter how treacherous it is, I still love riding in the rain. It is so lulling, peaceful. Sound is slurred by the shh-shhing of the water, which rolls in little estuaries from the treads of the tires. Every other minute or so you reach up and wipe away the beading rain that blurs the vision through the shield, only to have it re-collect in seconds. Breath fogs the view from inside, and when you crack the shield open a bit to dispel the moisture, rain pelts your lips. Your hands feel strangely distant on the controls, because of the addition of thick rubber or Gore-Tex; you feel insulated or blown up, like Michelin's Bibendum. What's going on out there seems a million miles away, though it's on top of you, and driving at you, and kicked up behind you in that poetically arcing stream from the spinning wheel. The thoughts rise and collect as they always do, but now they're a dry ceiling. If you're doing this at night, perils and isolation both are intensified: the headlights of cars coming toward you refract and brighten to a glare on your face shield; the buffeting wind coming off the passing vehicles pushes you sideways for a moment, and all you can do is hang on. Perhaps that's the source of the comfort I feel—lack of alternatives. Life simplified at long last.

The small glow emanating from the lighted dials is a portable beacon that remains both ahead and calmly with you. The sight of the instrument panel's little light in the greater dark puts me in mind of a tiny spaceship floating on its way through a benighted universe of unfathomed spread. The headlight glances off the slick leaves at the edge of the road, and what is beyond that quick beam waits there for you to arrive upon it and briefly launch it into existence before consigning it back to what is behind in the black.

With the dampened sound, thoughts become louder. The only thing beside yourself that you can hear, somewhere beneath you, is a steady throb of engine. It is all there is to keep you anchored to the world. All the rest, all the earth, is rain.

This is so untroubled a state of affairs that sometimes catatonia wants to overtake me—in spite of all the ways I try to remind myself about the dangers of believing what it is convenient to believe. I recall riding up the New Jersey Turnpike in a dead rain near midnight on a Sunday, the traffic as unceasing as the storm. I had been doing sixty in the same lane for what seemed like forever, which is what the turnpike is all about. Then I needed to change. I did it as I had dozens of times before on this same road, when it was dry. This time, crossing the lane divider and those handy little reflectors put there for the safety of cars, my rear wheel met the plastic and for a second spun. It was in that class of events that are simple and quick, so immediate they seem to precede their own occurrence, as when your foot slips in a dream and thus makes a cliff appear. I woke up to a moment of blinding panic, then it was over. For a mile or two my heart was near my gullet, and I thought about all the possibilities that could have been realized. I'd like to say that for the rest of the ride I was more careful, and I probably was to the degree that anyone can manage life's risks, but I still couldn't begin the accounting of everything that hadn't occurred to me yet, a voodoo list that I believed once mastered would deliver me from evil. There is so much that must remain incalculable, a fact better accepted than kicked against. It is a hoary lesson repeated, if I would listen, in every revolution of the wheels.

Does all this sound like a rhapsody? I both mean it to and don't. There are two bikes in the world that belong to me. One is the real one, which sits in the garage on Union Street with a rear-drive leak and clapped-out front suspension begging for new springs. This is the one I've done about 35,000 miles on, a white Moto Guzzi Lario, two cylinders with four valves per head, small and lean with sixteen-inch wheels front and back, Italian-red rims. I've spent what must amount to a couple of seven-day weeks in the rain on it. This is the bike I have finally finished payments on, have been up to Canada and down to the Gulf Coast on, wish for the Al-Can highway on. The other is the perfect vehicle, the bike of the mind. This is the motorcycle that is lavish in its gifts and lessons. Sometimes I fear it; often I dream about it; sometimes I love it with longing as if it were already gone.

Here, now, on the cusp of winter, I walk the sidewalks of Brooklyn and descend into the subway to wait. Down there, all of a sudden, I walk into an ambush of memory: a peculiar dead end somewhere, in a coal town in Pennsylvania at dusk a couple of years ago when, following the route signs to a more familiar road, I found myself heading into a cul-de-sac near a deserted town park and a cemetery up the hill beyond. The road ended smack at the burying ground's driveway. I turned about and did the circuit again, just to make certain I hadn't misread the signs, which I obviously had, but right now there seems something more imperative about that dead end. I never thought about it until this moment, at the Seventh Avenue station, and now my mind is filled with it. The purple light at the edge of the fall sky, the dark trees rising up, the road disappearing among the graves.

Or it comes to me, another time, that I'm in Tennessee at night. It's so black I don't know what's on either side of the road, behind the shallow vault of trees and pavement illuminated by my headlight. The road seems to tilt downward into the cold and dark green, although I know it's flat. Up ahead is the cauldron from which they sell the boiled peanuts, its bright steam, then more blackness beyond. It feels, in my recollection, as if nothing preceded this particular moment. But I can surely feel the cold right through my clothes, view the scene coming toward me.

Sometimes I get a couple of those weirdly floating moments in a day, as I'm going about my business. Then I'm quickly cut loose and adrift in this sea of arbitrary memory. The thing is, the only thoughts that come to me like this are memories of riding. Nothing else survives the precise weight of those sensations. Each moment of those 35,000 miles seems to be catalogued in some deep archive, and occasionally the wind flips up one of the index cards they're each on and it's suddenly there, bobbing at the surface of consciousness, along with a ghost perception of the temperature and smell of the air. This is the perfume of the past. Future scents wait by the road.

© Martin Dixon

Cool Breeze of the Untouchables at the Imperials Bike Blessing

from

ONE MAN CARAVAN

robert e. fulton

between Damascus and Baghdad lie six hundred miles of Syrian Desert across the sands of which I was now ready to point the motorcycle in what I considered one of the crucial stages of my undertaking. Physically I was in good shape. So was the machine. But mentally—that was another story. My attempt to get reliable information concerning the desert route seemed about as futile as the quest of Diogenes. Instead of a lantern I carried only the simple statement: "I am planning to cross the desert from Damascus to Baghdad on a motorcycle. What about the roads?"

"Easy! Simple!" declared a Damascus Frenchman.

"Impossible! Absolutely out of the question!" countered an Englishman.

"You can cross!" "You can't cross!" "The way's almost hard as concrete!" "There's only sand a foot deep. . . ."

Boiled down it came to the old adage that you can't know the truth until you've sought it yourself. There was no other solution to the problem of getting information about the desert. Somehow it didn't strike me as a very happy one.

Yet the desert had a strange lure; seeming to draw one like a lodestone—drawing men instead of metal. There to the East, outside "the oldest city in the world," lay the age-old stamping ground of the Arabs, the desert highway to far-off Cathay, the trail of Marco Polo, the path to a thousand riches—riches the like of which for centuries poured across that route between two continents.

I felt the lure and the attraction and was frankly afraid. Yet with all my fears something seemed to be pushing me along, almost telling me what to do next . . . somehow getting things done. Yet, there were obstacles— plenty of them. First of all, the Damascus police.

"Cross the desert on a motorcycle? Sapristi! C'est défendu!" the prefecture officials snorted. They sought to find in their rules and regulations a specific law which forbid it. But all their efforts came to naught.

Finally they played their ace-in-the-hole: their right to declare my vehicle "unfit." But there, too, they were stymied, since the overhauling job on the machine had been done by the official mechanics of the Nairn Brothers.

These brothers Nairn were two Australians—Anzacs—who had remained in the Near East after the World War to go into business for themselves. It was they who figured that the time had once again come to reopen the ancient desert highway between Damascus and Baghdad, one virtually closed since the days of the Crusades and Vasco da Gama's rounding of the "Cape." So the brothers Nairn took a plow and started across the desert to lay down a route from the Persian Gulf to the Mediterranean. The plow was necessary so that in case they got lost the furrow would lead them back to their starting point. Thus began the Nairn Transport Company.

When I inquired of company officials about the route, they were most anxious to inform me that my crossing could be made simply and expeditiously if I used the Nairn service. All I would have to do would be to follow their six-wheel bus and they would take all responsibility for my safe conduct—price, ten pounds, or fifty American dollars.

Ninety percent of those crossing the Syrian Desert pay the Nairn organization for this service. Automobile drivers invariably join one of the convoys for safe keeping and assistance "in case."

I figured it might be worth the $50.00 to have a safe convoy, even though it might not be as adventurous a journey. But it was one of the drivers who let out the cat. A rugged Australian, old-timer to the desert, McQueen by name, pushed me into a corner.

"Listen, lad," he said gruffly. "If you come along, just because you pay the ten pounds don't think you'll be riding behind me the whole way. I'll toss that machine of yours up on the roof as soon as we're out of town. I'm telling you this, so you won't be complaining later. I've a schedule to maintain and those two wheels can't keep up with six."

Which led me to turn down the Nairn offer of convoy, save $50.00 and apply to the police for clearance papers. Naturally, when I informed the authorities that the Nairn shops had checked my machine, there was nothing they could say about its being unfit. If the Nairns didn't know their business, then who should?

And so, reluctantly they stamped my papers . . . and explained a few of the desert's laws.

"You may go only on a Monday or a Friday, convoy days," they said. "Then the desert is patrolled and one is reasonably safe from marauding Arabs. It is absolutely forbidden to go at any other time!"

"And be sure of your gas and oil."

"And take plenty of water."

"And carry sugar for food. It has the most energy value and requires the least amount of space."

"And you better get a headstart with *that* machine. Go out to Khan Abu Shamat for the night. It's only forty miles, virtually on the desert's edge . . . but every mile counts once you're on the 'blue'!"

For the first sixteen miles out of Damascus I was traveling on pavement, the main highway to Aleppo. But at the sixteen-mile mark, where the road turns northward, it was just possible to make out the message on a weather-beaten old sign: "Baghdad, 792 Kilometers →" pointing right out into the "blue." Suddenly I realized why the desert was known as such. Blue was the way I felt as I rolled into the ditch, gave a last furtive look at the smooth highway and started dodging stony patches. But at least the surface was hard and there was an informal line of telegraph poles standing as reassuring sentinels every fifty yards.

In the golden glow of the sunset the little Khan stood out like a treasure house. The French flag flew over the tiny border post, though the actual frontier is some hundred miles to the east, a mere technicality in that desert vastness. At about 5:30, a little over two hours out of Damascus, I entered the mud-walled enclosure and was courteously welcomed by the Commandant, although, as he explained it, this whole procedure was "strictly out of order."

Almost immediately after my arrival, the trumpet sounded clear and crisp, and probably carried for miles over the silent waste. The doors creaked on their hinges, massive bars fell into place, a guard mounted the wall, and the little fort was ready . . . ready for whatever the night might bring.

"So you're going to cross the desert," began the Commandant in the confidence of his little quarters. The lamp wick needed trimming, the flickering flame betraying only a crude wooden table, twin iron beds, a dresser and some broken chairs. The old soldier's shadow grew immense as he drew close to the lantern and paused to fill his pipe.

Time and the desert had made their mark on him. His eyes were dull with years of desert sun, his beard gray with its companionship. But withal there was that kindliness which comes only with such association. His rugged, outdoor life had kept him in condition and his fingers nimbly filled the bowl.

There was no sound but the steady, rhythmical thud of the sentry's pace on the starlit roof above. The atmosphere was charged with a sense of tense excitement. But I was still too happy with the way I had found the desert that afternoon to be much worried. True, it had looked barren, but the surface had been quite hard and in comparison to Turkey it was a dream. If it would only continue like that all the way. . . .

"No doubt you are wondering what you will find, out there." The Commandant said it for me.

"Well, it would be useless for me to try to tell you. The desert tells a different story every time one ventures on it . . . and that's saying a good deal considering how many times I've been out there! It will certainly not tell you the same one that it does to me, not alike to any two persons. But I can tell you what it has held for many others."

Leaning forward into the light, he put his elbows on the table and enveloped himself in smoke like an old woman enveloping herself in a shawl as she prepares to weave a tale. For a moment again there was only the steady rhythm of the sentry's pace. Thump! Thump! Thump!—or was it the pace of my heart?

"Not very long ago, about six months, I should say, a group of Englishmen arrived here at dawn. They had been detailed to deliver a fleet of eight cars, new machines straight from a British factory, to Baghdad. They were a gay and fun-loving lot, I knew several of them from seeing them repeatedly pass in and out of here. They knew the desert all right . . . if anyone can ever know it.

"We had a drink or two on the house and finally, with the customary 'Cheerio,' they disappeared over the horizon. Of course everything was in order. It was a convoy day and the patrol had started before them. It ran its course to the frontier and returned by sunset 'without incident' . . . and for two days the desert was silent.

"Then one noon the trumpet sounded and the lookout reported a great dust cloud rising on the horizon. Careening over the desert, as though driven by a drunk, came an automobile, and out of it poured, or rather fell, the eight Englishmen. Or isn't an Englishman an Englishman without his clothes?" The Commandant's eyes blinked good-naturedly.

"They were hardly recognizable—looked like so many insane bushmen. Their only attire, aside from a lot of cuts and bruises, consisted of automobile upholstery, stuffing from the cushions, canvas from the top, rugs from the floor.

"And lucky they were, that they knew the desert or they probably would never have come out alive. Perhaps you haven't heard of the British Army that was surprised while bathing in the Tigris. If you had you would not have forgotten it. The Arabs took neither guns, ammunition, nor food—only *clothes*. The result was that before the naked soldiers could reach shelter, the sun turned them into so many raving lunatics shooting one another down.

"It seems that these chaps met with some other automobiles on the desert. They were fired upon by the Arab occupants, outnumbered and stripped of everything. Finally the Arabs smashed to pieces whatever cars they could not drive away, then vanished. Of the remaining wrecks, the enterprising victims were able to construct one machine and so limp back to life."

The old soldier looked at me squarely. His point was obvious. There was no answer. I could only stick out my chin and look squarely back. Slowly he began to smile.

"Well, I can see you are determined to go," he finally said. "I could tell you such stories all night but I can see it would make no difference. Youth . . . ah, youth!"

He leaned back in his chair, his hands behind his head, and puffed great circles. What brilliant images did he see in the dim shadows of the rafters, images of his own younger days, the sentry's measured tread seemingly counting back the years? I would have given a lot to see them too. . . . How much more would he have given for what I saw? But that is "the veil beyond which we cannot see." For a long time there were no words. Then the years rolled back and we were again in the present, he was again Commandant.

"Well, since that's the case, and I'm glad it is," he smiled, "take a tip from an old-timer—an old-timer whose hair was turned gray seeing it come true. Tomorrow, Heaven grant it, you will be hundreds of miles from here. You will be out in the middle of the blue, the vast, mysterious, cruel, yet magnificent blue. I hate it, yet I love it. It has been my life and will probably be my death. But that is another story. The point now is that you will be out there — alone."

He put all the emphasis on that last word.

"And to a man *alone* in the middle of the blue this is my advice: If you break down out there, sit down! Stay with your machine! It is solid, black, and big enough to be seen. If you stay near it the patrol *may* find you. But if you leave and try to walk out of it, you will never come through alive. My advice is based on many a sad lesson. Remember, just don't try to walk out of it!"

As I lay on one of the iron beds and things began to fade into a haze, the words of the Commandant were still with me: "Don't try to walk out of it. If you break down, sit down!"

The sentry's steady pace pounded out the words on the roof; the flickering light wrote them on the walls; the stars screamed them to the heavens; the clock ticked off the syllables: "If you break down, sit down! Don't try to walk out of it . . . *don't try to walk out of it!*"

THERE WAS A clatter of feet outside. Someone was shaking me. The voice of the Commandant barked in the still-dark quarters. "Vite, vite!" I rose quickly, obeying. "Follow me," he ordered as I stumbled towards the door rubbing my sleep-filled eyes. We mounted a ladder to the parapet and turned eyes westward. Through a cut in the castellated wall I could see a golden glow intermittently lighting the dark sky. Vague at first, it rapidly brightened. Suddenly four beady eyes, blindingly brilliant, popped over the hill. Like two heads of a dragon, they approached one another, separated, and came together again as, side by side, they writhed and wriggled over the intervening space.

The *dawn patrol!*

I felt a shiver of fear and excitement.

"Attention!" Almost before the Arab guard could jump into line there was a command "Halt" from one of the heavy machines which, with brakes squealing, tires skidding, slipped into their berths before the little outpost.

"*Mon Capitain! A votre service.*"

"*Bon jour, Monsieur le Commandant.*"

It was a dream. Surely it must be. Or was I alive? This little fort and those massive rolling arsenals; those ominous, oily-barreled machine guns gleaming in the lantern light and catching the first rays of the dawn . . . could it be real? The dancing stars, the picturesque Arab guard . . . surely some fantastic illusion. And down there in the courtyard stood a motorcycle, so tiny and so frail compared with the two machines and their gun mountings. It stood down there on two wheels, a speck in all this vastness . . . *alone*.

But my sudden abstraction was as suddenly dispelled by the hurry and bustle around me. The dawn patrol could not wait long. It had a job to do. The Commandant was standing beside me as I poured gasoline and oil into the tanks, fuel he offered from his own private supply. The Capitain and his Lieutenant were puffing tranquilly at cigarettes, talking with the Commandant. They gave me no more than a few stares; kept looking always toward the two Chenard-Walker cars on which they rode their patrol, like scouts keeping their eyes on their horses.

In one of the cars rode the Capitain, an Arab driver at the wheel and two Arabs at the guns. The Lieutenant commanded the other with the same arrangement. All were wrapped in red-tassel-decorated kaffiyeh and all wore great goggles to protect their eyes against the bite of the sand, the rip of the wind and the glare of the sun. My goggles, too, were in place.

A word of thanks, a salute, and, as if moved by powerful springs, the patrol suddenly sprang into action like demons headed for an urgent meeting with the Devil. Kicking the starter and shouting an "Au revoir" at the Commandant, I was after them.

The speeding cars churned a suffocating wake of dirt and flying stones. Into the bargain, they knew where they were going, had four wheels under them, and the road was not strange to them. A mile, two miles; I tried to plunge ahead and keep them in sight. But it was no use. They were on their way to the frontier a hundred miles away. There they would turn and whiz back to Damascus. I hit a couple of soft sand holes and had to slow down. There was a faint speck on the horizon. That was the patrol cars. The speck disappeared. I never saw them again!

It is wholly possible that the patrol passed me on its way back from the frontier; or perhaps it stopped somewhere and *I* passed it. The desert is quite rough and rolling. There are innumerable *wadis*—dried-up river beds—and low hills. The road itself is, after all, no road but a route, an imaginary line across the waste. It makes little difference whether one travels five miles on one side or ten on the other. The terrain is the same. One has only to keep going east and watch for the sign posts.

Signs? Of course. On the Syrian side they are black wooden and placed so as to be visible one from another. During the day they are relatively easy to locate, but after dark . . . Being wood and of several years' standing many of them are now on the verge of collapse. Twice in the next fifty-seven miles I lost track of them and went scurrying about to find them. I couldn't afford to do that often. Every drop of gas and oil was precious. But the mental ease was worth the extravagance.

The next habitation I was due to see after leaving Khan Abu Shamat was Fort Descharpentrie, the last French outpost on the desert, in which there were billeted a wireless operator and a few guards. To reach the Fort it was necessary to watch first for a low mud flat. There I found the water had so thoroughly leveled and the sun so thoroughly baked the dirt that the going was like traveling on smooth steel. Smooth for about a mile and then suddenly there would appear a fissure wide enough to swallow a camel. The very first such crack brought my speed down to ten miles an hour—and pronto.

After the mud flat came the "80-Mile Hills" and Fort Descharpentrie is just beyond, in the Wadi Saba Biar. It appeared about a mile to north-ward, easy to locate because of its radio masts. I pushed on without fur-ther investigation. Pushed is the word, since beyond the 80-Mile Hills the going became rough. There were camel skeletons and bad gullies. There were more mud flats, too, and at noon I crossed the provisional Syrian-Irakian frontier. This I knew only because the wooden Syrian signs suddenly disappeared in favor of substantial black and white metal ones. There is no formal demarcation, but my mileage meter and map also convinced me that this was correct. From then on I completely gave up looking for the patrol cars. I was beyond their dead-line.

The Irakian sign-posts have been wisely painted black and white which makes them discernible by day or night. The only thing wrong is that unlike the Syrian posts which are visible one from another, they are erected at fixed intervals of five kilometers, irrespective of whether the spot is at the top of a hill or bottom of a gully, with the result that one whose very existence seems to hang on the sight of a post spends many "non-existent" hours scanning the hilly horizon for something which is standing in a river bed.

My maps told me that I had eighty miles, more or less, to Rutbah Wells, the desert's half-way mark, where I planned to stay the night. It was already late afternoon; my muscles were tired and taut from con-stantly fighting soft and sandy spots which would be under me without warning. But it was the mental hazard which was the principal bogey. Lying in back of my mind every minute, like a cold ball of lead, was the constant fear that something might happen to the motorcycle; a piston might seize, a head crack, a tire blow . . . or what if I capsized and broke a leg or an arm? In a fatigued brain there is no restraining imagination and a thousand mental tragedies took place before anything really hap-pened. And then it was only a short circuit which refused to light my headlamp. This within twenty-five miles of Rutbah. Without lights I was as though blind. It took me two hours of guessing and groping to find the cause of the trouble, repair it and start wearily, every nerve taut, over the remaining miles into Rutbah Wells. When I saw the first red glimmer of the little light atop the radio tower, and recognized it as such, it was as though I had been given a reprieve from a slow torturing death.

The British officer who greeted me was as astonished as I was fagged. His eyes actually popped. I must have been a pretty sight; caked with dust and grime from head to toe, the only proof that I was a white person being the two large circles around my eyes, where the goggles had protected the skin. All I recall is that I fell on a bed and was dead to the world until the next morning.

When I awoke I felt as though I had passed through the scrimmage lines of a dozen football teams and had been caught between the centers at each play. A faint feeling of nausea overcame me each time I tried to rouse enough interest to look over the motorcycle. I felt I never wanted to see the thing again. I needed rest and decided to take it and not start until the next morning. The Britisher in charge of the fort was pleasant and chatted affably. By noon I felt some of my "push" returning. I looked over the machine, refueled at a dollar a gallon for gasoline, and was given an Arab to show me the sights of Rutbah Wells. The chuckle I got out of meeting my guide did much to snap me out of the doldrums. I hadn't quite believed my ears when I heard him call, in good English, to a scampering youngster: "Oye! String Bean!"

"Yes, it is a strange name," explained the British officer. "But you would find more and stranger if you remained here at Rutbah. The Arab, you see, likes to name his children in some logical, simple sequence. One, for example, might name all his offspring after fish: Salmon, Shark, Trout, Bass, Minnow, and the like; another after trees, another after metals, and so on. In this case it is simply the bean family. His first child is called Lima Bean; the second String Bean, the third Baked Bean and the fourth and latest, from long association with Englishmen, alas—Old Bean."

It was the dignified father of all the Beans who showed me the sights. It didn't take long, but it was interesting while it lasted, especially the original wells, over two hundred feet deep, dug by the Roman Legions on one of their phenomenal marches to heaven-knew-where.

The fort itself, of brick, was erected by the British and Irak governments in consort. There was a radio station; a good storage section containing sufficient provisions to withstand a month's siege; an emergency landing field where planes of the British, French and Dutch airlines operating between Europe and the Orient occasionally stopped, and that was all. The front yard was approximately a thousand miles long by five hundred miles wide, the back yard double that size.

Another twelve hours of sleep worked wonders for my spirits and at sunrise I kicked the starter and was off. For seventy-five miles out of Rutbah the going was comparatively smooth and hard and I made good time. Then, just before one of the tricky mud flat passages, I started to spot wrecks of the desert. Previously there had been many camel bones, bleached skeletons. But now on every side there were burned, rusted automobile chassis: Fiats, Dodges, Buicks, a Staer, even a Rolls-Royce. Within twenty miles of each other there were two crashed airplanes. It was depressing. It wasn't difficult to imagine the skeleton of my motorcycle in the same condition as the others and it gave me the jitters. Minutes began to seem like hours as the sun climbed to its mid-day peak. It seemed as if all time and creation passed.

Brown and dusty desert; the charred, rusted wrecks from which the occupants probably never even had a chance to "walk out of it"; more and more emptiness, that was all. Monotony! *Monotony!*

On the water there is always the lapping of waves against the boat, in the wilderness the rustling of leaves, but out on the "blue" it is so silent, so empty, all is so vast that one can almost hear one's heart beat. The roar of the motor sounds like some insignificant pip-squeak hung in space and trying to wake the universe.

As the day wore on the sound became more alarming. When I started that morning, the steady drone of the exhaust had been deep and chesty. But now, after half-a-dozen hours of desert driving, it seemed to fill with static, the machine began to wobble, the tires seemed flat, the whole engine seemed on the verge of falling apart, collapsing.

It wasn't the machine, it was nerves; strung tight, pulled tighter by the constant thought of "what would happen if something happened?"

I decided to stop and try to eat. They had fixed a box lunch for me at Rutbah Wells. I had smiled when they pointed out a generous slice of Angel's Food cake which had been included. Momentarily it lightened my spirits to contemplate the weirdness of sitting in that great emptiness unpacking a piece of Angel's Food cake. But it was not enough to give me an appetite. Devil's Food is all that came to mind. And what I saw next completely robbed me of my appetite. Not a hundred yards away, over the shoulder of a low hill there suddenly popped a roaring large motor car. It fairly jumped toward me as I jumped up, spilling the box lunch.

"Arabs!"

The story of the Commandant struck the gong. I thought of running. . . . But where? I stood as if glued to the spot. Not until the big car came to a stop beside me, did I move. Five burly men tumbled out.

"What in hell?"

"Well, I'll be . . ."

"I'd like to know where in . . ."

One was an Englishman, a second a Persian, and the three remaining passengers were just plain Americans, the ones who didn't bother to restrain themselves. They were jabbering away at me with shouted questions before they'd touched the ground.

We had a regular pow-wow and Old Home Week. Good-naturedly they advised me that I was a fool, an idiot, and several other categories of mankind for trying to cross the desert on a motorcycle. They had to cross in the motor car for business, but I was just doing it . . . for what? They were generous in replenishing my water bottle and also filled my gas tank. They brought out sandwiches and fruit and we talked and munched and all was fine. Here were businessmen, men of trade and barter. They traveled by automobiles, they wore occidental clothes and spoke a strange language but they were no different from the merchants who for centuries have traveled with the caravans trading two goats for a cow, rolls of silks for bags of wool.

The meeting was . . . marvelous. No other word describes it, for it buoyed my spirits and sent them soaring. The time came to push on and one of the party who'd been doing business with the Anglo-Persian Oil Company stepped forward.

"Wait a minute, young man," he said. "Wait just a minute. I'm interested in this trip of yours. When you come through Indianapolis look me up."

His card read, "Edward Herrington, President, Marmon-Herrington Motor Truck Company."

"That's interesting," I commented. Then I told him of my father's connection with the motor truck industry. The man almost exploded.

"What! You don't mean to tell me you're Bob Fulton's son? Why . . . why, I worked with him for years!"

He beamed, he glowed, he chortled and all but kissed me on both cheeks! Suddenly the desert seemed like home . . . crowded with life and activity. In fact, even the sand had a positively friendly look.

ALTHOUGH I WAS on the most bleak and back-breaking terrain for thirty miles after bidding good-by to Colonel Herrington and his companions, the lift I got from the encounter with the-man-from-home seemed to work miracles.

The route lay through "Bad Lands," every whit as desolate as those of Nevada, Arizona, and New Mexico. Yet the fissures, the straight up and down bluffs of drab earth standing menacing in cruel contour impressed me as just another "sight" to record. Ramadi, the Iraq frontier post, seemed just around the corner.

The going was rough and treacherous and there was an increasing number of rusted, burned chassis strewn along the way. There were many more *wadis* to negotiate, the river beds proving hot-boxes into which to descend. The temperature on the open stretches never varied from a blistering 95 degrees Fahrenheit.

But the "Bad Lands" were hardly out of sight when there was a new sensation. The air began to reek with a foul stench. At first I thought I was approaching oil refining plants which give off what is perhaps the "thickest" stink of anything in the world—excluding, as I soon discovered, bituminous lakes. These natural smells beat the oil refinery variety by a wide margin. The bitumin, a variety of tar, was not, unfortunately, used to build even a few miles of highway. Indeed not, for the way remained pristine in its desert awfulness. Even smelly bitumin would have been better than chuck holes.

The sun was setting as I reached the frontier post (over 250 miles beyond the actual frontier): Ramadi hugging the ancient Euphrates. Here was water—and (at certain seasons of the year) in fatal abundance. Ramadi is known as the City of Floods, today and since time beyond recording. City? Rather, it is a tiny town of mud, replete with dust, dogs, and Arabs. And yet it has water, it has palms—slender palms and not many in number, bending under the bitumin-laden wind.

I observed those palms more closely than they had any right to expect for Ramadi is said to be the spot from which Noah started his maritime meanderings aboard the Ark. Those palms, to this day, are of just the right size and type to build an Ark of the number of cubits described in the Bible.

As for the odor—I even sniffed at it voluntarily while surveying the palms, for those same bitumin deposits are supposed to have furnished Noah the tar with which to calk the seams of his Ark.

Today the Arabs use the sticky bitumin to calk and waterproof their strange "praus" and the still stranger "gufa" boats. Who wouldn't laugh at the thought of some smart university crew and its bewildered cox trying to control one of those strange craft. Built of wicker, they are round and like overgrown baskets. The cane is then smeared with a thick coating of bitumin, and it's all like going rowing in a laundry hamper.

But, most interesting of all, there is a Khurdish legend that tells of Noah's landing on Mt. Ararat, which the local Arabs maintain is in Khurdistan to northward, and dispatching each of his sons in a different direction. One of them, on traveling westward, came into the desert and there, "Holy Jehovah, what horror was this? Sinners yet alive?"

The "sinners" listened in amazement to the fellow's frenzied tale of deluge.

"Flood? Flood?" they knew nothing of a recent flood. After all, every year, even to this day, in the spring and summer when the snows of high Persia begin to melt, there are innumerable floods in the Tigris-Euphrates valley.

And so, putting their heads together, these ancient rehabilitators of the earth decided to build a tower . . . and surely as it rose, people from far away would see it and come to learn the cause; and thus they could gauge their worthy task of propagation.

So the tower rose, and the people came. But unfortunately the Arab is a nomad, a bedouin, one that for centuries has wandered over the desert virtually alone, with just his family and his herds. Thence his individualism of temperament and of tongue. Living thus, each family naturally develops its own vernacular, its own dialect, one so much its own that two desert Arabs often understand each other only with the greatest of difficulty.

And so, as they assembled there came about a vast confusion of tongues . . . and, for us, a modern interpretation of that ancient story of the tower that Babel didn't build.

But modern Ramadi at best is not even a shadow of its historic self. I was much too tired, to say nothing of being tired of dust and dusty villages, to dig out more of the "city's" past glory. Baghdad was now too close at hand; Baghdad of the "Hundred and One Nights," Baghdad of every child's dreams, and Baghdad with a desert-motorcyclist's idea of a modern hotel, a bath-tub, and a big meal. Soup, steak (even without onions), mashed potatoes, string beans . . . and ice cream. Who said there was no Santa Claus? Truly a childhood Baghdad. And only seventy-five miles away, I was going to be there for lunch. I could hardly wait for sunrise.

Out of Ramadi the road followed the Euphrates for thirty-two miles to Al Falluja. Slender palms, gracing the river bank, rested the eye after five hundred miles of open desert riding. At Al Falluja the road crossed the river and, once again, commenced the march of telegraph poles.

Only forty-three miles of unirrigated desert remained to Baghdad . . . yet it took eight hours to cover that distance. Without so much as a puff of warning a pea-soup dust storm enveloped me. With a fifty-mile-an-hour velocity the wind cut diagonally across the track. Visibility was reduced to a matter of feet, the sky turned into a great sheet of yellow-brown wrapping paper.

My luncheon hour at Baghdad's best hotel came and went as dust did its best to substitute and the clock slowly turned. Bucking at every step, I crawled along. By three o'clock, with the increase of traffic, I knew I was nearing the city. Soon trucks were thundering by me, hooting their horns raucously; there were donkeys and camels and humans. Though the going was nerve-jangling, the dirt biting and the wind so strong as to make steering a job in itself, yet how could one completely forget that there would soon be a hot tub in the best hotel room money could buy; that serving boys would be bringing large and fluffy towels and there would be a shave, a suit of linens brought up for inspection, a fine dinner, and, as a grand finale, that very evening there would be the lights of Baghdad?

It was four in the afternoon when the desert highway finally gave way to bitumin pavement and before me loomed a traffic circle. I might have been coming out of the Holland Tunnel from Manhattan and heading for Philadelphia, for there was a traffic circle like any other traffic circle in the world. Roads went off this way and that—and I went in the direction of "West Baghdad." West Baghdad! East Chicago, South San Francisco, North Tarrytown . . . West Baghdad!

A sign advised me at the next corner that I had to turn right for uptown. I went across the Maude Bridge, over pontoons spanning the Tigris, and hummed along, my uncertain thoughts humming, too, and, in spite of it all, my heart beating faster.

I was in Baghdad. I was approaching New Street, the main street of Baghdad. A turn to the right and then . . . CRASH! For an instant I didn't realize what had happened. I had hopped clear as the motorcycle went over. A little boy of eight or nine lay sprawled over the front wheel. He had dashed off the curb, directly into me and lay there screaming to heaven. The noise reassured my fast beating heart. They were screams of fright, rather than agony. Two policemen, in their dusty faded uniforms, immediately appeared. The little boy scrambled to his feet. Through the grime on his hands and face and his bare legs I sought to find signs of cuts, of blood. There were none. Suddenly realizing the presence of the two policemen his mouth reopened. But instead of screaming he just left it open, rolled his eyes and then, as though propelled from a gun, disappeared from the scene, dodging between a cart and two trucks. Dragging the machine to the side of the street, I kicked the starter. The engine roared, and still the policemen had said nothing. One even walked away. But the other stood there looking me over carefully.

Could it be otherwise than that I should fulfill my destiny and complete one more figure of the pattern which seemed to have been drawn for my wanderings? It certainly couldn't. Finally he motioned that I should follow. Guess where? For the twenty-seventh time since leaving London I was ushered into a jail. But I had met the desert, and it was mine.

Scorpio Rising

Kenneth Anger, 1963 Photofest

THE GRANDSTAND COMPLEX

horace mccoy

tony Lukatovich had finished the Florida season a few points ahead of me, but I had got them back (with plenty to spare) the first four weeks in Los Angeles. That L.A. track was made to order for me. I had so much confidence in it, and in my JAP motor, that after the first week I stopped wearing the steel cap on my left foot and the polo belt I used to protect my abdomen. This made it more dangerous for me in case of a bad spill, but it looked spectacular to the crowds. You have to be a showman to be a success in motorcycle racing. Finally, to live up to the publicity I was getting in the newspapers, and to prove that my winning of last year's national championship was no accident, I discarded my crash helmet, substituting a simple leather helmet such as aviators used to wear. Everybody said I was a damn fool for doing this. If my head ever smacked the track or the guard rail at fifty-five or sixty that leather helmet would have been absolutely no protection. My skull would have cracked like an eggshell. I knew that and so did the crowd. The majority came out just to hear somebody's skull crack (you may not think you can hear a skull crack with all those exhausts popping, but you can, you most certainly can) or to see somebody's brains spilled in the dirt, but so far the customers had been disappointed. At the end of the first four weeks I was the big favorite in L.A. I was out in front in individual points, and with the Long Beach team matches coming up, and the national awards but a month away, I looked like a cinch to repeat the championship.

Tony Lukatovich was very jealous of my popularity and you would have thought that every point I collected was a year off his life. He had been the runner-up in the national last year and he had definitely made up his mind he was not going to finish second again. I don't think he wanted the championship title as much as he did the glory that went with it. He was a grandstander, a great grandstander. He was a great rider, too, but it was the cheers of the crowd he wanted. These were meat and drink to him. Give him a crowd big enough and let them all root for him and he was the greatest motorcycle racer who ever lived. He would pull turns and slides and finishes that none of the others of us would even dare think about. In Florida when he was leading in points and was the star attraction, where the crowd was for him to a man, he was a broadsiding maniac. He was more than that; he was a genius.

But the Florida track was short, one sixth of a mile, and the L.A. track was longer, one fifth of a mile. Those seventy-two yards made a difference. On the longer track Tony's judgment, his intuition, was a fraction bad. His timing slipped just enough to keep him from winning consistently.

"It's only your imagination," I told him one day, lying, trying to cheer him up.

"I haven't got any imagination. You're the guy who's got all the imagination. You go to hell," he said.

"All right, if that's the way you feel about it," I said. "I was only trying to help you out."

"I don't need any help from you," he said. "You go to hell."

After that he got nastier and nastier and finally I stopped speaking to him at all. Then he began taking all sorts of reckless chances on the turns and doing trick riding in the homestretch, trying to show up the rest of us. But instead of impressing the crowds with his ability he only gave them the idea that he was a wild man out there trying to kill some of the other riders.

I never did get really sore at him because I knew what was the matter. He simply wanted to become a favorite with the customers and get them pulling for him. He was starving for lack of glory. But the harder he tried the worse he looked. In every race I was knocking his ears down. I was concentrating on piling up all the points I possibly could so that if I had a spill that put me in the hospital I would have enough points to coast to the championship. I didn't expect to go to the hospital; I mean I wasn't looking forward to it, but in motorcycle racing you never can tell, especially when you have a wild man who hates your guts riding behind you.

Tony was trying so desperately to win, was looking so bad, the committee notified him that unless he got back some of his old-time form they would have to give him a handicap. This was like telling Joe Louis that unless he improved they were going to match him with Barney Ross. Tony raved and yelled and screamed and put on an act in front of the stands, challenging the committee to a fight, individually or collectively, kicking up the dirt and throwing his equipment all over the infield. He rushed over to the loudspeaker microphone and was trying to make a speech to the crowd when Jack Gurling, the promoter, collared him and threatened him with a suspension. That cooled Mr. Lukatovich, but I knew from the look of his face that there was blood on the moon.

That night after the races he came over to my room. I invited him in, thinking he probably wanted to talk things over.

"The team races with Long Beach are next week," he said.

"That's right," I said.

"And you and I race again as the number-one team?"

"I suppose we do," I said.

"And if we win this time we get permanent possession of the cups?"

"That's right. We've got two legs on 'em now and if we win this time we get permanent possession. Did you get back your cup from your mother?"

Tony always sent all the trophies and cups he won back home to his mother in Ohio, so she could show the neighbors how well he was going.

"No, I didn't," he replied.

"You didn't? Don't you think you ought to get it?"

"I can't," he said. "It would break her heart. She thinks it's mine already."

"It probably will be," I said, "but if we should happen to lose it might be embarrassing for you not to have the cup."

"We won't lose," he said. "But I didn't come over here to talk about that. I want to talk about us—you and me."

"Go ahead," I told him.

"Do you think you're a better rider than I am?" he asked.

"How do you think I won the championship last year—with cigarette coupons?"

"You think you are then?"

"I don't think anything about it. I know damn well I am."

"Do you think you've got as much nerve as I have?"

"I wouldn't know much about that. But I've got more skill, which is a damn sight more important."

"All you've got is a swelled head," he said. "Why have you got it in for me?"

"You must be daffy," I said. "I haven't got it in for you. The only trouble with you is you're jealous. As long as you're the fair-haired boy with the fans and get all the newspaper publicity, everything is roses. The moment somebody else does, you curl up. You can't take it, Tony."

"Is that so?" he said, jumping up, grabbing me by the coat lapel.

"Sit down," I said. He had that blood-on-the-moon look on his face again. "I don't know what's eating you," I said, "but whatever it is, I don't want any part of it. Suppose you beat it."

He said nothing, standing there and looking at me with his eyes glittering.

"Go on, beat it," I said. "Whatever grudges we've got we'll settle out there on the track."

"That's exactly what I want to do," he said. "That's exactly why I came here. I'm going to make you a proposition. I'll see how much nerve you've got."

I knew this was going to be something that was very screwy.

"There's no doubt," he said, "that we're the two best motorcycle racers in the world."

"That's right. I'm the best and you're the second best," I said.

"Okay. We'll make a bet on it."

"You know I don't bet," I said.

"Not money," he said smiling, shaking his head. "Not money. You. Bet yourself."

"I don't get you," I said.

"Your life. You," he said. "You and I race together in the team matches. If you win I'll kill myself. If I win you kill yourself. That'll leave the winner the biggest star in the game."

"Nothing doing," I said.

"Why not? There's nothing new about duels—they've been fighting them for hundreds of years. The other day I read in the paper about a couple of miners in Europe fighting a duel with sledgehammers. That's all this is—a duel. With motorcycles."

"This is the goofiest thing I ever listened to," I said. "Nothing doing."

"I told you I had more nerve than you did," he said.

"It's not a question of nerve—"

"Oh, yes, it is."

"Oh, no, it's not. It's that grandstand complex of yours. You'd rather be dead than to be second best."

"I'm slowly dying anyway," he said.

"You go right ahead and die," I told him. "Me, I'm having a fine time living."

"Well, then, it's all settled," he said, turning to go.

"Let's shake hands on it," he said, sticking out his hand.

"Why should I shake hands with you?" I asked. "You hate my guts."

"Sure, I do, sure, I do," he said, smiling. "But that's got nothing to do with it. Gentlemen always shake hands when they make a bet."

"I haven't made any bet," I said, getting sore.

"Oh, yes, you have. The team race Friday night—the race for life. Whoever loses kills himself."

He stood there smiling, his hand stuck out, waiting for my shake.

"Beat it the hell out of here," I said.

"Is it yes or no?" he asked, not moving.

"Beat it—" I said.

"All right, I'll beat it. But this is going to ruin you. I'm going to spread the word around to everybody the newspaper reporters and everybody, that you're yellow. I'm going to tell them about the proposition to fight a duel with motorcycles and how you were too yellow to take me up on it because you thought you might lose and have to kill yourself. This'll ruin you."

Suddenly it dawned on me that he was right. This would ruin me. People wouldn't stop to figure it was a screwy proposition, they'd really think I was yellow. Soon they'd have me believing it myself.

"You polack ——— —— — —————," I said, stepping over, hitting him in the face. He grabbed me, trying to hold on, but I shook him loose and began punching him in the head with my fists. He grabbed me again and we fell over a chair, breaking it, wrestling on the floor. I finally climbed to my feet, dragging him with me, and started punching him in the face some more. Then he grabbed me again, trying to hold on. I got loose and hit him back of the ear and he fell to the floor unconscious, his arms doubled under his stomach.

"Well," my mind said, "you've knocked him out and where did it get you? He's still got that axe over you. The only way to stop whatever is going to happen from actually happening is to cut the guy's tongue out.

The minute he starts talking everybody will think you are yellow and they'll all go over to his side. . . . It looks like you'll have to accept the challenge."

"I suppose so," I replied to myself.

"The thing to do," my mind said, "is to win."

"I'll win, all right," I said. "I certainly don't want to have to commit suicide."

I got a wet towel out of the bathroom and rolled Tony over and began rubbing his face and wrists and pretty soon he came to.

"I'm okay," he said, sitting up.

"There's just one thing," I said. "If I do win this race how do I know you won't welsh?"

"Don't worry," he said, pushing himself up off the floor. "I won't welsh and neither will you. We'll shake hands like gentlemen do."

He stuck out his hand. I took it.

"All right, you polack — — — — — — — — — — — — —," I said. "Now beat it."

THERE WAS A big crowd out for the team races, many of them coming from Long Beach to back their own riders. There was a lot of money bet on the races this year by the Long Beach fans because our second, third and fourth teams were weaker than usual. The men who had been our number-two team last year, and who had won easily, both had been killed on the Florida track. Tony and I looked like cinches to beat our men, but we weren't so sure about the other teams.

About 7:30 that night Tony came in the shed where I was tightening up my chain.

"How do you feel?" he asked. It was the first time he had spoken to me since the fight.

"Swell," I said, "just perfectly—damn swell. How do you feel?"

"I feel fine," he said.

"You won't feel so fine when Gurling finds you," I said. "He's been asking me questions about your cup."

"Look," he said, "everything will be all right if we win. One of us has *got* to win. I told Gurling my mother had mailed the cup but that it just hadn't got here yet."

"Suppose we lose?" I asked.

"We can't lose," he said. "One of us has *got* to win. Not only for the cup, but for another reason, too. Did you keep your dinner down tonight?" he asked, leaning over.

"What was that?" I asked suddenly, turning around, pretending I had heard something. "That was a peculiar noise. Is anybody rattling dice in here? Oh, excuse me," I said, looking at Tony. "It's you."

"Me?" he said, surprised.

"It's your teeth I hear," I said.

"You go to hell," he said, crossing to where his mechanics were checking his motor. . . .

The first event on the program was a handicap race for Class B riders, boys who had ridden only a few events. The next event was a four-lap heat, the first three to transfer to Event 7, the handicap semifinals. I won this race in 1:05:10, pretty good time. The third event was an exhibition by some local trick-riding jockies. Tony was in Event 4, the first three in this also to transfer to Event 7. He won the heat in 1:06 flat. Events 5 and 6 were for novice riders.

Tony and I were the only ones to start from scratch in Event 7, one of the two feature races of the night. This event was run in two heats, the first three in each heat to transfer to the final event, four laps, the points to count toward the national championship.

Tony and I sat in our saddles on the scratch line, saying nothing, six feet apart, while the announcer introduced us. I got the most applause. I looked at Tony, winking.

"It won't be long now," he said, winking back.

"Don't let him get your goat," my mind told me.

"Fat chance," I replied.

The starter's gun popped and my two mechanics shoved. My motor caught on the first shove.

"Good old JAP," I said to myself, giving her the gun.

There were two men in front of me. They were both handicap men. One had started from thirty yards ahead of the scratch line and the other from twenty-five. I wasn't much worried about them; they were kids on the way up, and I knew I could outgut them in a pinch. But I went right after them anyway, not taking any chances. I trailed them a full lap before I could cut down the handicap and on the backstretch I hung on their tails waiting for a hole at the turn. One of them skidded a little and I shot through. I trailed the leader down the stretch, but I took him on the front turn and went ahead. In a moment I got a flash out of the corner of my eye and I knew it was Tony making his bid. I hugged the inside railing, hoping he didn't lose his head and crash me. Tony was a maniac when he was desperate. With some riders you can make a close race out of it and give the fans a good finish and a run for their money, but not with Tony. Stay just as far in front of him as you possibly could, was my motto.

I beat him into the finish by a length. I went on around the track and went through the gate into the pits.

There was one other event before the team race—the race that meant the finish for either me or Tony. I had six or seven minutes before we were to go out, so I walked around, trying to tell myself there was nothing to get nervous about. I got a hot dog and a bottle of pop, trying to put my mind on the movies or women or something, anything except what depended on the outcome of the duel. The taste of mustard in the hot dog nauseated me and for a minute I thought I would have to check my dinner. I gagged on the pop, finally throwing it away, too.

"What the hell is this?" I asked myself. "Why am I so nervous? I've never been nervous before. I can beat that guy any day in the week."

"Let's go," said one of my mechanics.

"It's not time yet," I said.

"Sure, it is," he said. "The other race is finished. Come on—"

There was more applause when I came out onto the track. Tony and the Long Beach riders were already there, Red Dooley and Paul Jarvis, two top-notchers, not champions yet, but a couple of boys who were getting better every hour. I gave my motor to my mechanics, moving up to the starting line where they were waiting to toss for positions. Tony and I both lost and had to take the second and fourth positions. The Long Beach crowd whooped it up at this.

"Toss for us," Tony said to the starter. "You call it," he said to me.

"Never mind," I said. "You can have two."

"Okay," he said, not even thanking me.

"That was a silly thing to do," my mind said a moment after I had uttered the words. "Why didn't you toss with him? Number four is on the outside, the worst position on the track. You've deliberately put yourself in a hole in the most important race you ever rode in your life."

There was a lot of yelling . . . and then we were off. The others got away first. My motor didn't fire at once.

"Good God!" I thought.

My mechanics shoved again, harder, and this time the motor caught. The others were going into the turn, twenty yards ahead. This was a terrific handicap to give good riders and I knew I was up against it.

I settled down to business, telling myself not to get panicky, and eased into the first turn. But on the backstretch I opened up, swinging high on the outside to keep my goggles from fouling from the dirt the front riders were kicking up. At the turn I dropped down into the slot, figuring Paul Jarvis, just in front of me, would be a little too anxious and would go in a little too fast to hold his line and would therefore slide a little.

He did. He left two feet between him and the inside railing and I went through without shutting off. But the impetus carried me to the outside again and I had to shut off and skid to keep from hitting the wall. I laid my left toe on the ground, pulling my motor over at an angle of about thirty degrees. I heard a gasp go up from the stands. I eased my handlebars over, opening up in the homestretch.

Tony was in second place, a full length behind Dooley. I was still twenty yards back of Tony. I was in a rotten spot. We had three laps left, just three, and I knew I was going to need everything I had to win this race. My motor was all right now that she was rolling—it was the best racing JAP in the world. This time it was up to me.

I took the front turn wide open, laying my motor over my left knee, listening for that first faint *whirr* that tells you the traction is slipping. When you hear that you want to get it up in a hurry, else you will have the whole thing suddenly in your lap.

. . . I fought and fought, took chances I had never taken before, used all my skill, all my anticipation, but I was getting nowhere. I had managed to cut off a few yards, but I was not close enough to make my bid. I felt satisfied this was the greatest race I had ever ridden. I would have been in front by the same distance I was now behind if I hadn't lost that one or two seconds getting started.

On the third lap Tony took the back turn wide open, a stupid thing to do, and lost a couple of yards in a slide. I picked up this much on him, going down the stretch so close that my front wheel almost touched his rear wheel. On the front turn of the last lap Dooley made his first mistake—he hit a patch of soft dirt that he should have spotted before now, and slid across it. It was a very short slide, but for an instant his back wheel spun and in that instant Tony and I had pulled up on him. It happened in the tick of a clock.

We went into the backstretch at top speed. Tony knew I was behind him and tried to shake me off, but I held on, hoping he would slide in the turn so I could take him. This was my final chance to win; if it didn't happen I was a gone gosling.

I eased over to the right a trifle to get set for the jump. Dooley was swinging wide now, trying to play safe, and I saw Tony follow him over.

"He's crazy to take a chance like that," I thought.

Just then Tony's front wheel hit Dooley's rear wheel and both motors went over, riders and all. One of the wheels struck the concrete guard rail, leaving a shower of sparks. Suddenly, the sky filled with flame. It was right in front of me.

"Good God, I'm going to pile up!" I thought, twisting my handlebars over, turning my head so the crash wouldn't put out my eyes. . . . My motor twisted and kicked and I had that awful cold feeling in the bowels that a man gets when he realizes the thing he is riding is suddenly out of control. . . . Then my wheels gripped and I righted myself and saw the starter in front of me waving the checkered flag, the winner's flag, giving the signal to me.

"CAN I DROP you some place?" a reporter asked, coming out of the morgue with me.

"No, thanks," I said.

"Too bad about Tony," he said. "Jesus, there wasn't much left of his face, was there? Those spokes are as bad as a meat grinder."

I looked at him steadily, trying to focus my eyes on him, but not being able to.

"Tony called me up just this afternoon," he said. "It's a funny thing, but he had a hunch something like this was going to happen."

"He did?" I said.

"Yes," the reporter said. "It was a good story. I used it as a feature in the Bulldog. It's out now. Read it. As a matter of fact, it was written especially for you."

"I'll get it," I said.

"Well . . . you sure I can't drop you some place?"

"I think I'll walk around a little," I said.

At the corner I was stopped by the traffic light. There was a stack of morning papers piled up by the lamp post. "TWO DIE IN MOTORCYCLE RACE," the headline said. "Tony Lukatovich and Red Dooley killed in Long Beach—L.A. team match. . . ." I stopped, looking down at the paper. "Motorcycle Champion Resigns Career after Fatal Smash; Vows He Will Never Race Again," said a heading.

"I didn't say that," I said to myself, trying to figure the whole thing out. The next moment I knew what the reporter meant. "My God!" I said to myself, turning the corner, walking down the street very fast. . . .

HARLEYS, CHOPPERS, FULL DRESSERS, AND STOLEN WHEELS

ralph "sonny" barger

If anybody deserves anything in this whole bike-riding world, it's Sonny. He led the way. You see people wearing their fucking patches, 'Ride to live, Live to ride.' Yeah, right. As soon as the shit comes down, their bike is the first thing they sell. Sonny is the one who pushed the bike-riding lifestyle. There wasn't an outlaw type of lifestyle as there is today until he created it.

—Oakland Hell's Angels president Cisco Valderrama

i've always been crazy about motorcycles. When I was a kid, the Oakland motorcycle cops used to park in front of my house, waiting to catch drivers rolling the stop sign on the corner. Oakland Police Department cops rode Harleys and Indians, the latter a V-twin flathead. Man, I was in awe of their bikes. Even though I really didn't like cops, I'd walk up and talk with them just as an excuse to look at their bikes. Once, one of the motorcycle cops was kick-starting his bike and my dog King freaked out and bit him. Figuring they would throw King in the pet slammer, I grabbed him and ran off. Later that night the police knocked on our door. Luckily my father smoothed things out, and they allowed us to keep King if we promised not to let him leave the house until his rabies quarantine expired.

Motorcycles became the thing to ride in California after World War II. A lot of the GIs coming home from the Pacific who didn't want to return to some boring life in Indiana or Kentucky chose to stick around California. A motorcycle was a cheap mode of transportation, kind of dangerous and perfect for racing and hanging out. Plus they could ride together, just like they were back in the service again. California and its sunshine became the center of motorcycle culture, and for years there were more motorcycles registered in the state of California than in all the other states combined.

I bought my first motor scooter, a Cushman, when I was thirteen. Cushmans had small wheels and the motor mounted on a tin scooter-type frame. An oval box on top of the frame served as the seat. After you kick-started them, little gearshifts and a two-speed shifter made them go. We could throttle those suckers up to forty miles per hour. Mustangs looked like miniature motorcycles with a Briggs & Stratton motor and a fairly small gas tank. During the early fifties when Cushmans and Mustangs were really popular, a brand-new Mustang cost a few hundred bucks, but a used Cushman went for around twenty dollars. So we rode Cushmans.

I was bored stiff with school. I wanted to ride. A guy named Joe Macco drove demolition derby hardtops for a Signal gas station around the corner from where I lived. Joe was twenty-one (old and wise to a fourteen-year-old like me). They called the cars hardtops. They were those neat little '32 Fords. We'd weld a roll bar over the top of these Fords and nobody cared if they got wrecked or not. Joe and his buddy Marty let me paint the numbers on the hardtops, and on Saturday nights we'd all go down to the races at the Cow Palace in San Francisco and watch Joe smash up those wrecks.

My brother-in-law Bud (sister Shirley's husband) bought used cars and fixed them up for extra cash. Bud and Shirley had a big backyard filled with old heaps that he would buy on the cheap and we'd both work on. I liked working on cars, but I really dug motorcycles. Compared to a car, a bike is a much more personal thing. You can pull the motor off, spread it all out on your workbench, and not have your head stuck down in the hood of some big hunk of steel.

A trailer rental shop opened up next door to my house, and the guy who ran the yard owned a bike too. He let me work for him, and he would take me out for rides on his Norton motorcycle. Riding the Norton, I realized how much more powerful they were than Cushmans or Mustangs.

I saved my dough and bought my first real motorcycle when I was eighteen after being discharged from the Army. The average motorcycle rider was still a little older than I was. I was always the younger guy riding out in front with my friends, most of whom were in their middle twenties. The big bike companies in those days were BSA, Triumph, Norton, Harley-Davidson, and Indian. I went for the Harley and got myself a used 1936 model that, counting tax and license, set me back $125. Gasoline was nineteen cents per gallon, so now I had a cheap way to cruise the streets of Oakland. I was finally on the loose.

Motorcycles were built on rigid frames then, which meant they would vibrate when you rode them. When you hit bumps or a pothole there wasn't a lot of flex on the frame. The constant vibration caused a lot of parts and pieces to come loose and fall off, sometimes when you were riding. You had to constantly wrench up your bike just to keep it shipshape.

Messing around with motorcycles is something I do best. It seems I've been working on motorcycles all my life, modifying them, chopping them, customizing them to my own taste, then changing my mind, breaking them down, and starting over again.

The original Harleys were flatheads. A flathead literally means the head of the engine is flat and it has valves on the side like a flathead Ford engine. My 1936 Harley had overhead valves, instead of valves on the side going up and down. These were called knuckleheads, because they had a big aluminum block on the side where the pushrods went, looking like a knuckle. In 1948, Harley changed over to a tin cover called a panhead, which evolved in 1966 to an aluminum cover called a shovelhead. Different engine heads never overlapped on Harleys; when they changed, they changed across the board. In 1984, Harley converted to a different-looking engine they call an Evolution head.

Harley has enjoyed a huge share of the large-bike market for decades. They control about fifty percent of cruiser sales, with Japanese bikes making up the other half. As a result, they often act a little high and mighty toward their customers.

An official at Harley-Davidson was once quoted as saying, "Enough bikes is too many, and if we make enough, we lose mystique." While they keep saying they're building more and more each year, up until a couple of years ago I believe Harley-Davidson intentionally held back production to stir up demand. Now there are companies like Titan, American Eagle, and American Illusion imitating Harley's Softail model. That's the fifties-styled bike all these new riders want. Softail-type bikes look like rigid-frames but really aren't, and they don't necessarily ride "soft" either. Although they're equipped with shock absorbers, if you ride them over fifty-five miles per hour on the open road you're not going to experience a smooth ride. The motor is not rubber-mounted; it's not much different from a 1936 Harley in the ride. They still tend to break and vibrate if you ride them too fast. For riders who just want to ride down to the bar every Saturday night, the Softail is Harley's best selling bike for modern times, and the design incorporated the cool look of the chopper. In 2000, Harley came out with an 88B motor that is counterbalanced and does not vibrate.

Titan, American Eagle, and American Illusion make what they call "clone bikes," and although some of these models are manufactured in America, they often don't make their own engines and are just copies of Harleys.

But Hell's Angels started riding Harley-Davidsons mostly because, unlike today, they didn't have much choice. In 1957, it was either ride a Harley or settle for a Triumph or BSA. They'd already stopped building Indians. It's always been important for Hell's Angels to ride American-made machines. In terms of pure workmanship, personally I don't like Harleys. I ride them because I'm in the club, and that's the image, but if I could I would seriously consider riding a Honda ST1100 or a BMW. We really missed the boat not switching over to the Japanese models when they began building bigger bikes. I'll usually say, "Fuck Harley-Davidson. You can buy an ST1100 and the motherfucker will do 110 miles per hour right from the factory all day long." The newest "rice rockets" can carry 140 horsepower to the rear wheel, and can easily do 180 miles per hour right out of the box. While it's probably too late to switch over now, it would have been a nice move, because Japanese bikes today are so much cheaper and better built. However, Japanese motorcycles don't have as much personality.

I ride a Harley FXRT because it's their best model for people who put on a lot of miles. Harley doesn't make them anymore, but they're the best of both worlds—it's a good bike for long distances and also handles and corners well on the short runs. It's not as heavy as their other dresser models, but they ride a little faster, and they still come with saddlebags for traveling. But my FXRT is lucky if it does ninety, that is, until I work on it. After you work on it, you make it unreliable. I always say, the faster a Harley, the less reliable. New Triumphs can do a quarter mile in ten seconds. If you get a Harley street bike to run a quarter mile like that, it's a bomb. The worst thing about it is that once you get a Harley going that fast, you can't stop it. Right now, Hell's Angels are stuck with Harleys, or maybe we're stuck with each other. Someday we'll be smart enough to walk away.

A Harley FXR is the bike of choice for most Hell's Angels today. FXRs have a rubber-mounted motor on a swing-arm frame. A swing arm means the frame houses left and right shock absorbers in the back section for better road flex. Harley developed the FXR as a reaction to bike riders like the Hell's Angels who preferred more stripped-down bikes. The FXR and the FXRT are basically the same bike. The FXR is more stripped-down, while the FXRT was designed as a touring bike with saddlebags and a fairing, which is the plastic piece that holds the windshield and reduces the wind on the rider.

The FXR is an efficient bike for speed and distance. For years, most Hell's Angels usually rode rigid-frame bikes. Nowadays, they're switching over to FXRs because they're riding out of state more, going longer distances, and riding faster.

As far as what Harley manufactures, the FXR handled and rode the best, so everybody bought them. After 1993, Harley-Davidson stopped making the FXR. When the 1999 limited series came out, they were list-priced at $17,000. Because of demand, the shops sold them for as much as $25,000. The Dyna Glide has since replaced the FXR. In my opinion it's not as good a bike because it doesn't handle as well as an FXR.

What it's really all about with a Harley-Davidson is the sound . . . everybody loves that fucking rumble. Another thing Harley owners really crave about their bikes is the low-end torque, the raw power coming out of the gate. It runs out pretty quick once you get up past ninety miles an hour. Most Harley riders don't care about high speed, they'd rather have that low-end torque, the one that gurgles down in your groin and gives you the feeling of power. The Japanese bikes, while they *have* the power, they don't quite have the *feeling* of power. You can hook a rope up to a Harley and pull a Mack truck. You can't do that with a Japanese bike. Even though the power is there, you'd tear the clutch right out.

In the early sixties, Honda had an ad, "You meet the nicest people on a Honda." That really turned the Hell's Angels off and knocked Harley for a loop with the average consumer. Honda had such tiny bikes, 50cc and 100cc bikes, the biggest one being a 450cc. Later, when they started coming out with 900, 1100, and 1200 and even those big 1500cc bikes, man, that's some machinery Harley can't touch. Kawasaki and some of the Japanese sport bikes have better brakes and more horsepower and handle easier.

What Harley has is brute horsepower. A brand-new Harley comes with about forty-nine to fifty-two horsepower to the rear wheel. After I've done a little work on mine, I'll get eighty-one horses to the rear wheel.

Up until 1984, Harley-Davidsons were famous for leaking oil. Even when they were brand-new, they leaked, and dealers had to put pieces of cardboard under them in the showroom. Early Harleys came with oil leaks because the tin primary cases had ineffective cork gaskets around them. Sometimes the motors weren't machined properly. If you didn't start your bike for a week, the oil accumulated through the oil pump and into the crankcase. Once you started it, it spit oil all over the ground. After stricter quality control and extra research and development at the factory, they eventually took care of the problem with the new Evolution motor.

If you fix an older Harley right, they won't leak. You'll *never* find a drop of oil under my bike because I refuse to believe motorcycles have to leak. What I do is make sure all the seals are quality, that everything is sealed up right. If I see oil seeping, I wash the parts and replace the gaskets. I guess I'm a bit of a fanatic. The only time you'll see a drop of oil under my motorcycle is after I've run it hard at high speeds. One drop comes out of the breather tube as a result of condensation a while after stopping. I probably could solve that by installing a one-way PCV valve that only lets the engine breathe in, keeping the oil from leaking out. But I'd rather let that single drop continue to leak, because I still want my engine to breathe out.

With speed limits being raised across the United States, I recently installed a RevTech six-speed transmission by Custom Chrome, Inc., in my bike. Having a sixth gear instead of a normal five-speed is like an overdrive and it's really nice. You can hit ninety-five miles per hour and not have your engine rev up. It relieves stress on the motor. If you're doing ninety-five on the highway and turning 5,000 revolutions per minute, you can now do the same speed and only be turning 3,500 RPM. I'm also awaiting my eighty-eight-cubic-inch CCI RevTech motor to go along with the six-speed transmission.

Harley-Davidson has yet to convert to six speeds, while some Jap bikes are already going up to seven speeds. I believe most Harley riders will want to convert to six speeds. When we had three speeds, riders wanted four. When Harley went to four speeds, people dreamed about five-speed motorcycles. Harley six-speed bikes are only a matter of time.

Even though average Harley enthusiasts like the Softail and drive short distances, they'll instinctively want what the Hell's Angels want—

faster horses and more efficient overdrive. Motorcycles went to bigger motors (from eighty inches to eighty-eight to ninety-five) because riders like the Hell's Angels kept pushing for more. When the rubber meets the road, the yuppies and the RUBbers (rich urban bikers) will want what we want.

HELL'S ANGEL "CHOPPERS" were born when we started taking the front fenders off our bikes, cutting off the back fender, and changing the handlebars. When you watch *The Wild One*, check out the bikes. Lee Marvin and his crew were riding Harleys and Indians with cut front fenders. They hadn't gone to smaller tanks or different wheels. When the Hell's Angels came along, we started taking our bikes apart, improving them and fucking with Harley's formula designs.

When you'd buy a new motorcycle it came equipped with standard features. First we would take the windshields off, then throw out the saddlebags and switch the big old ugly seat (with springs) with a smaller, skinny seat. We didn't need all of those lights either. We converted the oversized headlight to a smaller beam, replaced the straight handlebars with a set of high bars, and replaced the bigger gas tanks with small teardrop-shaped tanks. We used old Mustang motorcycle gas tanks until the mid-fifties, when we started using narrow Sportster gas tanks. The tanks were changed for looks, because the wide and thick stock tanks on a Harley covered up the top of the motor. The design of the bike became radically streamlined, the curvature of the body narrow and sleek. It looked cooler if the front end was longer with a skinny front wheel. Plus you could see the whole motor, a real extra for a street machine.

Next we'd toss the front fender, then cut the back one or make an even thinner fender from the tire cover mount of a 1936 Ford. That made a beautiful back fender for a Harley with a sixteen-inch tire, and it was practical too.

The standard color on Harley frames used to always be black. The gas tank and fenders would be another color. When we built our own bikes we made the frames the same color as the gas tanks and molded it so you didn't see any welding marks. We'd chrome every part we could and install dual carburetors. The results of all the customizing we did were a lot of trophies at the competitions.

I painted myself like a pumpkin to match the new orange of my motorcycle on Halloween night at the Fillmore, 1968. Someone who worked at the Bay Bridge brought me some orange spray cans, so I painted my bike with what soon became "Oakland Orange." It was kinda a bright racing orange. During the Oakland Hell's Angels' 1960s days, orange became a very popular color, and a lot of Oakland members painted their bikes that color. Forget the symbolism, it was free paint.

We painted our death heads and designs on the gas tanks. Tommy the Greek, an old car painter in Oakland, was our man. You immediately recognized Tommy the Greek's designs because he had a very distinctive flame design. Big Daddy Roth picked up on Tommy's style too. Von Dutch was another artist whose customized paintwork was admired, especially in SoCal. There were other artists like Len Barton in the Bay Area, Gil Avery in Fresno, Art Hemsel, and Red Lee who were well known for painting cool designs on gas tanks. Arlen Ness, who is one of the leading sellers of bike parts today, got his start as a bike painter. When the Harleys came fresh from the factory, guys like Arlen would take them apart and paint everything one color to match, using fancy shades like candy-apple red.

As opposed to choppers, "full dressers" are motorcycles that keep all of the original manufacturer's pieces on, plus they add accessories like fancy Plexiglas windshields, mud flaps, leather saddlebags, aerials for their radios with raccoon tails on them, extended fenders with a lot of chrome, and *lots* of lights. Too much useless gear, man. The street term for full dressers is "garbage wagons," and in the old days you'd never catch a Hell's Angel on one of them. The casual weekender who was going down to visit his mother-in-law usually rode a full dresser. Or maybe off-duty cops.

These days if I was just a long-distance rider, I'd go for the Harley-Davidson Road King. The Road King is better than Harley's Dyna Glide for long distances. The Road King is a rubber-mounted, stripped-down version of the full dresser. It still has saddlebags and the fairing, but doesn't have stuff like a radio and the big passenger seat.

The Hell's Angels crafted a whole different type of motorcycle. Just like Corvette and Thunderbird helped create the sportscar look for Ford and Chevy, we created the chopper look from Harley-Davidsons. Hell's Angels didn't buy a lot of parts. We made them. I made the first set of high bars that I ever had from the chairs of those old chrome tables in the fifties with Formica tops. You'd get a set of those chairs and they were one inch thick and already bent. You cut off the two ends of the chair, and bang, you had a set of high bars.

Some of the other ways we'd modify our bikes were when we took the rigid front end of one bike, cut it off, took another rigid, cut *it* off, and welded them together to make the front end six inches longer. By extending the front end of the bike out, the frame dropped lower. Then we'd install the narrow fenders, grab rails, and sissy bars. We made our own sissy bars and foot pegs, molding them out of metal, bending and welding them to our own specifications. By the late 1960s and early 1970s, we might chop a bike to make it sit lower, but we didn't usually cut the frame. It only seemed that way since our seats sat way back, right up on the rear fender.

The only parts we had to buy were for the internal engine and transmission parts. I've probably spent half of my life in a garage so I always have a garage full of spare parts. We'd cut down the fly-wheels on the left side to make them lighter so the bike would take off quicker. For top-end performance for the long hauls, a heavier flywheel was better, but it was important to us to take off quick.

It was a macho thing to have what we called suicide clutches and jockey shifts, where you would shift gears with your left hand and operate a clutch system with your left foot. Before bikes had electronic ignitions, we would install magnetos to eliminate the need for batteries and coils. A magneto generates electricity for the spark plugs when you kick-start the bike. It was just another way to slim down our choppers.

For the quick takeoff as well, we put in new cams and solid push rods, installed bigger valves and new pistons, punched out the carburetor, and put closer-ratio gears inside the transmission with bigger sprockets to make our motorcycles accelerate faster. Everything had to do with takeoff.

The back wheels were changed to an eighteen-inch wheel, and a twenty-one-inch was used for the front. From the axle down, an eighteen-inch rim with a 450×18 tire leaves four and a half inches of tire from the rim to the ground. A twenty-one-inch wheel leaves you only about two and a half inches of tire, so while it really doesn't raise or lower the bike that much, it makes it significantly narrower and faster because of less tire on the ground.

The best deals for bikes were used Harley-Davidsons that the police departments sold. By the way, they still auction them today. Two hundred bucks in the sixties would buy about six or seven thousand dollars in bikes and parts today. The highway patrol—in the days of shovelhead engines—would put twenty thousand miles on bikes before rebuilding them. After forty thousand miles, they'd send them to their academies. Their reasoning was they thought the bikes suffered too much metal fatigue. When the academy was through with them, they'd auction them off, which is when we would buy them. One of the reasons Hell's Angels have stayed loyal to Harley-Davidsons is that a Harley can always be rebuilt, no matter what happens to it—unless it catches on fire and burns. That's why you can still see 1936 Harleys on the road today. They are indestructible if you maintain them.

In the early sixties, the serial number on a motorcycle didn't really matter. They were on the left side of the engine case, and if the number matched your pink slip, you were okay, whether it was a factory number or inscribed with a punch. The cops then didn't give a shit if you had lights or license plates. Once bikes started getting stolen, the law got more particular. The vehicle registration laws tightened up and there started being a few more rules. Now even frames have ID numbers.

A lot of the guys in the club would experiment with different things. We'd move our brake to the middle of the bike, replacing the old one with a hydraulic model. Harley-Davidson picked up on that modification and put it on all of their stock bikes. We also changed the kickstands by taking them off the front of the bike and moving them to the middle. Then Harley started doing that on their Sportsters and later on the Big Twins. For kick-start mechanisms, one of the things I always did was cut the kick-start pedal in half and add an inch and a half so you could start a lot easier. To make a motorcycle start, you have to spin the motor enough, and the faster you spin the motor, the easier it starts. If, like me, you weighed 150 pounds and you leaned into the pedal, that extra inch and a half would increase the kick. If you weighed over 250 pounds like Junkie George or Big Al, starting a bike was a snap.

We designed and built a bike that ran damn smooth, using the least amount of parts and accessories. Choppers were stripped down for speed, looks, and ultimate discomfort. After we got through with them, they weren't the easiest bikes to ride, but what the hell, at least we looked cool. It became a style and look: a bitch bar (sissy bar) so your chick could lay back. When we'd ride down the street, people would check us out—and that was what it was all about.

The government started getting nervous about motorcycle clubs chopping up their bikes. Laws were passed, and as club members started raking bikes and putting on long front ends, the highway patrol helped pass laws regulating handlebar height. For a while, we ran with no front brakes. We didn't need them. A small spool wheel with nice long spokes and no front brakes looked real nice. Then a law was passed requiring front brakes. Some of our handlebars were well over shoulder height. The law was uptight and arbitrary that handlebars should be at shoulder level and no higher. They claimed you couldn't control the bike if your handlebars were too high, which is nuts. We tried to explain to lawmakers that above-shoulder-level handlebars were more comfortable on long rides. The dumb-fuck politicians didn't even consider that's how the everyday person controls their car. Look at people as they drive their cars and notice how they place their hands: On top of the steering wheel—well above shoulder level. It's natural. But I guess since we the Hell's Angels did it, they had to get us for something.

In the early days of motorcycling, nobody even thought about wearing a helmet. Now, of course, there are laws in many states. While I was in jail in 1991, California finally passed its helmet law. In the sixties, I was instrumental in keeping the helmet law off the books. There was a San Francisco assemblyman named John Foran who crusaded relentlessly to pass the first helmet law. I was always in his face, fighting him, and for three or four years, I beat him every time. The final time we clashed, he came up to me and said, "You know, Sonny, next year I'm presenting a bill in front of the assembly that says only *you* have to wear a helmet."

As a club it became our personal mission, so we rode to Sacramento to fight their laws on the steps of the capitol building. It always brought out the news cameras when the Hell's Angels helped lead the battle against helmet laws, because the motorcycle industry was too chickenshit to wage a visible fight against the California assembly. The motorcycle industry was caught in a huge public relations dilemma. They didn't want to see the law passed either, but they were afraid of looking like they weren't safety-conscious. Motorcycle manufacturers never wanted the law passed, because wearing a helmet implied that a motorcycle wasn't safe. The Hell's Angels didn't mind being labeled the bad guys should the law pass. We were used to it.

IT'S FUNNY WHEN you think about it now, but in order to look cool and have our own look, we cannibalized Harleys to the point where Harley dealers didn't even want us near their shops. We'd destroyed the original Harley design and image by taking stuff off "their" bikes and replacing them with our very own parts. Some Harley-Davidson shops refused to sell us anything. Members used to have to send in their old ladies to pick up parts.

To Harley-Davidson, we made motorcycle riding look bad. Even if we did, we also made them tons of dough for the notoriety of us riding Harley-Davidsons. In the 1950s, people were so intimidated by Harleys that if you rode one sometimes you wouldn't get waited on in restaurants or they wouldn't give you a room at a motel.

I think the Hell's Angels are responsible for a lot of the current designs and workmanship on modern motorcycles. When you look at current custom Softail motorcycles (not the full dressers) you see a lot of our design innovations. Our chopper motorcycles inspired even kids' bicycles, like the Schwinn Sting Ray with its banana seat and gooseneck handlebars. It was only a matter of time before everybody on top would cash in on selling custom motorcycle parts. Custom motorcycles and bike-riding gear has become a bigger business than ever. Thank the Hell's Angels for that.

STOLEN BIKES HAVE always been a major, let's say, preoccupation with clubs like ours. The Hell's Angels have a rule that with any bike riders who come over and party with us, you cannot steal their motorcycle if it's parked in front of the clubhouse or in front of a member's house. Now that's fair, isn't it? In 1967, three Angels, Big Al Perryman, Fu Griffin, and Cisco Valderrama, stole twenty-seven motorcycles in one day. It's gotta be some kind of world record. The story goes that there were twenty-seven bikers from this nameless club from California that came down to party with the Richmond Hell's Angels one weekend. The clubhouse got raided and everybody went to jail. Cisco needed a twenty-one inch skinny front wheel, but he knew we had this rule not to steal any bike stuff parked in front of the clubhouse. Cisco knew about the party and all the jailing that went on, so hey, who was gonna miss a front wheel? But a rule is a rule. That's when Big Al and Cisco came up with the scheme of stealing all the bikes. Fuck the front wheel, they wanted the whole enchilada. They rolled all the bikes down the block and parked them there overnight. The next day they figured they were fair game — they weren't in front of an Angels clubhouse anymore and nobody else had stolen them. Fu drove them down in Cisco's '65 Impala convertible and they started bringing them back two by two to Oakland and stashing them at Fu's house. When they were through they had a bike shop, twenty-seven to be exact, all for one lousy front wheel. They stripped them all down and now they had a big — a really big — parts shop.

Then I found out about it.

Cisco and Big Al were in trouble again. They'd fucked up. I told them they'd crossed a thin line between right and wrong, so I made them return every bike. Actually, since they had already been stripped down, we had to have each guy come over to Fu's house and pick up his stolen motorcycle in a box.

But what goes around comes around, because one year later, in 1968, my bike, my honey, my pride, my joy, got ripped off, and boy was I pissed.

Sweet Cocaine. I couldn't believe anybody would steal my beautiful hand-built bike. *Sweet Cocaine* was featured on the album cover of the *Hell's Angels '69* soundtrack. I built it from the ground up, and never a wrench was turned on that bike without the sweet sniff of cocaine. When I finished that bike, I built a miniature Sportster version of the same model for my girlfriend Sharon, calling hers *Little Cocaine.*

I was in Hayward at a jewelry store buying my sister a ring when I heard two ladies who were working in the store talking.

"He must be in his car, because I don't see his motorcycle."

"Are you referring to me?" I asked them. "My bike's right outside."

I walked outside, and sure enough *Sweet Cocaine* was gone. The two ladies had called the cops, but when the police showed up, I told them I had walked to the store. There must have been some mistake. Inside, my guts were on fire, but on the outside I didn't want any cops involved in the search. I remained calm. I got on the phone and called for an emergency meeting with the club.

"Everybody looks for my bike," I told everyone in a rage. "Nobody, and I mean nobody, rides a motorcycle in this town until I get *Sweet Cocaine* back."

Sharon manned the phones at home while everybody else scoured the area. The first calls came in and someone reported seeing a pink Cadillac near the jewelry store. I went from bar to bar, grilling people, asking about the bike, the Cadillac, anything. I wanted the fucking thing back *now*. Meanwhile, every known bike thief was calling. Rick Motley, one of the better-known bike thieves—now dead—called the house and told Sharon he would rather have the Army, the Navy, the Marines, and the Green Berets after him than Sonny Barger and the Hell's Angels looking for *Sweet Cocaine*.

Then we got a vital lead. The Cadillac proved to be a dead end. Some delivery guy outside the jewelry store had seen a guy riding away on a bike, wearing a vest with only a bottom rocker. With a rough description of the guy and the color of his patch, we narrowed it down real quick to a club called the Unknowns. We knew which bar they hung out in, so we raced over there and grabbed up a couple of them fast and asked them what their prospects were up to. Prospects are prospective members who'll do anything, anytime, to anyone just to get into a club. I asked about their prospects because they were crazy motherfuckers with no brains, no history, and usually no future. According to one of the members, yeah, a couple of prospects were tearing down a bike they had just stolen. I told them, "That bike is mine, motherfucker, and you're going to help me get it back."

The prospects who stole the bike didn't know whom it belonged to. The guys who *told* them to steal it probably knew it was mine. I had the registration by the back license plate in a clear round glass tube. The guys tearing it down for parts that night had everything unbolted, but when they got to the registration holder, they knew they were in deep,

deep shit. Rather than return *Sweet Cocaine*, they dumped it into the Oakland Estuary.

We rounded up everybody who was responsible, tied them up, and took them over to my house on Golf Links Road. Sharon was supposed to keep an eye on them, but it was a good thing we tied them up because it was so late at night Sharon kept falling asleep clutching her gun. Every half hour or so, the front door would open and another accomplice was tossed into the living room. When we found the last guy the punishment began. One at a time we bullwhipped them and beat them with spiked dog collars, broke their fingers with ball peen hammers. One of them screamed at us, "Why don't you just kill us and get it over with?"

Then we took their motorcycles, sold them, and disbanded their club.

Moral of the story—don't get caught stealing a Hell's Angel's bike, especially if it's the president's.

© Martin Dixon

from

THE MOTORCYCLE DIARIES

ernesto "che" guevara

LET'S GET THINGS STRAIGHT

this isn't a tale of derring-do, nor is it merely some kind of 'cynical account'; it isn't meant to be, at least. It's a chunk of two lives running parallel for a while, with common aspirations and similar dreams. In nine months a man can think a lot of thoughts, from the height of philosophical conjecture to the most abject longing for a bowl of soup—in perfect harmony with the state of his stomach. And if, at the same time, he's a bit of an adventurer, he could have experiences which might interest other people and his random account would read something like this diary.

So, the coin was tossed, turned somersaults; sometimes coming up heads, sometimes tails. Man, the measure of all things, speaks through my mouth and recounts in my own words what my eyes saw. Out of ten possible heads I may have only seen one tail, or vice versa: there are no excuses; my mouth says what my eyes told it. Was our view too narrow, too biased, too hasty, were our conclusions too rigid? Maybe so, but this is how the typewriter interprets the disparate impulses which made you press the keys, and those fleeting impulses are dead. Besides, no one is answerable to them. The person who wrote these notes died the day he stepped back on Argentine soil. The person who is reorganizing and polishing them, me, is no longer me, at least I'm not the me I was. Wandering around our 'America with a capital A' has changed me more than I thought.

Any book on photographic technique can show you the image of a nocturnal landscape with the full moon shining and the accompanying text revealing the secret of this sunlit darkness. But the reader doesn't really know what kind of sensitive fluid covers my retina, I'm hardly aware of it myself, so you can't examine the plate to find out the actual moment it was taken. If I present a nocturnal picture, you have to take it or leave it, it's not important. Unless you actually know the landscape my diary photographed, you've no option but to accept my version. I now leave you with myself, the man I once was . . .

PRODROMES

It was an October morning. I'd taken advantage of the holiday on the 17th[1] and gone to Córdoba. We were under the vine at Alberto Granado's, drinking sweet maté,[2] commenting on the latest events in this 'wretched life', and tinkering with La Poderosa II.[3] Alberto was grumbling about having had to quit his job at the leper colony in San Francisco del Chañar and how badly paid he now was at the Hospital Español. I'd also had to quit my job but, unlike him, I was happy to leave. Still, I was restless too, mainly because I was a dreamer and a free spirit; I was fed up with medical school, hospitals and exams.

Our fantasizing took us to faraway places, sailing tropical seas, travelling through Asia. And suddenly, slipping in as if part of our fantasy, came the question: 'Why don't we go to North America?'

'North America? How?'

'On La Poderosa, man.'

That's how the trip came about, and it never deviated from the general principle laid down then: improvisation. Alberto's brothers joined us and a round of maté sealed our pact not to give up until our dream was a reality. Next came the tedious business of chasing visas, certificates and documents, and overcoming all the hurdles modern nations put in the way of would-be travellers. To save face, just in case, we decided to say we were going to Chile. My main task before leaving was to take exams in as many subjects as possible; Alberto's to get the bike ready for the long journey and study the route. At that stage the momentousness of our endeavour hadn't dawned on us, all we could see was the dusty road ahead and us on our bike devouring kilometres in the flight northward.

DISCOVERING THE OCEAN

The full moon, silhouetted over the sea, showers the waves with silvery sparks. Sitting on a dune, watching the continuous ebb and flow, we each think our different thoughts. For me, the sea has always been a confidant, a friend which absorbs all you tell it without betraying your secrets, and always gives the best advice—a sound you can interpret as you wish. For Alberto, it is a new, oddly perturbing spectacle, reflected in the intensity with which his gaze follows every wave swelling then dying on the beach. At almost thirty, Alberto is seeing the Atlantic for the first time and is overwhelmed by a discovery which opens up infinite routes to all points of the globe. The fresh breeze fills the senses with the power of the sea, it transforms all it touches; even Come-back[4] gazes, his funny little snout aloft, at the silver ribbon unfurling before him several times a minute. Come-back is a symbol and a survivor: a symbol of the bond demanding my return; a survivor of his own mishaps—two crashes in which his little bag flew off the back of the bike, being trodden underfoot by a horse, and persistent diarrhoea.

We're in Villa Gesell, north of Mar del Plata, being entertained by an uncle of mine, and taking stock of our first 1,200 kilometres—supposedly the easiest, yet they've already taught us a healthy respect for distances. Whether we make it or not, it's going to be tough, that's obvious already. Alberto laughs at his minutely detailed plans for the trip, according to which we should already be on the last lap when in fact we're only just starting out.

We left Gesell well stocked with vegetables and tinned meat 'donated' by my uncle. He asked us to send a telegram if we reach Bariloche so he can buy a lottery ticket with the same number as the telegram; a bit of an exaggeration, we thought. Others added, 'The bike's a good excuse for jogging,' and so on. We're determined to prove them wrong, but a natural apprehension keeps us from advertising our mutual confidence.

Along the coast road Come-back keeps up his affinity for aviation but emerges unscathed from a fresh head-on bang. The bike is very hard to control because the extra weight on a rack behind the centre of gravity lifts the front wheel at the slightest lapse in concentration and sends us flying. We stop at a butcher's and buy some meat to grill and milk for the dog, who won't touch it. I begin to worry more about the animal's health than the cash I'd coughed up for it. The meat turns out to be horse. It's incredibly sweet and we can't eat it. Fed up, I chuck a bit away and the dog wolfs it down in no time. Amazed, I throw it another piece and the same thing happens. The milk regime is lifted. In Miramar, in the midst of the uproar caused by Come-back's admirers, I enter a . . .

. . . ROMANTIC INTERLUDE

It isn't really the purpose of this diary to recount the days in Miramar where Come-back found a new home, at one of whose residents in particular the name was directed. The trip hung in the balance, in a cocoon, subordinate to the word which consents and ties.

Alberto saw the danger and was already imagining himself alone on the highways and byways of America, but he said nothing. The tug of war was between her and me. For a moment Otero Silva's poem[5] rang in my ears as I left, I thought, victorious:

> I heard on the boat
> Wet feet splashing
> And felt faces dusk with hunger
> My heart a pendulum between her and the street
> What strength broke me free from her eyes
> Loose from her arms
> She stood tears clouding her grief
> Behind rain and window pane
> But unable to cry: Wait
> I'll go with you!

Afterwards I wasn't sure if driftwood had the right to say 'I succeeded' when the tide threw it up on the beach it sought; but that was later. Later is of no interest to now. The two days I'd planned stretched like elastic into eight and with the bitter-sweet taste of the goodbye mingling with my inveterate halitosis I finally felt myself wafted away on the winds of adventure towards worlds which I fancied stranger than they were, in situations I imagined much more normal than they turned out to be.

I remember the day my friend the sea decided to come to my aid and rescue me from limbo. The beach was deserted and a cold wind blew towards the land. My head lay in the lap which tied me to these shores. The whole universe floated rhythmically by, obeying impulses from my voice within, lulled by everything around. Suddenly a stronger gust of wind brought a different voice from the sea; I lifted my head in surprise, it was nothing, a false alarm. I settled my head back, returned my dreams to the caressing lap again, when I heard the sea's warning once more. Its vast discordant rhythm hammered at the fortress in me and threatened its imposing serenity. We felt cold and left the beach, fleeing the perturbing presence which refused to leave me. On that small stretch of beach the sea pranced about indifferent to its eternal law and spawned the note of caution, the warning. But a man in love (Alberto used a juicier, less literary word) is in no condition to listen to that kind of signal; in the great belly of the Buick the bourgeois side of my universe was still under construction.

The first commandment for every good explorer is: An expedition has two points; the point of departure and the point of arrival. If you want to make the second theoretical point coincide with the actual point, don't think about the means (the expedition is a hypothetical space which ends where it ends, so there are as many means as there are means to an end, that is, the means are limitless).

I remembered Alberto's exhortation: 'The bracelet or you're not who you think you are.'

Her hands disappeared in the hollow of mine.

'Chichina, that bracelet . . . Can I take it to guide me and remind me of you?'

Poor thing! I know the gold didn't matter, despite what they say: her fingers were merely weighing up the love that made me ask for it. At least, that's what I honestly think. Alberto says (a bit mischievously, I feel), that you don't need very sensitive fingers to weigh up the twenty-nine carats of my love.

CUTTING THE LAST TIES

Our next stop was Necochea where an old university friend of Alberto's had his practice. We made it easily in a morning, arriving just at steak time, and received a cordial welcome from the friend and a not so cordial one from his wife who saw danger in our resolutely bohemian ways.

'You qualify as a doctor in a year's time yet you're going away? And you've no idea when you'll be back. Why?'

Not getting a precise answer to her desperate whys and wherefores made her hair stand on end. She treated us courteously but her hostility was plain despite the fact she knew (I think she knew) victory was hers, that her husband was beyond 'redemption.'

In Mar del Plata we'd visited a doctor friend of Alberto's who had joined the Party,[6] with all the privileges that entailed. This one in Necochea remained faithful to his—the radicals—yet we were as remote from one as from the other. Radicalism, which had never been a tenable political position for me, was also losing its grip on Alberto who had been friendly at one time with certain of the leaders he respected. When we mounted our bike again, after thanking the couple for giving us three days of the good life, we journeyed on to Bahía Blanca, feeling a little lonelier but a good deal freer. Friends were expecting us there too, friends of mine this time, and they also offered us generous and cordial hospitality. We spent several days in this southern port, fixing the bike and wandering round the city. These were the last days when we did not have to think about money. A rigid diet of meat, polenta and bread would have to be followed to the letter to stretch our pathetic monetary resources. Bread now tasted of warning: 'I won't be so easy to get soon, man.' And we swallowed it with all the more gusto. Like camels, we wanted to store up reserves for what lay ahead.

The night before our departure, I came down with quite a high temperature, which made us a day late leaving Bahía Blanca. We finally left at three in the afternoon, under a blazing sun which was even hotter by the time we reached the sand dunes round Médanos. The bike, with its badly distributed load, kept leaping out of control and spinning over. Alberto fought a stubborn duel with the sand which he insists he won. The truth is that we found ourselves resting comfortably on our backsides in the sand six times before we finally got out on to the flat. We did get out, however, and this is my comrade's main argument for claiming victory over Médanos.

Setting off again, I took the controls and accelerated to make up for lost time. A fine sand covered part of the bend and, wham: the worst crash of our whole expedition. Alberto came out unscathed but the cylinder trapped my foot and scorched it, leaving an unpleasant souvenir for a long time because the wound didn't heal.

A heavy downpour forced us to seek shelter at an *estancia*,[7] but to reach it we had to go three hundred metres up a muddy track which sent us flying another couple of times. The welcome was magnificent but the toll of our first experience on unpaved roads was alarming: nine spills in a single day. However, lying on camp beds, the only beds we'd know from now on, beside La Poderosa, our snail-like abode, we looked into the future with impatient joy. We seemed to breathe more freely, a lighter air, an air of adventure. Faraway countries, heroic deeds, beautiful women whirled round and round in our turbulent imaginations. But in tired eyes which nevertheless refused sleep, a pair of green dots representing the world I'd left mocked the freedom I sought, hitching their image to my fantasy flight across the lands and seas of the world.

REMEDY FOR FLU: BED

The bike snorted with boredom along the long accident-free road and we snorted with fatigue. Driving on a gravel-covered road had changed a pleasant spree into a heavy chore. And a whole day of tacking turns at the controls had by night-time left us with a greater desire to sleep than to make the effort to reach Choele Choel, a biggish town where there was the chance of free lodging. We stopped in Benjamín Zorrilla and settled down comfortably in a room at the railway station. We slept like logs.

The next morning we got up early, but when I went to fetch water for our maté, a strange sensation ran through my body followed by a shiver. Ten minutes later I was trembling uncontrollably like a man possessed. My quinine tablets were no use, my head was like a drum beating out strange rhythms, weird colours passed shapelessly round the walls and some desperate retching produced a green vomit. I spent the whole day in that state, unable to eat a thing, until the evening, when I felt fit enough to climb on the bike and, dozing on Alberto's shoulder, reached Choele Choel. We went straight to see Dr Barrera, the director of the little hospital and a member of parliament. He received us amiably, giving us a room to sleep in. He put me on a course of penicillin which lowered my temperature within four hours, but whenever we talked about leaving the doctor shook his head and said, 'For flu: bed.' (That was the diagnosis, for want of a better one.) So we spent several days there, being looked after like royalty. Alberto took a photo of me in my hospital garb. I looked awful: gaunt, huge eyes, a beard whose ridiculous shape didn't change much in the following months. It's a shame it wasn't a good photo; it documented our changed circumstances, our new horizons, free from the shackles of 'civilization'.

One morning the doctor didn't shake his head in the usual fashion and that was enough. We were gone within the hour, heading west towards the lakes, our next destination. Our bike struggled, showing signs it was feeling the strain, especially in the bodywork which we constantly had to fix with Alberto's favourite spare part—wire. I don't know where he picked up this quote, which he attributed to Oscar Gálvez:[8] 'Where a piece of wire can replace a screw, give me the wire, it's safer.' Our trousers and hands were proof that we sided with Gálvez, at least as far as wire was concerned.

Night had fallen and we were trying to reach human habitation: we had no lights and spending the night in the open is not pleasant. We were going along slowly with a torch when there was a strange noise we couldn't identify. The torch didn't give enough light to find the cause of the noise so we had to camp right there. We settled down for the night as best we could, put up our tent and crawled into it, hoping to smother our hunger and thirst (there was no water near by and we had no meat) with some exhausted sleep. However, in no time the evening breeze had turned into a violent gale which uprooted our tent and exposed us to the elements, to the worsening cold. We had to tie the bike to a telegraph pole and, putting the tent over it for protection, lie down behind it. The semi-hurricane prevented us from using our camp beds. It wasn't a pleasant night at all, but sleep finally triumphed over the cold, wind and everything else, and we woke at nine in the morning with the sun high over our heads.

In the light of day, we discovered that the famous noise had been the front part of the bike frame breaking. We now had to fix it as best we could and find a town where we could weld the broken bar. Our friend, the wire, solved our problem provisionally. We packed up and set off not knowing exactly how far we were from the nearest habitation. Imagine our surprise when, coming out of the next bend, we saw a house. They received us very well and appeased our hunger with exquisite roast lamb. From there we walked twenty kilometres to a place called Piedra del Águila where we could weld the part, but it was so late by then that we decided to spend the night in the mechanic's house.

Except for a couple more minor spills which didn't damage the bike too much, we continued calmly on towards San Martín de los Andes. We were almost there, and I was driving, when we took our first tumble in the South on a beautiful gravel bend by a babbling brook. This time La Poderosa's bodywork was damaged enough to make us stop and, to cap it all, we had what we most dreaded: a punctured back tyre. To be able to mend it, we had to take off all the luggage, undo all the wire securing the rack, then struggle with the wheel cover which defied our pathetic crowbar. This flat tyre (lazily done, I admit) lost us two hours. Late in the afternoon we stopped at an *estancia* whose owners, very welcoming Germans, had in the past put up an uncle of mine, an inveterate old traveller whose example I was now emulating. They said we could fish in the river flowing through the *estancia*. Alberto cast his line, and before he knew what was happening, he had a fleeting form glinting in the sunlight jumping about on the end of his hook. It was a rainbow trout, a beautiful fish, succulent and fleshy (at least it was when baked and seasoned by our hunger). I prepared the fish while Alberto cast his line again and again, but he didn't get a single bite despite hours of trying. It was dark by then, so we had to spend the night in the farm labourers' kitchen.

At five in the morning, the huge stove which occupies the middle of this kind of kitchen was lit and the whole place filled with smoke. The farm labourers passed round their bitter maté and cast aspersions on our own 'girlish' maté, as they call sweet maté in those parts. They weren't very communicative on the whole, typical of the subjugated Araucanian race, still wary of the white man who in the past brought them so much misfortune and still exploits them. When we asked about the land and their work, they answered by shrugging their shoulders and saying 'don't know' or 'maybe', which ended the conversation.

We also had the chance to gorge ourselves on cherries, so much so that when we went on to the plums I'd had enough and went to lie down to digest it all. Alberto had some so as not to seem rude. Up the trees we ate like pigs, as if we were in a race to the finish. One of the owner's sons seemed to think these disgustingly dressed and apparently famished 'doctors' a bit odd, but he said nothing and let us eat to our heart's content, to the point where we had to walk slowly to avoid kicking our own stomachs.

We mended the kick-start and other minor defects and set off again for San Martín de los Andes where we arrived just before dark.

---

1. At that time this was a national holiday to commemorate Juan Perón's release from prison in 1945. General Perón was President of Argentina from 1946 to 1955 and from 1973 until his death in 1974.
2. This is the Argentine national drink, a herb tea which is passed round, drunk from a gourd through a long metal utensil with a silver tip.
3. A Norton 500 motorcycle, literally 'the powerful one'.
4. In English in the original, this is the name of a little dog Ernesto is taking to his girlfriend Chichina, who is on holiday in Miramar, as a symbol of his return.

5. Miguel Otero Silva, left-wing Venezuelan poet and novelist, was born in 1908. The free version of the poem is by the translator.
6. The Peronist Party.
7. A farm or cattle ranch in Argentina.
8. An Argentina champion rally driver.

Photofest

Mary Murphy in publicity still from *The Wild One*, 1954

GREAT ESCAPE

eric burdon
with jeff craig

when I was on the West Coast and had some time off, I'd flee L.A. for the mighty desert surrounding Palm Springs. Back then, the clean air and the big white sand dunes were straight out of Beau Geste. The great dunes are gone now, blitzkreiged by the mighty yellow Caterpillars for housing and golf courses, but the area is still spectacular: the mountains are magenta, black and blue, and the hot sun keeps the skies open even when it's raining in L.A.

Back in the late '60s, a girlfriend of original Animals guitarist Hilton Valentine settled in the fledgeling community of Palm Desert. An accomplished artist who continues to live and work in the area, Ming Lowe at that time had a little house and studio which became a refuge from the madness of Hollywood. It was a great meeting place for artists and travellers attracted to the desert.

I'd arrive in my old El Camino, rifle in the rack, my collie dog Geordie and my dirt bike in the back. Riding the open desert at twilight in the winter, seeing the landscape blur by, was as seductive as anything

I've known. Two hours east of L.A., it could have been North Africa . . . it could have been any one of the exotic deserts. It was California at its best, and it's where I became a running mate of one of my screen heroes, Steve McQueen.

The first time I ran into Steve—and I mean just about literally ran into him—was when I was on a borrowed Harley from one of Frank Zappa's boys, headed down Sunset toward the beach. I was flying along in Brentwood when a traffic light turned yellow. I didn't want to run the light and started to brake hard, only to encounter a wet patch of pavement under one of the giant trees. In the left lane there was a green Porsche, and the driver saw what was about to happen. He was paying attention to what was going on around him and really knew what he was doing as he spun the Porsche out of the left lane, leaving me room to skid by. When I made the corner, the pavement was dry and I came to a stop safely. When I looked back, there was McQueen, a quick flash of white teeth before the Porsche sped away.

When I rented a house at the north end of Palm Springs in 1969, I was thrilled to find out McQueen lived nearby. My secretary had been out for a wild ride with him on the back of a Triumph motorcycle that he'd had specially doctored for the sand. She had been so impressed that she convinced me to connect with McQueen the following weekend.

There was something really strange about seeing him just mucking around in the sandbox. This guy had a smell of gasoline, black powder and pot that seemed to drift behind him everywhere he went. I told him it made me imagine him as a young Erwin Rommel and at times he'd adopt a mock German tone to his American accent.

We always had girlfriends around, fresh from out of town, making their first trip to the desert. We'd run them out into the dunes toward the east end of the valley, me on my 350 Yamaha and Steve on his desert Triumph.

All along the valley, tamarisk trees had been planted as windbreaks. They were a clear mark of where civilization ended and the desert began.

"Step this way," I'd say, pushing the branches aside for the girls, their bare feet landing in warm, silky sand, the black sky above with a billion stars and a thumbnail moon. There must have been a hundred nights like this.

There were two things you didn't ask Steve about. One was Charles Manson. McQueen was friends with Sharon Tate and Roman Polanski and was supposed to visit her on the night the Manson gang entered and slaughtered the home's occupants. Later on, Steve's name was found on the list of celebrities that Manson wanted to kill.

The other thing you didn't ask Steve about was the big motorcycle jump stunt in his great war film The Great Escape. Due to insurance restrictions, he'd not been allowed to film the scene himself and it was always a sore point with him. Instead, his riding buddy and stunt double Bud Egans had done the jump. I had no doubt that Steve could have done it, however. One time we went out riding together he took me to an area where there was a large sandy berm at the edge of a long wooden fence. Without prompting, he told me it was roughly the same kind of jump as in Great Escape. He didn't offer any more information and I didn't ask. As I rode my bike around the berm, Steve didn't think twice about it and hit the thing throttle open, piloting his Triumph into the air.

It was skill. And it was balls. As Bette Davis once asked him, "Why do you ride those motorcycles like that and maybe kill yourself?"

Steve's answer: "So I won't forget that I'm a man and not just an actor."

On one of our many trips out to the dunes—the day of Ike's funeral in April, 1969, in fact—we stood looking at Mount Eisenhower off in the distance. Steve pulled a joint out of his pocket and fired it up. As he exhaled, he said "You know, there's a rumor that Ike had secret meetings with space aliens. Some people even think he was a space creature himself."

I laughed and McQueen said, "No, I'm not joking. Who else could have won the war? Who else could have beat the Germans?"

Tough, gruff . . . and he had a great sense of humor. Though Steve wasn't given to deep, introspective conversation, he was also a little self-conscious about his image at this time. Despite great reviews and box office—his film, *Bullitt,* was concerning him. He said he was uneasy about having taken on the role of a cop, thinking it might jeopardize his image as a rebel.

"You got nothing to worry about," I told him. "Bullitt IS a rebel—he's a hip cop."

A few years later, after he'd married Ali MacGraw, the two of them were out cruising Palm Springs. He told me they'd dropped in at the grand opening of a new restaurant in town, Melvyn's (now a legendary celebrity hangout), and were turned away by the owner without a second glance.

"You really are judged by what you look like," Steve said, somewhat surprised at the time, since at that time he was the biggest and highest-paid movie star in the world.

Courtesy Ted Markland

Steve McQueen with Ted Markland.

The restaurant's owner, Mel Haber, is truly a gentleman, one of the most charming businessmen in the Palm Springs area, and remembers feeling bad after turning them away, not knowing who they were.

"It was our opening night, and everybody was beautifully dressed and they came right up on the motorcycle," he remembers these days. "Later on my parking attendant asked about Steve McQueen and Ali Mac-Graw and I said they never showed up. That's when I realized!"

Of course, Steve and Ali seemed to take it in stride and later did dine at Melvyn's, sans motorcycle.

Before I'd met McQueen, we each had been big fans of the legendary Von Dutch, and had frequented his San Fernando Valley shop. Von Dutch was a top automotive artist, gunsmith, engineer, innovator and great friend of McQueen. His design ideas would become an influence on great artists such as Robert Williams and be the basis of the California Kustom Kar Kulture that's still going strong today. His most popular single piece of art, the Flying Eyeball concept based on an ancient Middle Eastern cultural icon, would become the working title for my 1994 band.

If you're a real cult film fan, you might know that Von Dutch painted all the houses in the way-out film *Angels from Hell*, which starred my longtime buddy Ted Markland—who played the guy in the wheelchair in *One Flew Over the Cuckoo's Nest*. Von Dutch did a great paint job on Ted's personal bike, as well. All gold with Egyptian symbols all over it. Back before I met Steve, he and Ted used to run in the hills off Mullholland Drive in Hollywood.

After I met Steve, the more we saw of each other the more I liked him. I was amazed to see that such an action hero in the cinema would be, in the 1960s, accepted by people of the hip persuasion as well as the straights. But we never talked about the war—and since he didn't volunteer, I didn't ask.

Through his corporation Solar, he'd developed a plastic for gas tanks, and he wanted to show me his new design one morning. So I rode my dirt bike out over the giant dunes and met him with a couple of members of his crew, who were helping with his specially designed dune buggy—powered by a Porsche 911 engine.

I climbed into the bucket seat, a special design that Steve received a patent for. He showed me how to strap down the racing safety harness. As the massive rear tires dug into the white sand I was pinned backward. It was all I could do to clench my teeth and hang onto the roll bars, screaming, as we headed east toward Indio. Then, a quick turnaround to the left and we headed back toward the San Jacinto mountains at the west end of the valley and soon were tearing up the walls of one of the big dunes.

"See," he yelled over the racket of the engine, "we don't need no gas gauge, all I've got to do is look over my shoulder and I can see how much gas there is in the tank."

"Yeah," I agreed, "it's fantastic."

"So simple. I can adapt these tanks for dirt bikes as well. All you gotta do is glance down and you know where you're at."

"Cool," I yelled over the din of the engine, hanging on for dear life.

As we reached the crest of the dune, my tongue was stuck on the roof of my mouth. We came off the top of the dune and he gunned the engine. I held on for dear life as we flipped. The roll bar connected with the sand. He cut the engine and we came to a screeching halt. I was laughing hysterically. Steve turned to me and through his yellow-tinted glasses, he squinted at me, his mouth open, "Sshhh . . . quiet."

We both listened—to what, I'm not quite sure. One of the rear wheels was still spinning. He turned to look at the gas tank, the gasoline still slopping around inside. "Hey," he said, "it works."

With that, he unhooked one of the button-down clasps on his blue jean shirt pocket, pulled out a joint, stuck it in his mouth and lit up, taking a huge hit before passing it to me. "Now you can laugh," he said.

"What are we going to do now?"

"C'mon. Help me roll it over. It shouldn't be a problem."

MCQUEEN WAS FEARLESS. His old buddy Mike Egans once told me a great story about Steve getting busted by Hollywood cops. They'd been trying for ages to trap Steve as he screamed up and down Mullholland in the Hollywood Hills. It's a crowded residential area now, but back in the '60s it was still the wilds, and a lot of us used to tear up and down the winding street from the coast on up high into the hills. I had an old Jensen, and McQueen proudly raced his rare D-Model Jaguar—basically a Le Mans racer that was technically not street legal, something he got around with a bit of fame and intimidation at the DMV, I'd imagine.

For most of us speeding along the same route, the cops just let us go—one told me once that they'd wait until we crash . . . no sense in risking their own lives chasing us. With McQueen, though, the stakes were higher. It was a game. They'd set speed traps and do everything they could to nab him on his midnight runs, but his Jag ran circles around the cops' old clunky Fords.

Until one night: trapped by a line of cruisers, McQueen finally got nabbed. It was all fun and games until the cops hauled him away to a Hollywood police station and threw him in a cell. At first, he kept laughing that it was all a game of cat and mouse, and that they weren't really going to throw the book at him . . . they were just pissed since it took so long to catch him. The longer he sat in the cell, though, the more worried he got that maybe he really was facing some charges. The one thing that meant everything to him was his driver's licence.

Then one of the cops came in an opened his cell door.

"You're right, we are just fucking with you. You're free to go."

It did get McQueen to stop doing his midnight runs up and down Mullholland in the Jag, however.

Probably the best story I ever heard about McQueen was also from Egans. By the time Steve had terminal cancer, he'd amassed a great collection of nearly 200 motorcycles, 50-some cars and 5 planes stored at the Santa Paula airport north of L.A.

One day, near the end of his life, Steve showed up at Von Dutch's workshop. He picked up a .45 automatic, checked to see that it was loaded, stuffed it into his belt and walked out. He got into the cockpit of his PT-17 Stearman biplane, taxied down the runway and took off out over the Pacific.

Von Dutch figured that was the last he'd ever see of McQueen . . . or the plane. Not a bad way for a living legend to take his leave of the world.

Hours passed, Von Dutch recalled, when finally out of the dusk came the sound of a sputtering plane engine running on empty. McQueen dropped down out of the sky and landed the biplane, taxiing back to its parking space in front of the hangar.

As McQueen got out of the plane, Von Dutch said "Chicken shit."

"Fuck you," McQueen replied. "I just didn't want to scratch it."

In the years since running with Steve in the desert, I've been through my share of Harleys. I gave up riding for a few years in the 1990s because of chronic neck pain—and in protest of California's 1992 mandatory helmet law. But by the year 2000, I couldn't resist temptation and got back in the saddle with a new Harley.

The dunes of the desert are a distant memory, but on still evenings, as the sun sets over the west end of the valley and I cruise quiet back roads, the thought of Steve McQueen is never far away.

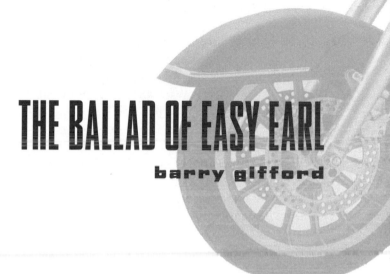

THE BALLAD OF EASY EARL

barry gifford

"earl, my man, it's a goddamn good thing you got a big dick," Easy Earl Blakey said aloud, as he sat alone in his car on the side of the road by Irish Bayou, " 'cause you sure must have a tiny motherfuckin' brain."

He had no idea what time it was, but Earl figured it had to be well past midnight by now. He had been driving aimlessly around the city since fleeing Alfonzo's Mexicali, and finally pulled over due to fatigue. What had gone down back there? he asked himself. All he could remember was that there had been some kind of an argument at the other end of the bar, and then the gun spinning along the mahogany into his hand. He had heard someone coming up behind him, turned and saw two guns pointed in his direction. After that, Earl's mind was blank. He knew he had fired the revolver, though, even if he could not clearly recall having done so. Something in his brain had just snapped when he'd seen those pistols pushed toward his face.

He took a deep breath, then lit up a Kool. There was so little traffic out here, he thought, looking up at the crescent moon. If he shot himself, it might be two or three days, maybe a week, before his body would be discovered. Earl sat and smoked. When he had had enough of it, he tossed the butt out the window, then picked up the revolver and got out of the car. Earl walked over to the bayou and threw the gun into the water. He stood there for a minute, listening. All he heard were airplane engines droning overhead. Earl went back to the Mercury, got in and cranked it up. Where to? he wondered, and started driving.

For some reason, the image of Willie Wong entered Earl's mind. Willie Wong had been a boyhood pal of Earl's. They had grown up together in the Eighth Ward and remained friends until Willie's death at the age of twenty-one. Willie had been a normal Chinese-American kid; he had studied hard in school and worked regularly at various jobs to help support himself and his parents, who owned a small grocery store on St. Claude Avenue. Then, when Willie was eighteen, he saw the movie *The Wild One*, which starred Marlon Brando as a devil-may-care, hardcase motorcycle gang leader. Willie fell in love with the image personified by Brando, and he bought a thirdhand Triumph Bonneville, allowed his lank black hair to grow long, wore a leather jacket, engineer boots and oily Levi's. He also started smoking, something else he never had done before, and it was rare to see him riding around on his bike without an unfiltered Lucky Strike dangling from his lips. Willie even invented his own nickname, "the Wild Wong," and encouraged everyone he knew to call him that. Only his parents refused to honor this request, continuing to address him as they always had, by his Chinese name, Zhao.

The Wild Wong was killed on a wet Thursday evening when a drunken driver in a brand-new SAAB sedan cut too closely in front of Willie's Triumph on Chef Menteur Highway and clipped the front wheel, catapulting the Wild Wong headfirst into a roadside ditch, breaking his back and neck. At Willie's funeral, Earl had been surprised to see that the Wong family had dressed their son in his biker clothes to be viewed in an open casket. He had been certain that the Wongs would have cut Willie's hair and put him into a suit. As he passed the casket, Earl had noticed that an unsealed package of Lucky Strike cigarettes had been placed in Willie's left hand.

Why he thought at this difficult moment in his own life of the Wild Wong, Earl did not know. Something had happened to Willie when he'd seen that movie, and his life had been changed irrevocably. Now, Easy Earl knew, nothing would be the same for him, either. That was it, he supposed. Something a person never could imagine took place and then the world looked completely different.

The image of Willie Wong lying in his coffin twenty-five years ago would not go away, and Earl drove fast on the deserted road in his Monarch with the headlights off.

"Whoooeeee! Willie Wild Wong, you dumb motherfucker!" Earl shouted. "I'm comin' to find you, brother, ready or not!"

© Martin Dixon

This properly performed "endo" is very difficult to control. Jaguars Bike Blessing.

from

ALL SHOT UP

chester himes

three minutes after the Buick had squeezed into the Alley, a small black sedan skidded about the corner into 112th Street from Lexington Avenue.

Grave Digger was driving with the lights dimmed, and Coffin Ed was keeping a sharp lookout among the parked cars for the Buick.

The heater had suddenly begun to work, and the ice was melting on the windshield. The wind had shifted to the east, and the sleet had stopped. The tires sang softly in the shifting sleet on the asphalt street as the car straightened out; but the next moment it began going off to the right, so Grave Digger had to steer slightly left to keep it on a straight course.

'I got a feeling this is a wild-goose chase,' Coffin Ed said. 'It's hard to figure anybody being that stupid these days.'

'Who knows?' Grave Digger said. 'This boy ain't won no prizes so far.'

They were halfway down the block of dilapidated old houses and jerry-built tenements when they spied a motorcycle with a sidecar turn into the other end from Third Avenue.

They became suddenly alert. They didn't recognize the vehicle; they knew nothing of its history, its use or its owner. But they knew that anyone out on a night like that in an open vehicle bore investigation.

The rider of the motorcycle saw them at the instant they saw him. He saw a small black sedan coming crabwise down the otherwise deserted street. As much trouble as he had gone to over the years to keep out of its way, he knew it like the plague.

He wore dark-brown coveralls, a woolen-lined army fatigue jacket, and a fur-lined, dark-plaid hunter's cap.

The seat had been removed from the sidecar, and in its place were two fully-tired automobile wheels covered with black tarpaulin.

When Coffin Ed spied the tarpaulin-covered objects, he said, 'Do you see what I see?'

'I dig you,' Grave Digger said, and stepped on the gas.

If the tires had been smaller, the rider would have swallowed them the way peddlers swallowed marijuana cigarettes when the cops closed in. Instead he gunned his motorcycle straight ahead, switching on the bright light to blind the two detectives, and leaning far over to the right side out of line of fire. Motor roar filled the night like jet planes taking off.

Simultaneously Grave Digger switched on his bright lights. Coffin Ed had his pistol out and was fumbling with the handle to the window, trying to get it down. But he didn't have time.

The two vehicles roared straight toward one another on the half-slippery street.

Grave Digger tried to outguess him. He saw the joker leaning to his right, overtop the sidecar. He knew the joker had them figured to figure he'd be leaning to the left, balancing the sidecar for any quick maneuver. He cased the joker to make a sharp last-minute turn to the right, braking slightly to make a triangle skid, and try to pass the car on the left, on the driver's side, opposite the free-swinging gun of Coffin Ed.

So he jerked the little sedan sharply to the left, tamped the brakes and went into an oblique skid, blocking off the left side of the street.

But the joker outguessed Grave Digger. He made a rollover in his seat like a Hollywood Indian on a pinto pony, and broke a ninety degree turn to his own left and gunned it to the limit for a flying skid.

His intention was to get past the sedan on the right side, and to hell with getting shot at.

Both drivers miscalculated the traction of the street. The hard, sleety coating was tricky; the tires bit in and gripped. The motorcycle sidecar hit the right-rear fender of the sedan at a tangent, and went into a full-gunned spin. The sedan wobbled on its rear wheels and threw Grave

Digger off balance. The motorcycle went over the curb behind a parked car, bouncing like a rubber ball, bruised the rider's leg against a rusty iron stairpost and headed back in the direction it had come from.

Coffin Ed was stuck in the half-opened window, his gun arm pinioned and useless, shouting at the top of his voice: 'Halt or I'll shoot!'

The rider heard him over the roar of the motor as he was fighting to keep the vehicle on the sidewalk and avoid side-scraping the row of stairposts on one side and the parked cars on the other.

The sedan was across the street, pointed at an angle toward the opposite curb, but headed in the general right direction.

'I'll get him,' Grave Digger said, shifting back to first and tramping on the throttle.

But he hadn't straightened out the wheels from his sharp left turn, and, instead of the car curving back into the street, it bounded to the left and went broadside into a parked Chevy. The Chevy door caved in, and the left-front fender of the little sedan crumpled like tin foil. Glass flew from the smashed headlamp, and the rending sound of metal woke up the neighborhood.

The thing to have done was to back up, straighten out and start over.

Grave Digger was so blind mad by this turn of events he kept tramping on the throttle and scraped past the Chevy by sheer horsepower. His own crumpled left-front fender caught in the Chevy's left-rear fender, and both broke loose from their respective cars.

He left them bouncing in the street and took off after the motorcycle that had bounced back into the street and was making a two-wheeled turn north up Third Avenue.

It was pushing four-thirty in the morning, and the big transport trucks were on the streets, coming from the west, through the tunnels underneath the Hudson River, and heading north through Manhattan Island toward upstate New York—Troy, Albany, Schenectady or the Boston road.

A trailer truck was going north on Third Avenue when Grave Digger made the turn, and for a moment it looked as though he might go underneath it. Coffin Ed was leaning out the window with his pistol in his hand. He ducked back, but his gun was still in sight when they passed the driver's cabin.

The truck driver's eyes popped.

'Did you see that cannon?' he asked his helper.

'This is Harlem,' his helper said. 'It's crazy, man.'

The white driver and the colored helper grinned at one another.

The motorcycle was turning west into 114th Street when Grave Digger got the sedan steadied from its shimmy. The melting ice on the windscreen was blurring his vision, and he turned on the wipers. For a moment he couldn't see at all. But he turned anyway, hoping he was right.

He bent too sharp and bumped over the near-side corner curb. Coffin Ed's head hit the ceiling.

'Goddam, Digger, you're beating me to death,' he complained.

'All I can say is I've had better nights,' Grave Digger muttered through clenched teeth.

They kept the motorcycle in sight until it turned north on Seventh Avenue, but didn't gain on it. For a time it was out of sight. When they came into Seventh Avenue, they didn't see it.

Three trucks were lined up on the outside lane, and a fourth was passing the one ahead.

'We don't want to lose that son,' Grave Digger said.

'He's passing on the sidewalk,' Coffin Ed said, leaning out his right-side window.

'Cut one over his head.'

Coffin Ed crossed his left arm to overtop the window ledge, rested the long nickel-plated barrel atop his left wrist and blasted at the night. Flame lanced into the dark, and three blocks ahead a streetlamp went out.

The motorcycle curved from the sidewalk back into the street in front of the line of trucks. Grave Digger came up behind the truck on the inside lane and opened his siren.

At 116th Street Coffin Ed said, 'He's keeping straight ahead, Trying to make the county line.'

Grave Digger swerved to the left of the park that ran down between the traffic lanes and went up the left-hand side. The windshield wipers had cleared halfmoons in the dirty glass, and he could see an open road. He pushed the throttle to the floor, gaining on the motorcycle across the dividing park.

'Slow him down, Ed,' he said.

The park, circled by a small wire fence, was higher than the level of the street, and it shielded the motorcycle's tires. It was going too fast to risk shooting at the lamp. He threw three shots in back of it, but the rider didn't slow.

They passed two more northbound trucks, and for a time both lanes were clear. The sedan came up level with the motorcycle.

Coffin Ed said, 'Watch him close, Digger, he's going to try some trick.'

'He's as scared of these corners as we are,' Grave Digger said, 'He's going to try to crash us into a truck.'

'He's got two up ahead.'

'I'd better get behind him now.'

At 121st Street Grave Digger swerved back to the right-side lanes.

One block ahead, a refrigerator truck was flashing its yellow passing lights as it pulled to the inner lane to pass an open truck carrying sheet metal.

The motorcycle rider had time to pass on the inside, but he hung back, riding the rear of the refrigerator truck until it had pulled clear over to the left, blocking both sides of the street.

'Get a tire now,' Grave Digger said.

Coffin Ed leaned out of his window, took careful aim over his left wrist and let go his last two bullets. He missed the motorcycle tire, with both shots, but the fifth and last one in his revolver was always a tracer bullet, since one night he had been caught shooting in the dark. They followed its white phosphorescent trajectory as it went past the rear tire, hit a manhole cover in the street, ricocheted in a slight upward angle and buried itself in the outside tire of the open truck carrying sheet metal. The tire exploded with a bang. The driver felt the truck lurch and hit the brakes.

This threw the motorcycle rider off his timing. He had planned to cut quickly between the two trucks and shoot ahead before the inside truck drew level with the truck it was passing. When he got them behind him the two trucks would block off the street, and he would make his getaway.

He was pulling up fast behind the truck carrying sheet metal when the tire burst and the driver tamped his brakes. He wheeled sharply to the left, but not quickly enough.

The three thin sheets of stainless steel, six feet in width, with red flags flying from both corners, formed a blade less than a quarter of an inch thick. This blade caught the rider above his woolen-lined jacket, on the exposed part of his neck, which was stretched and taut from his physical exertion, as the motorcycle went underneath. He was hitting more than fifty-five miles an hour, and the blade severed his head from his body as though he had been guillotined.

His head rolled halfway up the sheets of metal while his body kept astride the seat and his hands gripped the handlebars. A stream of blood spurted from his severed jugular, but his body completed the maneuver which his head had ordered and went past the truck as planned.

The truck driver glanced from his window to watch the passing truck as he kept braking to a stop. But instead he saw a man without a head passing on a motorcycle with a sidecar and a stream of steaming red blood flowing back in the wind.

He gasped and passed out.

His lax feet released the pressure from the brake and clutch, and the truck kept on ahead.

The motorcycle, ridden by a man without a head, surged forward at a rapid clip.

The driver of the refrigerator truck that was passing the open truck didn't believe what he saw. He switched on his bright lights, caught the headless motorcycle rider in their beam and quickly switched them off. He blinked his eyelids. It was the first time he had ever gone to sleep while driving, he thought; and my God, what a nightmare! He switched the lights back on, and there it still was. Man or hallucination, he was getting the hell away from there. He began flashing his blinkers as though he had gone crazy; he mashed the horn and stood on the throttle and looked to the other side.

The truck carrying the sheet metal turned gradually to the right from faulty steering mechanism. It climbed over the shallow curb and started up the wide stone steps of a big fashionable Negro church.

In the lighted box out in front of the church was the announcement of the sermon for the day.

Beware! Death is closer than you think!

The head rolled off the slow-moving truck, dropped to the sidewalk and rolled out into the street. Grave Digger, closing up fast, saw something that looked like a football with a cap on it bouncing on the black asphalt. It was caught in his one bright light, but the top was turned to him when he saw it, and he didn't recognize what it was.

'What did he throw out?' he asked Coffin Ed.

Coffin Ed was staring as though petrified. He gulped. 'His head,' he said.

Grave Digger's muscles jerked spasmodically. He hit the brake automatically.

A truck had closed in from behind unnoticed, and it couldn't stop in time. It smacked the little sedan gently, but that was enough. Grave Digger sailed forward; the bottom rim of the steering wheel caught him in the solar plexus and snapped his head down; his mouth hit the top rim of the steering wheel, and he mashed his lips and chipped two front teeth.

Coffin Ed went headfirst into the safety-glass windshield and battered out a hole. But his hard head saved him from serious injury.

'Goddam,' Grave Digger lisped, straightening up and spitting out chipped enamel. 'I'd have been better off with the Asiatic flu.'

'God knows, Digger, I would have, too,' Coffin Ed said.

Gradually the taut headless body on the motorcycle spewed out its blood and the muscles went limp. The motorcycle began to waver; it went to one side and then the other, crossed 125th Street, just missing a taxi, neatly circled around the big clock atop a post at the corner and crashed into the iron-barred door of the credit jewelry store, knocking down a sign that read:

We Will Give Credit to the Dead

Easy Rider

Dennis Hopper, 1969. Photofest

LIFE STYLES: THE CYCLISTS

hunter s. thompson

early, with ocean fog still in the streets, outlaw motorcyclists, wearing chains, shades and greasy Levis roll out from damp garages, all-night diners and one-night pads in Frisco, Hollywood, Berdoo and East Oakland. The Menace is loose again, the Hell's Angels, the hundred-carat headline, running fast and loud on the early-morning freeway, low in the saddle, nobody smiling, jamming crazy through traffic at ninety miles an hour down the center stripe, missing by inches . . . like Genghis Khan on an iron horse . . . Frenchy, Little Jesus, the Gimp, Blind Bob, Gut, Buzzard, Zorro, Hambone, Clean Cut, Tiny, Terry the Tramp, Mouldy Marvin, Mother Miles, Dirty Ed, Chuck the Duck, Fat Freddy, Filthy Phil, Charger Charley the Child Molester, Crazy Cross, Puff, Magoo, Animal and at least a hundred more . . . tense for the action, long hair in the wind, beards and bandannas flapping, earrings, armpits, chain whips, swastikas and stripped-down Harleys flashing chrome as traffic on 101 moves over, nervous, to let the formation pass like a burst of dirty thunder.

BY MIDSUMMER OF 1965 the Hell's Angels were the subject of at least two scholarly theses and no doubt others were in the works. Yet all over California there were people whose real or imagined dealings with outlaw motorcyclists had been much too personal to allow for any abstract, sociological perspective on the menace. For every one who'd ever seen a Hell's Angel in the flesh there were half a thousand more who'd been frightened silly by the whooping of the news media. So it was no surprise when a certain amount of public tension built up as the Fourth of July weekend approached.

On that Friday night I called the Box Shop, where some Angels hang out. I'd been meeting with the Angels on and off for months, but I'd never been on a holiday run. Since this one had all the makings of a real boomer, I decided to go along. An Angel named Frenchy made sure I wasn't planning to bring anyone with me before he confirmed the site: "Yeah, it's Bass Lake," he said. "About two hundred miles east from here. I'm a little worried about going. There might be trouble. We're hoping we can just get together and have a good time, but with all this publicity I'm afraid every cop in the state will be there."

Bass Lake is not really a town, but a resort area—a string of small settlements around a narrow, picture-postcard lake that is seven miles long and less than a mile wide at any point. The post office is on the north side of the lake in a cluster of stores and buildings all owned by a man named Williams. The local populace was expecting the worst. The most optimistic forecast for their weekend called for drunken brawling and property damage, civic fear and possible injury at any moment. And if the brute cyclists lived up to their reputation—which was not unlikely—there was every reason to expect a holocaust of arson, looting and rape.

I was expecting the worst, too, when I drove east in my car on Saturday morning to join the run. Somewhere near Modesto, about halfway between Oakland and Bass Lake, I heard on the radio that roadblocks were being set up to prevent the outlaws from entering the resort area. This worried me. The idea that the Hell's Angels would ride two hundred miles for a party and then be turned back by a roadblock ten miles from their destination was absurd. There would surely be violence, a bloody clash on a major highway, with holiday traffic backed up for miles. The alternative was to let the Angels pass, and this, strangely enough, was what happened.

The local sheriff, a giant of a man named "Tiny" Baxter, had in fact set up a roadblock about a half mile from the center of town. It was his decision and he backed it with his three-man force and a half-dozen local forest rangers. At the same time, he had decided to avert disaster by adopting an unprecedented stratagem of conciliation.

By the time I got there the outlaws were stopped along both sides of the highway, and Sonny Barger, the president of the Oakland branch of the Hell's Angels and the Maximum Leader of Angels everywhere, was striding forth to meet Baxter. The sheriff explained to the Angel chieftain and his praetorian guard that a spacious campsite had been carefully set aside for them—Willow Cove, about two miles down the main road and right on the lake.

"If you play straight with us, Sonny, we'll play straight with you. We don't want any trouble and we know you guys have as much right to camp on this lake as anybody else. But the minute you cause trouble for us or anyone else, we're gonna come down on you hard—it's gonna be powder valley for your whole gang."

Barger nods, seeming to understand. "We didn't come here for trouble, Sheriff. The way we heard it, you had trouble waitin' for us."

"Well, what did you expect? We heard you were coming in for a rumble, to tear things up." Baxter forces a smile. "But there's no reason why you can't enjoy yourselves here like everybody else. You guys know what you're doing. There's nothing wrong with you. We know that."

Then Barger smiles, very faintly, but he smiles so seldom that even a grimace means he thinks something is very funny. "Come off it, Sheriff. You know we're all losers or we wouldn't be here."

Barger signaled his people to follow the ranger's Jeep and check out the proffered campsite. The strange procession moved slowly down the highway, then veered into the pines on a narrow trail.

There were no complaints. Willow Cove lacked only a free beer machine to make it perfect. A dozen of the Angels leaped off their bikes and rushed into the lake fully clothed. I parked under a tree and got out to look around. We were on a small peninsula jutting into Bass Lake and cut off from the highway by a half mile of pine forest. It was an idyllic kind of setting and a very unlikely place to set aside for an orgy. But it was, and the outlaws set about occupying it like a victorious army. Sheriff Baxter and the head forest ranger explained to Barger that there were only two conditions on their use of the site:

> (1) that they would leave it as clean and unlittered as they found it; (2) that they would keep to themselves and not menace campgrounds on the other side of the lake, which were full of tourists.

Sonny agreed, and the weekend's first crisis was over. The outlaw clan, which now numbered two hundred, was settled in a private kingdom, and there was nothing of substance to bitch about. Beyond that, the Maximum Angel was publicly committed to the task of keeping his people under control. It was an unnatural situation for Barger to find himself in. Instead of spending the weekend rallying his boozy legion from one piece of unfriendly turf to another, beset at all times by cruel authority wearing guns and badges, he now found his people in a pleasant cul-de-sac, in a state of rare equality with the rest of humanity, which they could only disturb by committing some deliberate outrage—by violating an agreement that The Prez had honored with his word.

Once the pact was concluded, Barger began to get a beer kitty going. He stood in the middle of the big clearing and called for donations. Sheriff Baxter left, but six deputies attached themselves to the camp on what appeared to be a permanent basis. I was talking to one of them when Barger joined us with a handful of money. "The sheriff said that place by the post office will sell us all the beer we want," he said. "How about using your car?"

I didn't mind and the deputy said it was a socko idea, so we counted out the money on the hood of the car. It came to $120 in bills and roughly $15 in change. Then, to my astonishment, Sonny handed me the whole bundle and wished me well. "Try to hustle," he said. "Everybody's pretty thirsty."

I insisted that somebody come with me, to help load the beer in the car . . . but my real reason for not wanting to go alone had nothing to do with loading problems. I knew that all the outlaws lived in cities, where the price of a six-pack ranges from 79 cents to $1.25. But we were nowhere near a city, and I also knew, from long experience, that small stores in remote areas sometimes get their pricing policy from *The Gouger's Handbook*.

Once, near the Utah-Nevada border, I had to pay $3 for a six-pack, and if that was going to be the case at Bass Lake, I wanted a reliable witness—like Barger himself. At normal city prices, $135 would fetch about thirty cases of beer, but up in the Sierras it would cover only twenty, or maybe fifteen if the merchants were putting up a solid front. The Angels were in no position to do any comparison shopping, and if they were about to be taught a harsh lesson in socioeconomics, I figured they'd be more receptive to the bad news if it came from one of their own people.

I mentioned this on the way to town, after Sonny and an Angel called Pete had agreed to come with me. "You'd of come back with it," Sonny said. "A person would have to be awful stupid to run off with our beer money." Pete laughed. "Hell, we even know where you live."

Barger, like the politician he is, hastened to change the subject. "I read that article you wrote about us," he said. "It was okay."

I was surprised. He didn't seem like the type to be perusing *The Nation* where the piece had appeared. Later, when I saw the club scrapbook, I realized that the Angels have a copy of everything ever written about them. They are as vain as high-school football heroes. Both the Oakland Angels and the Gypsy Jokers have massive scrapbooks dating back more than ten years and far more complete than the clipping files in either of San Francisco's newspapers.

"What are you doin' now?" Sonny asked. "Are you writin' somethin' else?"

"Yeah," I said. "A book."

He shrugged. "Well, we don't ask for nothin' but the truth. Like I say, there's not much good you can write about us, but I don't see where that gives people the right to just make up stuff."

We were almost to Williams' store. We made the turn at the bottom of the hill and I parked the car as inconspicuously as possible about thirty yards from the store. According to the deputy at the campsite, the sale was already arranged. All we had to do was pay, load the beer, and leave. Sonny had the cash, and as far as I was concerned I was just the chauffeur.

It took about fifteen seconds to understand that something had queered the plan. As we stepped out of the car a group of local vigilantes began moving toward us. It was very hot and quiet, and I could taste the dust that hung over the parking area. A Madera County paddy wagon was parked at the other end of the shopping center, with two cops in the front seat. The mob stopped short of the car and formed a bristling human wall on the boardwalk in front of the store. Apparently they hadn't been informed of the pending transaction. I opened the trunk of my car, thinking that Sonny and Pete would go in for the beer. If things got serious, I could jump into the trunk and lock it behind me, then kick out the back seat and drive away when it was all over.

Neither Angel made a move toward the store. Traffic had stopped and the tourists were standing off at a safe distance, watching. The whole scene reeked of Hollywood: the showdown, *High Noon, Rio Bravo*. After a long silent moment a burr-haired fellow took a few steps forward and shouted, "You better get out of here. You don't have a chance."

I walked over to talk with him, thinking to explain the beer agreement. I wasn't particularly opposed to the idea of a riot, but I didn't want it to happen right then, with my car in the middle and me a participant. It would have been ugly: two Hell's Angels and a writer against a hundred country toughs on a dusty street in the Sierras. Burr-head listened to my reasoning, for a moment, then shook his head. "Mr. Williams changed his mind," he said. And then I heard Sonny's voice right behind me: "We can change our minds, too." He and Pete had walked out to join the argument and now the vigilantes moved forward to support Burr-head, who didn't look at all worried.

Well, I thought, here we go. The two cops in the paddy wagon hadn't moved; they were in no hurry to break the thing up. Getting beaten by a mob is a very frightening experience . . . like being caught in a bad surf: There is not much you can do except try to survive. It has happened to me twice, in New York and San Juan, and it came within seconds of happening again at Bass Lake. All that prevented it was the suspiciously timely arrival of Sheriff Tiny Baxter. The crowd parted to make room for his big car with the flashing red light on top. "I thought I told you to stay out of town," he snapped.

"We came for the beer," Sonny replied.

Baxter shook his head. "No, Williams says he's running low. You gotta go over to the market on the other side of the lake. They have plenty."

We left instantly. Baxter may or may not have known what he was doing, but if he did, then he deserves credit for coming up with a subtle and ingenious strategy. He made a limited number of appearances during that weekend, but each one came at a critical moment and he always arrived with a solution. After the fixing of the beer crisis the Angels began to view him as a secret sympathizer and by midnight of the first day Barger had been made to feel almost personally responsible for the welfare of everybody in Bass Lake. Each time Baxter fixed something he put the Angels more in his debt. The strange burden eventually ruined Barger's holiday.

On the way around the lake we speculated about what sort of mob might be waiting at the next store.

"They were gonna stomp us," said Pete.

"Yeah, and that would have been it," Sonny muttered. "That sheriff don't know how close he was to havin' a war on his hands."

The other market was in the center of the main tourist area, and when we got there the crowd was so dense that the only place to park was between the gas pump and the side door. If trouble broke out we'd be hopelessly penned in. At a glance the scene looked even worse than the one we'd just been rescued from.

But this was a different crowd. They'd apparently been waiting for hours to see the Angels in action, and now, as the two stepped out of the car, a murmur of gratification went up. These were not locals, but tourists—city people from the valley and the coast. A curious crowd gathered as Sonny and Pete bargained with the owner, a short moon-faced man who kept saying, "Sure thing, boys—I'll take care of you." He was aggressively friendly, even to the point of putting his arm around Pete's grimy shoulders as they made their way to the beer vault.

I bought a paper and went to the beer and lunch counter at the far end of the store. I heard a little girl behind me ask, "Where are they, Mommy? You said we were going to see them." I turned to look at the child, a bandy-legged pixie just getting her permanent teeth, and felt thankful once again that my only issue is male. I glanced at the mother and wondered what strange grooves her mind had been fitted to in these wonderfully prosperous times. She was a downbeat thirty-five, with short blond hair and a sleeveless blouse only half tucked into her tight Bermuda shorts. It was a vivid tableau: On a hot California afternoon a sag-bellied woman wearing St. Tropez sunglasses is hanging around a resort-area market, trailing her grade-school daughter and waiting in the midst of an eager crowd for the arrival of The Hoodlum Circus.

A crowd of about fifty people gathered to watch us load the beer. Several teen-agers got up the nerve to help. A man wearing madras shorts and black business socks kept asking Pete and Sonny to pose while he backed off for panoramic sequences with his home movie camera. Another man, also wearing Bermudas, sidled up to me and asked quietly, "Say, are you guys really Nazis?"

"Not me," I said. "I'm Kiwanis."

He nodded wisely, as if he had known all along. "Then what's all this stuff you read?" he asked. "You know, this stuff about swastikas."

I called to Sonny, who was showing our helpers how to stack the cases in the back seat. "Hey, this man wants to know if you're a Nazi." I expected him to laugh, but he didn't. He made the usual disclaimers regarding the swastikas and Iron Crosses ("That don't mean nothin', we buy that stuff in dime stores"), but just about the time the man seemed satisfied that it was all a rude put-on, Barger unloaded one of those jarring ad-libs that have made him a favorite among Bay Area newsmen. "But there's a lot about that country we admire," he said, referring to prewar Germany. "They had discipline. They might not of had all the right ideas, but at least they respected their leaders and they could depend on each other."

The audience seemed to want to mull this over and in the meantime I suggested we get back to Willow Cove. At any moment I expected somebody to start yelling about Dachau and then to see some furious Jew lay Barger out with a campstool. But there was no sign of anything like that. The atmosphere was so congenial that we soon found ourselves back inside the store, eating hamburgers and sipping draft beer. I was beginning to feel almost relaxed when we heard motorcycles outside and saw the crowd surge toward the door. Seconds later, Skip from Richmond appeared, saying he'd waited as long as he could for the beer and finally had decided to seek it on his own. Several more Angels arrived, for the same reason, and the owner scurried around behind the bar, serving up the mugs with a nice enthusiasm: "Drink up, boys, and take it easy—I bet you're thirsty as hell after that long ride, eh?"

The man's attitude was very odd. As we left he stood by the car and told us to come back real soon, "with the other fellas." Considering the circumstances, I listened closely for a telltale lilt of craziness in his voice. Maybe he's not even the owner, I thought. Maybe the owner had fled with his family to Nevada, leaving the village loony to mind the store and deal with the savages in his own way. Whoever he was, the eager little person had just sold eighty-eight six-packs of beer at $1.50 each and guaranteed himself a booming trade for the rest of the weekend. Without spending a penny, he'd landed the West Coast's top animal act, a surefire crowd-pleaser that would put the traditional lakeside fireworks display in deep shade.

If nothing else, that weekend was a monument to free enterprise. It is hard to say what might have happened if the outlaws hadn't been able to buy beer, but the moon-faced man at the tourist market was the visionary who turned the tide. After the first purchase, the Angels were welcome or at least tolerated everywhere except at Williams' store—which even the vigilantes abandoned when it became apparent the action was across the lake. Williams was left holding the civic bag; he had taken a gutty stand, his image was all moxie . . . and on Monday night, when the Angels were gone, he knew he had earned the leisure that enabled him to go out to the lakefront and gaze off in a proud, wistful way, like Gatsby, at the green neon lights of the taverns across the water, where the others were counting their money.

BEYOND THE BEER crisis, memories of that weekend are hazy. I functioned, but not well; and after thirty or forty hours of steady drinking I turned into a zombie and stayed on my feet only because the Angels kept feeding me pills. If it were not for the tape recorder I might have returned to San Francisco thinking I'd spent the weekend at a bad movie in some ugly corner of Oakland. But those little brown reels did their work. I recall crouching in the car and describing various scenes to the microphone . . . and on the way back to the city I played the tapes back and was amazed.

It had all seemed right and natural at the time, but on the tapes there were many explosions, berserk screams and a constant booming of motorcycle engines. Voices kept interrupting my monologue, cursing the beer shortage. I heard girls laughing, the clang of beer cans on the roof of the car, and the interminable barking and howling of Pete's big redbone hound. The dog had been on other runs, and seemed to know the spirit. It rarely slept, and ate constantly of horsemeat, ten or fifteen cans a day. Six of these and twenty-two cases of beer were our cargo back to camp in the fading hours of Saturday afternoon.

The car was so jammed with loose six-packs that I could barely move my arms to steer, and each bump in the road caused the springs to drag on the rear axle. When we got to the Willow Cove turnoff the car wouldn't climb the dirt hill that led into the pines. I backed off and made a fast run at it, driving the junker straight into the hill like a cannonball. Our secondary momentum took us over the hump, but the crash pushed the right fender back on the tire. The car lurched just far enough down the trail to block it completely, and stopped just short of crashing into a dozen bikes which were en route to the store. It took some rough work with a bumper jack to get it moving again, and just as we freed the front wheel a purple truck came grinding over the crest and rammed into my rear bumper. The rhythm of the weekend was picking up . . . a huge beer delivery, the rending of metal, greedy laughter and a rumble of excitement when Sonny told what had happened at Williams' store.

We had been away about two hours, but the interim peace had been preserved by the arrival of several carloads of girls and beer. By six, the whole clearing was ringed with cars and bikes. My car was in the middle, serving as a communal cooler. During Barger's absence, the other chapter presidents had seen to the gathering of wood for a bonfire. The task fell to the newest member in each chapter, a tradition that nobody questioned.

Just before dusk a sudden scrambling tension swept over the camp. People had been coming and going for several hours, but with no sense of urgency. The odd welcome at the beer market had undermined the sheriff's edict about keeping away from the tourists, and many of the outlaws had ridden over to sample the hospitality. The atmosphere at

Willow Cove was festive. New arrivals were greeted with shouts, kisses, flying tackles and sprays of beer. The deputies were taking pictures. At first I thought this was for evidence, but after watching them urge the Angels to strike colorful poses and dive into the lake with their clothes on I realized that the cops were as avid as any first-time visitors to the Bronx Zoo. One told me later, "Hell, I wish I had a movie camera, this is the damnedest thing I ever saw. People wouldn't believe it unless they saw pictures. Wait'll I show these to my kids!"

To squelch any possibility of the Angels roaring drunkenly out of camp during the night, Sheriff Baxter and the Highway Patrol announced a ten-o'clock curfew. At that hour, anyone in camp would have to stay, and nobody else could come in. This was made official just after dark. The deputies were still trying to be friendly, and they assured the Angels that the curfew was as much for their protection as anything else. They kept talking about "bunches of townspeople coming through the woods with deer rifles." To forestall this, the police set up a command post where the Willow Cove trail joined the highway.

Meanwhile, a mountain of six-packs was piling up in the middle of camp. By the time it got dark the car was half empty, so I put the rest of the beer in the back seat and locked my own gear in the trunk. I decided that any symbolic alienation I might incur by securing my valuables was worth the risk of having them lost—which they probably would have been, for it was not long before the camp became like an animal pen. A reporter from the Los Angeles *Times* showed up the next day and said it "looked like Dante's Inferno." But he arrived about noon, when most of the outlaws were calm and stupefied from the ravages of the previous night. If the midday lull seemed that awful, the bonfire scenes might have damaged his mind permanently.

Or perhaps not, for the ten-o'clock curfew had a drastic effect on the action. By driving all the fringe elements out of camp, it forced the Angels to fall back on their own entertainment resources. Most of those who left were girls; they had seemed to be enjoying things until the deputies announced that they would either leave by the deadline or stay all night. The implications were not pleasant—at ten the law was going to pull out, seal off the area, and let the orgy begin.

All afternoon the scene had been brightened by six or ten carloads of young girls from places like Fresno and Modesto and Merced who had somehow got wind of the gathering and apparently wanted to make a real party of it. It never occurred to the Angels that they would not stay the night—or the whole weekend, for that matter—so it came as a shock when they left. Three nurses who had picked up Larry, Pete and Puff earlier in the day made a brave decision to stay—but then, at the last moment, they fled. "Man, I can't stand it," said one Angel as he watched the last of the cars lurch off down the trail.

Some Angels rushed off to the beer market when the curfew was first announced, but their hopes for a party with the tourists were dashed when the place closed right on the dot of ten. There was nothing to do but go back to camp and get wasted. The police were lenient with late arrivals, but once in, there was no getting out.

The hours between ten and twelve were given over to massive consumption. Around eleven I ducked into the car and worked for a while on the tape, but my monologue was constantly interrupted by people reaching through the back windows and trying to wrench the trunk open. For hours there had been so much beer in camp that nobody worried about seeing the end of it, but suddenly it all disappeared. Instead of one beer at a time, everybody who reached into the car took a six-pack. The stash had begun. It was like a run on a bank. Within minutes the back seat was empty. There were still twenty or thirty six-packs piled up near the bonfire, but these weren't for stashing. The cans were clipped off one at a time. Nobody wanted to start a run on the public beer stock. It would have been very bad form, and if the hoarding became too obvious, those who planned to drink all night might get violent.

Now there was no telling what any one person might do. Wild shouts and explosions burst through the darkness. Now and then would come the sound of a body plunging into the lake . . . a splash, then yelling and kicking in the water. The only light was the bonfire, a heap of logs and branches about ten feet wide and five feet tall. It lit up the whole clearing and gleamed on the headlights and handlebars of the big Harleys that were parked on the edge of the darkness. In the wavering orange light it was hard to see faces except those right next to you. Bodies became silhouettes; only the voices were the same.

It was obvious to everyone standing around the campfire that the beer mountain was almost gone. Within an hour or so, those with nothing stashed were going to be thirsty. This would cause tension, and the hoarders were among the most insistent that another beer run should be made. Otherwise, they would have to share their stash, or fight. Some people were too stoned and wasted to care about beer, but a hard core of about fifty drinkers intended to stay on their feet all night.

Luckily, some time around four a big contingent from the south rolled in with several more cases and the police, wisely, allowed them to come in. The rest of the night was a question more of endurance than enjoyment. Magoo, a twenty-six-year-old teamster from Oakland, stayed by the fire and kept stoking. When somebody warned him not to burn everything up on the first night, he replied, "What the hell? There's a whole forest. We got plenty of firewood." Magoo is one of the most interesting of the Angels because his mind seems wholly immune to the notions and tenets of twentieth-century American life.

JUST BEFORE DAWN at Bass Lake I crept into my car to crash, making sure to lock the doors and roll the windows up far enough so that nobody could reach in. The Angels are hell on people who pass out at parties, and one of their proudest traditions is the sleepless first night of any run. Several times when I was looking for somebody I was told, "He's hiding to crash."

Crashing means nothing more sinister than going on the nod, either from booze or simple fatigue. When this happens—if the unfortunate has not found a safe hiding place—the others will immediately begin tormenting him.

By the time I decided to crash that night there wasn't a sober human being in the camp and I knew I couldn't count on anybody saying, "Leave him alone—he wouldn't understand." More than half of the fifty or so outlaws still standing around the bonfire had lost all contact with reality. Some of them just stood there like zombies and stared vacantly at the flames. Others would brood for a while, then suddenly begin shouting gibberish, which echoed across the lake like the screaming of many loons. Now and then a cherry bomb would go off in the fire, blasting sparks and embers in all directions. And behind all the other sounds, as always, was the revving and booming of motorcycle engines. Some of the Angels would sit on their bikes for a while, letting them idle, then kill the engine and move out again to socialize. It seemed to give them new energy, like a battery charge. The last sound I heard that night was the peaceful idling of a hog (a Harley-Davidson) next to my car.

The next morning I woke up to the same noise, but this time it was deafening. Apparently some enemy had crept in during the night and screwed every one of the carburetor adjustments, causing them all to need retuning.

The rest of the stay at Bass Lake was relatively peaceful. Many of the Angels spent Sunday afternoon at the beer market, performing for an overflow crowd of tourists. They poured beer on each other, exchanged lewd chatter with the citizens and had a fine time keeping everybody on edge. Old men brought beer for them, middle-aged women called out insulting questions and the cash register at the market clanged merrily.

The only other incident of the run occurred on Sunday night just before the beer market closed at ten. The Angels who'd been there all day were totally drunk when it came time to go, but they insisted on doing it up right. Whenever they exit in a group, drunk or sober, they boom off like a flight of jet fighters leaving a runway—one at a time, in rapid succession, and with overwhelming noise. The basic idea is that individual launches keep them from running into each other, but the Angels have developed the ritual to the realm of high drama. The order of departure doesn't matter, but the style and rhythm are crucial. They carefully prime their carburetors so the bikes will start on the first kick. An outlaw whose hog won't leap off like a thunderbolt feels a real stigma. It has the same effect as a gun jamming in combat or an actor blowing a key line. This is about the way it went at the beer market. A big crowd gathered in the driveway to watch the finale. A photographer rushed around frantically, flashing his strobe light every few seconds. But the Angels were too drunk to carry it off. Some of them flooded their carburetors, then raged and cursed as they jumped repeatedly on the kick starters. Others went careening off simultaneously or veered into the crowd with wild yells. Many were carrying six-packs, which made control even more difficult. Those who'd flooded their engines tried to atone for it by screeching off on one wheel, gunning their engines mercilessly to get up a head of steam before springing the clutch. Buck, a massive Joker, crashed into a police car before he got out of first gear and was taken straight to jail, where he spent the next thirty days. Frip from Oakland went flying off the road and hit a tree, breaking his ankle and blocking traffic on the narrow lakeside road.

A large crowd gathered, all wanting to help. The only cop on the scene was a Madera County sheriff's deputy in a paddy wagon, but he claimed to have no authority and refused to call a private ambulance until somebody signed an agreement to pay the bill. This drew jeers and protests from the crowd. The photographer lost his head and began to curse the deputy. One of the four or five Angels on the scene went roaring off toward Willow Cove. Finally the photographer said he'd pay the ambulance bill, and the deputy made the call.

Moments later two helmeted deputies rushed onto the scene, each with a German shepherd on a leash. There was a flurry of yelling and pushing as people tried to get away from the dogs. A siren wailed somewhere down the road, but the police cars couldn't get through the traffic jam. Some of the police left their cars and ran toward whatever was happening, waving their clubs and shouting. "Stand back! Stand back!"

Barger's scout party arrived seconds behind the police. As they weaved between cars their headlights jerked around crazily, adding a new element of menace to the scene. I caught a glimpse of Barger shoving through the crowd toward the injured Angel.

Then Sheriff Baxter arrived and was trying to calm things down. He found Barger and assured him that an ambulance was coming for his boy. This appeared to solve things, although Sonny and a dozen other Angels stayed until Frip was packed off to a hospital. Dirty Ed lurked quietly in the background, looking dangerous but not making any violent moves. As for me, a cop at the accident said I was going to be arrested for vagrancy the next time he laid eyes on me.

It didn't seem worth arguing about, so I drove north for about an hour, until I was sure the Madera County line was somewhere behind me. Then I found a back road next to an airport and went to sleep. The next morning I thought about going back to Bass Lake, but I didn't feel like spending the day scrounging beers and listening to the same dull noise. I ate breakfast with a bunch of farmers in a diner on 101, then drove on to San Francisco. The *Chronicle* story on the Angels said police in Madera County were still undecided on what to do about a restraining order that had been served on the outlaws. Apparently something had gone haywire, for the order called for the Angels to appear in Madera County Superior Court on July 16 or be permanently barred from the county. "Police feared there might be trouble," said the article, because, unless the hearing was held that day, ". . . the gang threatened to remain in Bass Lake until July 16 or return on that date with reinforcements." County officials were faced with a choice between dismissing the order entirely or hosting another run—and Barger said they had every intention of going back to argue their case. Needless to say, the order was done away with. It had been a bummer from the start, and not even the cops charged with enforcing it knew what it meant. The final press comment on the Bass Lake saga appeared in the *Examiner*, under a small headline: "A Victory for Hell's Angels." It said the order had been dismissed at the request of the district attorney.

In retrospect, there was unanimous agreement that both the press and the police had done a spectacular job. There was massive publicity, a massive police presence and massive beer-drinking to justify all their concern. In a galaxy of nationwide riots and civic upheaval that long Fourth of July weekend, Bass Lake shone like a star of peace.

from

FREEWHEELIN FRANK

frank reynolds
with michael mcclure

it was the Fourth of July, 1966, run for the Hell's Angels Motorcycle Club newly brought together under the California rocker. We were heading towards Bass Lake. This is an annual run of the year, not always to the same place, but Bass Lake has been our scene on several Fourth of Julys. All seven chapters arrived at the lake in the early morning hours of the Fourth of July weekend.

There before our eyes was the special squadron of cops assigned to the Hell's Angels. Buckingham, the head of it, we got to know quite well in a very short time. This plain-clothes inspector is very clever and specially trained to keep track of us. He and his special little cops had made an agreement with us that we would not give this special squad any trouble about giving them our names and letting them check out our engine numbers. In the past there was always an all-out alert on the main runs of all chapters. This caused chaos and confusion among the cops for they would all head for the designated area.

In the early days we had been forced out of Reno. And the death of Lovely Larry, on the prior April run, is what really put the cap on getting this special little squadron of cops to take care of us. The place where Lovely Larry was killed was Assafocko Lake near San Luis Obispo. It was a specially called run in April because everybody wanted to get out on a spring run. As it turned out a large mob of cops of all kinds descended onto the area around the lake where we had camped. There were approximately three hundred of us, three-quarters on motorcycles. The cops had a field day with roadblocks. Many bikes were confiscated. The cops had planned this as one of their definite big steps in breaking up the Hell's Angels. With armies of policemen in helicopters they just figured they'd walk right in and show us how it is, and show us that State Attorney General Lynch wasn't fooling when he said, "All-out war on the Hell's Angels . . . Statewide investigation . . ." As I said sometime before, as Lovely Larry went through the roadblocks, one after another, they blew his mind because he hated cops when they pushed a man. And then the report said that he was run over by an unidentified motorist. There was no car cited. I mean how could there be—there were so many squad cars on the highway! And they drug him away by the feet—first-aid treatment California-Highway-Patrol style recommended by all . . . The whole country loves it . . . backs them up all the way. Well, so here we are. I've run it down so I don't have to go through it again. So we'll just jump right back to Bass Lake which is the next run after Larry's death.

And here we are with the special little squadron, like I say, checking out the motorcycles. This time they weren't so perked up and popping off at the mouth. I think all the cops and especially the assigned investigators well knew who carried the guilt of Lovely Larry's death. They sure made a definite change awful fast.

This time there was only one little roadblock leading into our special encampment area. If there were any cameras they were well hidden. Nobody saw any helicopters. The cops at the gate kept all outsiders away from us. The Gypsy Jokers were headed for Bass Lake too, along with scores of other motorcycle trip hangers-on. We had arrived first, naturally—it was our scene, as it will always be. But we told the cops to let all the other little outlaw clubs in. A lot of us had specially in mind the Gypsy Jokers, due to the fact that they had been branching out throughout the state. Whether it was a rumor started by one of our warmongers or not doesn't matter, but it was said, "The Gypsy Jokers are going to come together and branch out, and after organizing enough they are going to kick the ass of the Hell's Angels." Everybody was heated up over this story but, as they rode in, we stood back and smiled and waved them on in. For a whole afternoon we let em sit around and drink and speak to us. And then it went into the first night of the weekend when a few of their women on the mama level were dragged off without a sound being made, and a few of the tough-looking characters were accidentally dropped into the lake from the overhanging cliff. They were big and strong and they made it back up. Accidents in the quiet night.

It was a warm night and a little fog rolled off the lake. There were a lot of weeping willow trees, a lot of sycamore, alder, oak and even more evergreens. In the night it was pitch black only a few feet from the bonfire—a huge bonfire of tree trunks—yet a few feet away it was very dark. We hadn't planned anything the first night as far as putting it on the Jokers and the rest of these loose-like cats—here today and gone tomorrow—as to what the trip is that they're smelling up, with their short sleeves and makeup frowns and sneers. Because we had two days to go, we left that night up to our individual sex deviates, for all the perverts were havin a trick or treat. While the rest of us stood about the fire and discussed the mind trip in the future, on the level of chess-game Angels. Though it wasn't spoken of and stressed as a chess game we all knew it was to be. Meanwhile out in the tules in pairs of two and three, the loose, outlawed women who came with these hotdog characters were being tasted by all of our master deviates. These were their finest hours as they would gruel and grin going down to scarf their box and trying to make them wince and scream as much as possible. Every now and then you'd hear the slapping whapping sound of a long black bull-whip. On the other end of it always and forever—was Blind Bob. Blind Bob, the leading sexual insane Hell's Angel. Need I say what chapter he is from? The newspapers and the magazines all run him down but never will they ever ever get the point. If they knew they'd surely blow it. For I have never read or never heard of anything to likely ever compare to Blind Bobby.

He swings the black whip above his head cracking it in the faces of strangers or anyone he might want to see squirm, yet he never has ever cut the face of a person he knew had something going. But he'll cut the face of many a little girl who'll say, "No, *stop. I came to be here with you Hell's Angels of such colorful strength!* You men who make all the old ladies shudder and the children run out in the street. You're so brave! Don't hurt me!" And all the time most of them dig it. One out of a thousand, I should say, one out of a million is a rape case. Where they get on a bummer and think they want it this way—and in spite of it they will come back on us.

Blind Bob is mad at those pop bottle lenses of his glasses but he wears a constant grin. He always has two or three women with him all the time. They look like they're in a trance. They might even dig ripping off the clothes of another broad as he goes into his deep convulsions with his witchlike maids.

As Peter, our new president of the Frisco Chapter, says, "Every cat's got his part among us. We all cannot be the same." That's when I did tell him I agreed. He then applied chess game terms to what he had said: Some wicked knights and rooks . . . Though there's many chapters they sure come out in a gleam.

As the sun sprang up the morning air burst in a still whiteness, the black smoky clouds had changed the trees to darkness in the daylight. It looked as though a spell had been cast upon this part of Bass Lake which was our land. We would have claimed it whether or not given the permission which we had been given. Only one time did the cops walk in: a couple of sheriff's deputies and three of Buckingham's goons. They didn't get all the way into the circle before we saw their backs turned stepping away, a little bit swaggery as they tried to hold that chest-out chin-up stance, as they departed going out the same way they came in, not saying a word, leaving nothing but wrappers of tums for the tummy.

About the area lay sleeping bags stained with wine and blood, though just a few showed bloodstains, as proof of Bobby's whip and the other deviates. Many of the girls were specially chosen Gypsy Joker women of beauty who knew damn well what the trip was when they entered our gates. The first night, only the lame men lost their women. If they would not stand up and defend their women then the deviates led them away. Though it was not still and quiet they kept it from becoming sharp and loud. Professional is not a good enough word for this Hell's Angel kind of play. It's putting it down the way it is and people had better damn well see it. Yet for eleven years or more they been coming back. The country thinks it's got some production lines; they ought to line it up with our production line of women! It would make all those suburb cats howl. They'd be lighting bonfires in the parks on election day if it were a bummer.

Meanwhile the second day grew into the hot sun. There was a still-ness among all the outlawed, which is too good a word for the hotdog riders. They were getting a little worried. They were breaking the gates down trying to get out more than five at a time for breakfast, which was in the contract. We didn't want our gates broke down so we stopped them. By midafternoon of the second day all of the loose hotdog riders that were going to show up had shown up. There were so many different oddball clubs. I'd never be able to remember all of the odd names, such as Cross Men, Question Marks, etc. I could go on and on. All the strange clubs usually wear some kind of a skull on the back of their jackets. They try to get as near to copying us as possible. They're all the same as far as the way they dress, for they try to dress exactly as we do, but the trip is—they are only out to try to catch the eye of the public for a few days and then they go back to whatever trip they are really on. It is not a everyday trip for them, as it is for us, not for a lifetime.

On the lake many motorboats were wheeling around and capsizing as they veered from left to right. Many Hell's Angels were throwing their women into the water and holding them under, as if to baptize them Angel style—always naked. As the evening shadows started to move in the whole area was heavily clouded in marijuana smoke. Wood had been gathered for the night's fire. Cases of beer stood up in the air six feet high from the day's thievery and what money had been collected to buy wine and beer. This was the second night . . . it would be the most festive night of the three-day weekend. Many of the cherub-like Angels were already drunk and mad on wine. In their madness of not knowing why or giving a fuck why they began to swing on strangers, occasionally slapping the face of a strange broad. Then, if her old man would not do anything about it, they would rip him completely to the ground. For instance, one broad who stood about as if she was anxious for something to happen was suddenly yanked by her long black hair and shoved. Her old man, who was nothing but a hotdog rider, of the Jokers, looked around and, instead of sticking up for her, screamed at her, saying, "GET OVER THERE AND SIT DOWN!"

One Angel says, "DON'T TALK TO HER LIKE THAT," breaking a fifth of wine over his forehead. The Joker then slumped to his knees biting the dust—out of breath forever as he fell. His broad meanwhile was yanked and thrown upon the ground, one Angel saying to her, "You better get yourself a real old man!" Pulling her pants off her he poured wine all over her pussy. And then he got down and scarfed her box out licking the wine up. After he'd finished, he called out, "LET'S TURN HER OUT!" Many who liked the broad immediately got in line waiting their turn. In the background motorcycles roared like thunder as they raced down the dusty trails around and around the encampment. Occasionally one would hit a bare stump throwing rider and motorcycle into the air. No one received any broken bones during the whole weekend within the encampment. Everybody gets so loose and drunk and free on a run that they're so limber it is impossible to break a bone, I think. It was quite a usual thing to see an Angel walk over and steal the bike of a hotdog rider and go racing off into the woods, not caring if he wrecked it and himself both. Each chapter had at least one prospective member. Through the three-day meeting the prospectives of each chapter were put to the test to prove that their chapter was the best. And in turn each chapter tried to prove that its prospective was the stronger and could do the most out-of-sight things. For instance, they were all put in barrels and rolled off this long sloping cliff that runs down into the lake, as one trick in the Ceremony of Prospects. Bo from Oakland won when he didn't come up for five minutes. Bo is like a reincarnation of Houdini, but looks like a blond vicious Viking. There was so much activity going on that one could not observe all of it.

What looked like a barbarian sale of women began as the evening shadows closed in. Upon an orange crate women were being stood with their hands tied behind them and auctioned off. The sign read: CHICKS FOR SALE. WE ACCEPT ANYTHING. A tall lanky Angel by the name of Buzzard was the auctioneer. He would stand and describe the tall or shortlike broad, describing how she sucked and fucked. Quoting, "Here is a broad I have before me, who is not only a nympho, she is also a bisexual. She can take care of your old lady as well as you. What is my offer?" The beautiful broad with long brown hair and a large bust with slim hips was quickly yanked from the orange crate as the long black whip cracked around her neck and jerked her from it. This time it was someone else wielding Bobby's whip: it was one of Satan's Slaves, who are very good friends of the Hell's Angels. They are from the South—and are known for their sexual deviation, for yanking women right off the streets and taking them into their bars and raping them. The Satan's Slaves are number one when it comes to sexual diversion. They are of Satan himself.

As darkness crept in the trees seemed covered with black smoke. The moon was full and the howls of women as they were being raped rang out into the night. This was the biggest sex orgy we had ever had in our lifetime. Everyone by this time was covered with filth from falling in the lake and wallowing in the dust and sloshing wine over each other. The smell of sexual orgies reeked along with the honeywind of marijuana. In some jagged stumplike corners of the forest certain characters were rolling their sleeves up geezing their arms full of crystal and opiates, jacking themselves completely off the ground in their insane way. Everyone was completely mad! Stark raving crazy! The hotdog stand riders had had their bikes taken away, kicked up and revved over till the engines BLEW scattering metal all over the ground. Those who had remained clean were sloshed with wine and spit on! At times a turd would come slinging through the air—shit splattering upon each other's faces. No one was to remain without filth upon his body.

In order to leave our campsite one had to follow a long winding trail that led through the trees before coming to the roadblock and the road. As some of the riders tried to leave from time to time during the night, some of the wildest Angels who had hidden themselves up trees along the roadway would jump down off the branches right on top of the bike rider knocking him from his motorcycle, leaving him sprawled out unconscious along the side of the trail. Then they'd drag the motorcycle, the broad, and the rider off into the weeds. The Angels would climb back up into the trees to wait for the next Gypsy Jokers or hotdog riders trying to escape.

From the overhanging branch of one tree, a hotdog rider was hanging by his heel after being tied and strung into the air. For who knows what—it didn't really matter. Many caps of LSD had been brought. This was an insane forest with a now higher fire that was raging into the sky. The cops did not dare come in. If they had come in they would have been ripped clean of their flesh and probably eaten.

I was high on acid by this time myself, and I could not comprehend what was happening and it probably didn't matter. The sounds were like an African jungle during the great fire when all of the animals grow angry and mad on the rampage. Anyone who was not a Hell's Angel or a close friend was smashed and beaten. Graves were being dug. I don't know if anyone was buried or not.

All night long this insane wildness went on. A jazz band was brought in from a local nightclub and forced against their will to stand by the fire and play as loud as they could. Many harmonicas blew insanely into the night—music in wild distortion. Women who had been raped during the previous days now walked along as if in a deep trance, not caring if the world had ended or not. It was as though we all hoped someone would come in trying to resist what we had started so we could rip them from bone to bone. But not once did we turn against one another. This was the closest the Hell's Angels had ever been, and we could not get any closer than we were. We loved one another and we could not hurt one another. We only wanted to hurt *anyone* who was not one of us.

The officers all talked of how people hated us—and wanted to see an end put to us. "We must stick together. We must become as one! We are the Gods!" We cried out in insane anger.

"We must strike out against those who attack us!"

"All men wish to put an end to us! And can not!"

"When we stick together we are an army!"

"When we stick together we are a FUCKING ARMY!" George cried out. "No one can stop us!"

I had already fucked four or five women, maybe more—I had lost count. Now all I could do was suck pussy. If I did not like the woman, I bit her pussy. I was tired and worn-out. Finally I fell into a bed of hot coals which seemed to be warm. Then I went to sleep. When I awoke I was covered with black soot. My clothes had been burned but not my skin. Why, I don't know. It didn't really matter. We had all undergone a spell which we had created ourselves. It was day and time to start breaking camp. No one was stirring. Clothing lay about the ground stained and ripped. Bodies hung out of trees—some half in the water and half out. One of my nearby brothers slept inside a garbage can, his feet dangling out.

It was so still not even birds were singing. It was cold before the sun had crept over the mountain. I kicked a can trying to make some noise and found out my ears were completely plugged. When I slapped the side of my head to make them open up I heard the sound of a horn blowing. I looked about to see who was blowing it but saw no one. Then I heard the rustle of branches breaking as someone fell from a tree right into the midst of a pile of sleeping bags. Someone stood up and screamed, "You motherfucking sonofabitch motherfucker!!"

I noticed I had stepped on a hat, containing change and a couple of crumpled dollar bills, which had been passed around by Johnny Angel, collecting for booze—is what he had said—but really he was collecting for his own pocket. It is an old Angel tradition to collect money when you are broke. The idea comes from the church where they pass a collection plate around every Sunday. Always at the start of a run you will see somebody passing a hat around to the hotdog riders and people dropping change in it.—This is supposed to be for booze but it is to fill one's own pocket and to get some money to eat on. This is usually only collected from the hotdog riders, unless an Angel is fool enough to drop a coin into it, which I doubt.

Then we broke camp, leaving behind the rumble of rubbish. The two toilets were burnt to the ground and we had to pay seventy-five dollars to replace them. Many drunken bodies of hotdog riders were left behind to pick themselves up—if they ever did. The cops jumped back from the gates as we roared out—they, too, looked insane after the two days. We broke onto the road in a roar, and as our heads cleared in the morning summer air, we roared out of the valley back to our cities and towns in California, knowing that we had a lot ahead of us. Knowing that we had brought our minds close together over the three days, we were riding out like saints with many prophecies to be delivered. There was work to be done. We had to get on with it. The festival was over, the 1966 Fourth of July run for the Hell's Angels Motorcycle Club of California.

I don't know where the Satan's Slaves are from. They come out of the San Fernando Valley, in southern California, from San Gabriel or San Joaquin—who knows? We consider them friends because they're so loose. They go into things with no thought of fear or of being afraid or anything. On the runs they always come in a big group. They are feared by the law. So we have no reason to place them in the same category as the Gypsy Jokers and all of the other hotdog riders. They were offered a charter under the Hell's Angels, but did not want it because they had had the name of Satan's Slaves for so long that I guess they feel it would be bad luck to change names now. Pete says we have to watch out for them. Pete is a great man, a man that likes to see and has a great understanding of men. He likes to talk a lot. The Satan's Slaves have no feelings for the law, just as we have none. But they take more of a destructive attitude towards the law, one that will be their own destruction if they do not watch out and are not very careful. For instance, we heard on the radio once that the landlord had evicted one Satan's Slave from an apartment house in southern California. In turn the Satan's Slaves ran through the apartments, ripping them apart, throwing the furniture into the pool, completely demolishing the house. This is why the Hell's Angels respect them, because they don't take no shit like we don't. We take care of business and then let the people ask the questions. I think we leave a very good telltale essence behind us. Either have respect for a man or this is the way you'll end up. When one thinks about it it's true. Tell me this is not the way it is going to end up in the end *end*. Need I say more? Destruction is on the menu for everyone.

The Satan's Slaves have a top rocker and a bottom rocker on the back of their jackets. The top rocker reads: SATAN'S SLAVES. The bottom rocker gives the name of the place they're from, and in the center, where our death's head is, they have a bike coming forward with high handlebars and in between the handlebars is the face of a devil. Their colors are black and white where ours are red and white. Nobody knows too much about them. All we know is that they're usually along on the runs. And they ride off together when the run is over. As we do.

WE ONCE WENT to San Bernardino for an incorporation meeting, the reason was to form a corporation of the Hell's Angels. There was a lawyer there by the name of Jeremiah Castelman, who had many ideas about making money, which would make him richer than everyone, naturally. We were ready for him at the Berdoo Ranch, for the officers of the chapters had brought along a tape recorder. When the lawyer saw the tape recorder he balked and stammered and stuttered with many words. For an hour or so he ran down the ifs and ands and buts of how we could make money. In the end the only chapters that were behind him were two out of seven chapters, and funny it was to note that it was the southern chapters that were behind him—the Berdoo Chapter and the Dago Chapter, both from the South.

The South is where the money is with all the movie producers, and all the production cats that want to go on the Batman trip for the Hell's Angels. We told him to take his Hell's Angels T-shirts, boots, purses, bands, and what not and shove them straight up his ass. Ralph Barger told him, over the tape recorder, "When I'm ready to use this death's head on my back to make money—that's the day I quit the Hell's Angels." And quote, "Before I see anyone use this death's head to make money, I'll kill the motherfucker." And he meant it, just like we mean it, though it took only one of us to say it. We're not on no money trip. We hate money, and all that love it we hate.

The day will come when Blind Bob will be able to whip anyone who sells his soul for money. Right now he's just getting in practice. This earth is Hell, and when the fire comes Blind Bob is going to be ready to torture all those souls of destruction who fall for the Devil's Fortune and Fame. So you the people better rise up off of it and start getting with the real thing. On the back of my courtesy cards I write six words: on the top it says LIFE SOUL DEATH, on the bottom it says LOVE FORTUNE FAME. I link up LIFE and FAME with an arrow. I link your SOUL with LOVE and I link your DEATH with FORTUNE, with arrows going from one word to the other. Write the six words down and line them up to see which direction your soul is headed towards. In other words, as you read your papers and books, all you'll see and hear of is FORTUNE and FAME. Have you ever asked yourself what happened to Love?

Do you know that God is Love? What happened to the creators? They're now shoved into the gutter . . . and the blasted production line has taken over. The true people on this earth are the creative people like the poets, the teachers, the painters—anyone who creates with his hands. These are people of Love, not of Fortune and Fame. Satan created Fortune and Fame. He came to the world with it. While God is Love. His people are creators as he is. In the end they will come together and Fortune and Fame will be left to burn as it is written.

THE HELL'S ANGELS

tom wolfe

Kesey met the Hell's Angels one afternoon in San Francisco through Hunter Thompson, who was writing a book about them. It turned out to be a remarkable book, as a matter of fact, called *Hell's Angels, a Strange and Terrible Saga*. Anyway, Kesey and Thompson were having a few beers and Thompson said he had to go over to a garage called the Box Shop to see a few of the Angels, and Kesey went along. A Hell's Angel named Frenchy and four or five others were over there working on their motorcycles and they took to Kesey right away. Kesey was a stud who was just as tough as they were. He had just been busted for marijuana, which certified him as Good People in the Angels' eyes. They told him you can't trust a man who hasn't done time, and Kesey was on the way to doing time, in any case. Kesey said later that the marijuana bust impressed them but they couldn't have cared less that he was a novelist. But they knew about that, too, and here was a big name who was friendly and interested in them, even though he wasn't a queer or a reporter or any of those other creep suck-ups who were coming around that summer.

And a great many were coming around in the summer of 1965. The summer of 1965 had made the Hell's Angels infamous celebrities in California. Their reputation was at its absolutely most notorious all-time highest. A series of incidents—followed by an amazing series of newspaper and magazine articles, *Life* and the *Saturday Evening Post* among them—had the people of the Far West looking to each weekend in the Angels' life as an invasion by baby-raping Huns. Intellectuals around San Francisco, particularly at Berkeley, at the University of California, were beginning to romanticize about the Angels in terms of "alienation" and "a generation in revolt," that kind of thing. People were beginning to get in touch with Thompson to see if he couldn't arrange for them to meet the Angels—not the whole bunch, Hunter, maybe one or two at a time. Well, Kesey didn't need any one or two at a time. He and the boys took a few tokes on a joint, and the Hell's Angels were on the bus.

The next thing the citizens of La Honda knew, there was a huge sign at the Kesey place—15 feet long, three feet high, in red white and blue.

The Merry Pranksters Welcome the Hell's Angels

Saturday, August 7, 1965, was a bright clear radiant limelit summer day amid God's handiwork in La Honda, California. The citizens were getting ready for the day by nailing shut their doors. The cops were getting ready by revving up a squad of ten patrol cars with flashing lights and ammunition. The Pranksters were getting ready by getting bombed. They were down there in the greeny gorge, in the cabin and around it, under the redwoods, getting bombed out of their gourds. They had some good heavy surges of God-given adrenaline going for them, too. Nobody ever came right out front and said it, but this happened to be the real-life Hell's Angels coming, about forty of them, on a full-fledged Angels' "run," the sort of outing on which the Angels did their thing, their whole freaking thing, *en* mangy raunchy head-breaking fire-pissing rough-goddamn-housing *masse*. The Pranksters had a lot of company for the occasion. It was practically like an audience, all waiting for the stars to appear. A lot of the old Perry Lane crowd was there, Vic Lovell, Ed McClanahan, and the others. Allen Ginsberg was there and so was Richard Alpert and a lot of San Francisco and Berkeley intellectuals. *Tachycardia*, you all—but Kesey was calm and even laughing a little, looking strong as an ox in his buckskin shirt, the Mountain Man, and he made it all seem right and inevitable, an inevitable part of the flow and right now in this moment. Hell, if the straight world of San Mateo County, California, had decided to declare them all outlaws over an innocuous thing like marijuana, then they could freaking well go with the flow and show them what the saga called Outlaw was really like. The Angels brought a lot of things into synch. Outlaws, by definition, were people who had moved off of dead center and were out in some kind of Edge City. The beauty of it was, the Angels had done it like the Pranksters, by choice. They had become outlaws first—to *explore*, muvva—and then got busted for it. The Angels' trip was the motorcycle and the Pranksters' was LSD, but both were in an incredible entry into an orgasmic moment, *now*, and within forty-eight hours the Angels would be taking acid on board, too. The Pranksters would be taking on . . . Ahor, the ancient horror, the middle-class boy fear of Hell's Angels, *Hell's Angels*, in the dirty flesh, and if they could bring that dark deep-down thing into their orbit—

Kesey! What in the freaking—tachycardia, you all . . .

Bob Dylan's voice is raunching and rheuming in the old jacklegged chants in huge volume from out the speakers up in the redwood tops up on the dirt cliff across the highway—*He o o oy Min ter'I am bou-rine Man*—as part of Sandy Lehmann-Haupt's Non-Station KLSD program, the indomitable disco-freak-jockey Lord Byron Styrofoam himself, Sandy, broadcasting over a microphone in a cabin and spinning them for you—Cassady revved up so tight it's like mechanical speed man sprocket—Mountain Girl ready—*Hey, Kesey!*—Hermit grin—Page ablaze—men, women, children, painted and in costume—ricochet around the limelit dell—*Argggggghhhhh*—about 3 P.M. they started hearing it.

It was like a locomotive about ten miles away. It was the Hell's Angels in "running formation" coming over the mountain on Harley-Davidson 74s. The Angels were up there somewhere weaving down the curves on Route 84, gearing down—*thraggggggggh*—and winding up, and the locomotive sound got louder and louder until you couldn't hear yourself talk any more or Bob Dylan rheumy and—*thraaaaaaaggggghh*—here they came around the last curve, the Hell's Angels, with the bikes, the beards, the long hair, the sleeveless denim jackets with the death's head insignia and all the rest, looking their most royal rotten, and then one by one they came barreling in over the wooden bridge up to the front of the house, skidding to a stop in explosions of dust, and it was like a movie or something—each one of the outlaws bouncing and gunning across the bridge with his arms spread out in a tough curve to the handlebars and then skidding to a stop, one after another after another.

The Angels, for their part, didn't know what to expect. Nobody had ever invited them anywhere before, at least not as a gang. They weren't on many people's invitation lists. They figured they would see what was there and what it was all about, and they would probably get in a hell of a fight before it was all over, and heads would break, but that was about par for the course anyway. The Angels always came into alien situations black and wary, sniffing out the adversary, but that didn't even register at this place. So many people were already so high, on something, it practically dissolved you on the spot. The Pranksters had what looked like about a million doses of the Angels' favorite drug—beer—and LSD for all who wanted to try it. The beer made the Angels very happy and the LSD made them strangely peaceful and sometimes catatonic, in contrast to the Pranksters and other intellectuals around, who soared on the stuff.

June the Goon gave a Hell's Angel named Freewheeling Frank some LSD, which he thought was some kind of souped-up speed or something—and he had the most wondrous experience of his life. By nightfall he had climbed a redwood and was nestled up against a loudspeaker in a tree grooving off the sounds and vibrations of Bob Dylan singing "The Subterranean Homesick Blues."

Pete, the drag racer, from the San Francisco Hell's Angels, grinned and rummaged through a beer tub and said, "Man, this is nothing but a goddamn wonderful scene. We didn't know what to expect when we came, but it turned out just fine. This time it's all ha-ha, not thump-thump." Soon the gorge was booming with the Angels' distinctive good-time lots-a-beer belly laugh, which goes: Haw!—Haw!—Haw!—Haw! —Haw!—Haw!

Sandy Lehmann-Haupt, Lord Byron Styrofoam, had hold of the microphone and his disco-freak-jockey rapping blared out of the redwoods and back across the highway: "This is Non-Station KLSD, 800 micrograms in your head, the station designed to blow your mind and undo your bind, from up here atop the redwoods on Venus!" Then he went into a long talking blues song about the Hell's Angels, about fifty stanzas worth, some of it obscure acid talk, some of it wild legends, about squashing turtles on the highway, nutty stuff like that, and every stanza ending with the refrain:

> Oh, but it's great to be an Angel,
> And be dirty all the time!

What the hell—here was some wild-looking kid with the temerity to broadcast out over the highways of California that Angels were dirty all the time—but how the hell could you resist, it was too freaking madly manic—and pretty soon the Angels and everybody else were joining in the chorus:

Oh, but it's great to be an Angel,
And be dirty all the time!

Then Allen Ginsberg was in front of the microphone with finger cymbals on each hand, dancing around with a beard down to his belly and chanting Hindu chants into the microphone booming out over California, U.S.A., *Hare krishna hare krishna hare krishma hare krishna* — what the mollyfock is hairy krishna — who is this hairy freak — but you can't help yourself, you got to groove with this cat in spite of yourself. Ginsberg really bowled the Angels over. He was a lot of things the Angels hated, a Jew, an intellectual, a New Yorker, but he was too much, the greatest straightest unstraight guy they ever met.

And be dirty all the time!

The filthy kooks — by nightfall the cops were lined up along the highway, car after car, just across the creek, outside the gate, wondering what the fock. The scene was really getting weird. The Pranksters had everything in their electronic arsenal going, rock 'n' roll blazing through the treetops, light projections streaming through the gorge, Station KLSD blazing and screaming over the cops' heads, people in Day-Glo regalia blazing and lurching in the gloom, the Angels going *Haw — Haw — Haw — Haw*, Cassady down to just his hell of a build, nothing else, just his hell of a build, jerking his arms out and sprocketing around under a spotlight on the porch of the log manse, flailing a beer bottle around in one hand and shaking his other one at the cops:

"You sneaky motherfuckers! What the fuck's wrong with you! Come on over here and see what you get . . . goddamn your shit-filled souls anyway!" — laughing and jerking and sprocketing — "Don't fuck with me, you sons of shit-lovers. Come on over. You'll get every fucking thing you deserve."

The hell of it, men, is here is a huge obscene clot of degradation, depradation and derogation proceeding loose and crazed on the hoof before our very eyes, complete with the very Hell's Angels, and there is nothing we can do but contain it. Technically, they might have been able to move in on the grounds of Cassady's exposing himself or something of the sort, but no real laws were being broken, except every law of God and man — but sheer containment was looking like the best policy. Moving in on those crazies even with ten carloads of armed cops for a misdemeanor like lewd display — the explosion was too grotesque to think of. And the cops' turret lights revolved and splashed against the dirt cliff in a red strobe light effect and their car-to-headquarters radios were wide open and cracking out with sulphurous 220-volt electric thorn baritones and staticky sibilants—*He-e-e-ey Mis-ter Tam-bou-rine Man*— just to render the La Honda gorge totally delirious.

Meanwhile, the Angels were discovering the goddamnedest thing. Usually, most places they headed into on their runs, they tested people's cool. What are *you* looking at, mother. As soon as the shock or naked terror registered, they would be happy. Or if there was no shock and terror but instead somebody tried some brave little shove back, then it was time to break heads and tear everybody a new asshole. But these mollyfocking Pranksters were test-proof. The Angels didn't know what permissive was until they got to Kesey's. *Go with the flow!* The biggest baddest toughest most awfulest-looking Hell's Angel of them all was a big monster named Tiny. The second biggest baddest toughest most-awfulest-looking Hell's Angel was a big raw-boned guy named Buzzard, dark-looking, with all this dark hair and a beard, all shaggy and matted and his nose came out like a beak and his Adam's apple hung down about a foot, and he was just like an enormous buzzard. Tiny and Buzzard had a thing of coming up to each other when they were around non-Angels and sticking out their tongues and then licking each other's tongues, a big sloppy lap it up, just to shake up the squares, it really jolted them—so they came up right in front of this tall broad of Kesey's, Mountain Girl, and la-a-a-a-ap—and they couldn't believe it. She just looked right at them and grinned and exploded sunballs out of her eyes and started laughing at them, *Haw— Haw—Haw*, as if to say in plain language: What a bullshit thing. It was freaking incredible. Then some of them passed a joint around and they passed it to Mountain Girl and she boomed out:

"Hell, no! What the hell you doing putting your dirty mouth on this clean joint for! This is a clean joint and you're putting your dirty mouths on it!" Nobody in living memory had ever refused a toke from a joint passed by Angels, at least not on grounds of sanitation, except this crazy girl who was just bullshitting them blind, and they loved it.

It even got to the point where Mountain Girl saw Tiny heading into the mad bathroom with a couple of beer cans like he is going to hole up in there and drink a couple of cans in peace, but this is the bathroom all the girls around here are using, and Mountain Girl yells out to Sonny Barger, the maximum leader of the Hell's Angels, "Hey, Sonny! Tell this big piece of trash to stay out of our clean bathroom!"—in a bullshit tone, of course—and Sonny picks it up, "Yeah, you big piece of trash! Stay out of the clean bathroom! They don't want you in there!"— and Tiny slinks out the door, outside, in a bullshit slink, but he does it—

And that's it! It's happening. The Hell's Angels are in our movie, we've got 'em in. Mountain Girl and a lot of the Pranksters had hit on the perfect combination with the Angels. They were friendly toward them, maybe friendlier than anybody had been in their lives, but they weren't craven about it, and they took no shit. It was the perfect combination, but the Pranksters didn't even have to think of it as a combination. They just did their thing and that was the way it worked out. All these principles they had been working on and talking about in the isolation of La Honda—they freaking well *worked*.

Go with the flow—and what a flow—these cats, these Pranksters—at big routs like this the Angels often had a second feature going entitled *Who Gets Fucked?*—and it hadn't even gotten to that before some blonde from out of town, one of the guests from way out there, just one nice soft honey hormone squash, she made it clear to three Angels that she was ready to go, so they all trooped out to the backhouse and they had a happy round out there. Pretty soon all the Angels knew about the "new mamma" out in the backhouse and a lot of them piled in there, hooking down beers, laughing, taking their turns, making various critiques. The girl had her red and white dress pushed up around her chest, and two or three would be on her at once, between her legs, sitting on her face in the sick ochre light of the shack with much lapping and leering and bubbling and gulping through furzes of pubic hair while sweat and semen glistened on the highlights of her belly and thighs and she twitched and moaned, not in protest, however, in a kind of drunken bout of God knew what and men with no pants on were standing around, cheering, chiding, waiting for their turn, or their second turn, or the third until she had been fenestrated in various places at least fifty times. Some of the Angels went out and got her ex-husband. He was weaving and veering around, bombed, they led him in there under glare and leer and lust musk suffocate the rut but they told him to go to it. All silent—shit, this is going too far—but the girl rises up in a blear and asks him to kiss her, which he does, glistening secretions, then he lurches and mounts her and slides it in, and the Angels cheer Haw Haw—

—but that is her movie, it truly is, and we have gone with the flow.

So much beer—which is like an exotic binge for the Pranksters, beer. Mountain Girl and Kesey are up in the limelit bower and the full moon comes down through the treetop silhouettes. They are just rapping in the moonlight, and then Sandy wanders on up there and sits with them, high on acid, and he looks down and the floor of the forest is rippling with moonlight, the ground shimmers and rolls like a stream in the magic bower and they just sit there — a *buzzard!* Buzzard is wandering up the slope toward them and there in the moonlight in the dark in the magic bower he . . . *is* a buzzard, the biggest ever made, the beak, the deathly black, the dopply glottal neck, the shelled back and dangling wings, stringy nodule legs — Kaaawwwwwww! — and Kesey jumps up and starts throwing his arms up at him, like the way you would scare away a buzzard, and says,

"Aaaaagh! a buzzard! Hey! Get away, you're a buzzard! Get this buzzard out of here!"

It's a bullshit gesture, of course — and Buzzard laughs — *Haw! Haw! Haw!* — it is not real, but it is . . . *real*, real buzzard, you can see the whole thing with two minds — Kaw Kaw Kaaawwwww — and Buzzard jumps and flaps his arms — and the whole . . . connection, the *synch*, between the name, the man, the bird, flows together right there, and it doesn't matter whether he is buzzard or man because it has all come together, and they all see it . . .

They all see so much. Buzzard goes, and Sandy goes, and Kesey and Mountain Girl are in the moonlight ripply bower. By and by — where? — Kesey and Mountain Girl — and so much flows together from the lights and the delirium and the staticky sibilants down below, so much is clear, so much flows in rightness, that night, under the full moon, up above the flails and bellows down below —

THE HELL'S ANGELS party went on for two days and the cops never moved in. Everybody, Angels and Pranksters, had a righteous time and no heads were broken. There had been one gang-bang, but the girl was a volunteer. It was her movie. In fact, for the next six or seven weeks, it was one long party with the Angels. The news spread around intellectual-hip circles in the San Francisco-Berkeley area like a legend. In these circles, anyway, it once and for all put Kesey and the Pranksters up above the category of just another weirdo intellectual group. They had broken through the worst hangup that intellectuals know — the *real-life* hangup. Intellectuals were always hung up with the feeling that they weren't coming to grips with real life. Real life belonged to all those funky spades and prize fighters and bullfighters and dock workers and grape pickers and wetbacks. *Nostalgie de la boue.* Well, the Hell's Angels were real life. It didn't get any realer than that, and Kesey had pulled it off. People from San Francisco and Berkeley started coming by La Honda more than ever. It was practically like an intellectual tourist attraction. Kesey would talk about the Angels.

"I asked Sonny Barger how he picks new members, new Angels, and he told me, 'We don't pick 'em. We *recognize* 'em.' "

And everybody grokked over that.

Likely as not, people would find Hell's Angels on the place. The Angels were adding LSD to the already elaborate list of highs and lows they liked, beer, wine, marijuana, benzedrine, Seconal, Amytal, Nembutal, Tuinal. Some of them had terrible bummers—bummers was the Angels' term for a bad trip on a motorcycle and very quickly it became the hip world's term for a bad trip on LSD. The only bad moment at Kesey's came one day when an Angel went berserk during the first rush of the drug and tried to strangle his old lady on Kesey's front steps. But he was too wasted at that point to really do much.

So it was wonderful and marvelous, an unholy alliance, the Merry Pranksters and the Hell's Angels, and all hours of the day or night you could hear the Hell's Angels gearing and winding down Route 84 to Kesey's, and the people of La Honda felt like the plague had come, and wasn't there anything that could be done. More than one of the Pranksters had his reservations, too. The Angels were like a time bomb. So far, so good—one day the Angels even swept and cleaned up the place—but they were capable of busting loose into carnage at any moment. It brought the adrenaline into your throat. The potential was there, too, because if the truth were known, there were just a few of the Pranksters who could really talk to the Angels—chiefly Kesey and Mountain Girl. Mainly it was Kesey. Kesey was the magnet and the strength, the man in both worlds. The Angels respected him and they weren't about to screw him around. He was one of the coolest guys they had ever come across. One day, finally, Kesey's cool came to the test with the Angels and it was a strange moment.

Kesey and the Pranksters and the Angels had taken to going out to the backhouse and sitting in a big circle and doing the Prankster thing, a lot of rapping back and forth and singing, high on grass, and you never knew where it was going to go. Usually it went great. The Angels took to the Prankster thing right away. They seemed to have an immediate intuitive grasp of where it was going, and one time Kesey started playing a regular guitar and Babbs started playing a four-string amplified guitar and Kesey got into a song off the top of his head, about "the vibrations," a bluesy song and the Angels joined in, and it got downright religious there for a while, with everybody singing, "Oh, the vi-bra-tions . . . Oh, the vi-bra-tions. . . ."

And then Kesey and a few of the Pranksters and a lot of the Angels, including Sonny Barger of the Oakland Chapter, the maximum leader of all the Angels, were sitting around the backhouse passing around joints and rapping. The subject was "people who are bullshit."

There are certain people who are bullshit and you can always recognize them, Kesey was saying, and the Angels were nodding yeah, that certainly is right.

"Now you take——," said Kesey, mentioning one of the Angels who was not present. "He's a bullshit person."

A *bullshit person*—and man—

"Listen, Kesey," says Barger, 100 percent Hell's Angels. "——is an Angel, and nobody—*nobody*—calls an Angel a bullshit person."

—the freaking gauntlet is down. It's like forever and every eye in the place pins on Kesey's face and you can hear the blood squirt in your veins. But Kesey doesn't even blink and his voice doesn't even change one half tone, just the old Oregon drawl:

"But I *know* him, Sonny. If I didn't *know* him, I wouldn't call him a bullshit person."

Yeah—we-e-e-ell—everybody, Angels and Pranksters—well—Kesey *knows* him—there is nothing to do but grok over this statement, and everybody sits there, still, trying to grok over it, and after a second, the moment where heads get broken and fire gets pissed is over—*We-e-e-ell, ye-ah*—

Two or three days later it occurs to some of the Pranksters that they *still* don't know what the hell Kesey meant when he said that. He *knows* the guy. It doesn't make any sense. It's a concept with no bottom to it—but so what! At the moment he said it, it was the one perfect thing he could have said. Kesey was so totally into the moment, he could come up with it, he could break up that old historic push me, shove you, yeah-sez-who sequence and in an instant the moment, that badass moment, was over.

THE PRANKSTERS GOT pretty close to several of the Angels as individuals. Particularly Gut and Freewheeling Frank and Terry and the Tramp. Every now and then somebody would take one or another of the Angels up into the tree house and give them a real initiation into psychedelics. They had a huge supply of DMT. As somebody once put it, LSD is a long strange journey; DMT is like being shot out of a cannon. There in the tree house, amid the winking googaws, they would give the Angels DMT, and Mountain Girl saw some of them, like Freewheeling Frank, after they came down. They would walk around in no particular direction, listing slightly, the eyes bugged wide open, glazed.

"They were as naked as an Angel is ever gonna git," she told Kesey.

MY HELL'S ANGEL

diane wakoski

This will be a straightforward poem.
This will have no beautiful sidetracking, like flutes on a shell, to
    distract you.
This will have no digressions,
    like wet fern,
    like kelp dragging your feet down in water
    like ground glass between your teeth
    like ornamented crosses and velvet coats
    like rusty pistols
    or crusty bread
to disguise my feelings,
to silhouette and forget me.

This will be a poem without imaginary characters
a point in time, an encounter,
a poetic moment,

someone else talking,
without an elegant race horse
to distract you.

I am writing it
because I had an experience that was a poem.
Because I am a romantic
Because my life is unfulfilled and I am looking for
new experiences
Because I open myself up to poetry
Because everyone talks it
when they see how very well
I listen.

This year.
Now.
Summer.
Beach. Where I am. A lonely woman
Ripe, exotic, with a grace
few women have.
Infectious smile. Friendly. Open.
Warm if I like you.
Walking on the beach
I have heard poetry. I am expecting to see people.
There are two hours of sunset on the beach
and I go down to walk on it,
to see the tide come up high against the rocks and swirl
like my favorite paintings around
my feet.
I have forgotten all the men I love.
I remember that I am alone
But I have lots of things to do.
And I am wearing my purple bikini
with a crinkly white shirt over it because it is a cool sunset.
Cool sunset
remember that.

I walk down the beach. It is
empty.
I am thinking of the men I love.
I have forgotten the men I love.

They are blond.
They are dark.
They all have mustaches,
ride motorcycles,
mainly exist in my head.

Against the rocks,
in the last strong rays of sunlight
I see a man in levis,
with his shirt off,
a beard longish hair,
he is relaxed into the rocks,
a part of the beach. Beside him
are motorcycle boots, which he is not wearing.
I like men who ride motorcycles.
I like the way his levis fit.
I am an old Californian.
The beach turns me on.
I decide he is someone I would like to interest.
I walk out into the foam.
I play in the water.
I skirt him. I am a skirt,
but I am wearing a bikini. My legs are tan.
I have long hair. It blows in the sunset, the salty air.
My dark glasses give me the look of an ancient scarab.

He gets up and walks over to where I am playing
into the waves. He is small.
Very muscular. The kind of man I like,
with a straight nose. Scars, many scars on his
shirtless torso. I am already participating in a literary event.
He is a character in my sunset-on-the-beach play. I am curious
what he will say and do. I like him because I have created him
and then by accident found him there.

He asks me if I live here and I say no, I am here for the summer.
I ask him if he lives here and he says no, his bike is broken and
is in San Diego and he is staying here until he can get it fixed.

I know then that he doesn't just wear motorcycle boots.
He rides motorcycles. His arm is tattooed.
It says, "Apache."

He asks me
referring to the two gold loops in my pierced ears,
if I have another earring.
Laughing I say, no, why should I have three earrings.
I like to laugh. It is part of the sunset.
Part of a play. Part of the deepness I feel in my body
about being alive. I can always cry or laugh. I
can reach down and pull out the creased edges of my body this way.
I am in touch with the water. It laps my feet.
Sun glints off my eyeglasses. I am
happy to be alive. Happy to encounter life.

He asks me if I will give him one of my earrings.
What would I do with only one, I ask him, laughing again,
happy that there are people like me who ask for what they want
and really expect the world to give it to them.
He doesn't even answer such a silly question. Obviously
whatever I do with only one earring is my business, not his.
It is gold. It shines in my ear.
It reminds me of the man who pierced my ears.
It reminds me of my pierced heart, of a car called Pierce Arrow,
It reminds me that the sun is glinting off my smile,
that the small waves are around my feet and I'm talking to a man
with one hole in one ear, wearing levis, who rides a broken Harley,
on a beach at sunset in California
and that there is nothing in my life
but the sun glinting off my earring and that the earring
could be given away and nothing would change.
An ex-
change.
No change.
So I take the earring from my left ear, and I laugh
and I hand it to him.

He puts it in his ear.

Now I tell him I am a poet.
And he tells me about his life.
It is a life of challenge. He wants to challenge every man
to fight him. He wants to prove his body against every man.

■ ■ ■

He rides with the Angels he tells me,
and he tells me of fishing,
of hunting with only a knife,
of riding,
of the pleasure of being a longshoreman when he has to work,
of moving his body in the cold,
of comparing what he can do with men much taller and bigger than
        he,
he tells me of loading tuna on the icy boats, of only wearing his
T-shirt, he tells me of sleeping on the beach at night, of the
challenge of riding his bike in winter on the sleety streets, of
the wind of Chicago. His eye
has a scar in it. He fights men who offer to buy him a beer
and make fun of his beard. He is blond,
he wants to fight the world off,
I do not want to fight the world off, but I love
this stranger, with my gold earring glinting in his ear
wanting to fight off the world,
to prove he is half Apache,
born on the reservation in Arizona,
riding with a gang of men who talk poetry

Where are my roots, I ask myself,
scarcely getting a word into this monologue,
the man who talks like an angel,
rides with the angels,
and whom I will see this once on a sunset beach in California.
I look at the cliffs over the beach.
We talk about building houses.
He knows how to fight,
and to construct buildings.
The ice plant is dry, barely holds in the eroding cliffs.
California will fall into the ocean soon.
He won't be sleeping on a cliff or under it when California does this.

He likes the Black Panther, he tells me.
I laugh.
Ask him which ones.
He does not understand me.
We talk about the elegance of big cats.
This one is special he says. He would like to own one.

My only monologue is delivered then
on the beach
in the sunset,
the tide getting higher,
one ear empty of its gold, my hands
moving like a cat pawing at my long hair
which moves in the salty beach air.

Why do you want to own the panther, I say.
Aren't you contradicting everything you've told me about being
wild and loving things for their wildness, wanting everything
to be free, wanting to fight for everything, to prove who is
freest, who in control?
Why must you own it?
Why must anyone own something to love it?
Why can't you let it come and go?
I am so afraid of owning things and tell him

but he knows
because I've given him my gold earring
and someone who cared about his possessions
would not give such a thing casually away.
I gave it because I knew that it was part of the encounter,
the exchange,
that everything we have is that way.

The tide got so high, he had to pick up his jacket, his wrist watch
and run. He was waiting to meet his girl friend. We ran
to where we might find his girl friend. She came, I walked away.
It was nice talking to you, I said,
laughing,
walking away, exhilarated,
knowing there are people whose will to survive
gives them muscles far beyond their size.
I will always remember
his muscles,
his Apache tattoo,
his words about the joy of fighting and winning,
the sadness of his broken bike,
his candor in immediately asking for what he wanted,
the sun on the beach,

my hair blowing,
the sun on my face,
the tide around my ankles,
the sun on his straight nose,
the eroding cliffs,
his anger at people who wouldn't fight, who had no pride,
the sun glinting on my gold earrings,
the sun on the gold hair on my arm,
the sun glinting off the waves,
the sun which he'd wake up to in the morning, on the beach,
the sun he put in my heart
because he was so alive
and he shared some of it
with me.

Louisville. Kentucky. 1965. Bikerider crossing the Ohio River.

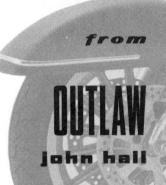

from

OUTLAW

john hall

"The Spirit of the Lord is a raging fire in the breast of the
faithful that devours the impious."

Saint Thomas Munzer

the Pagans Motorcycle Club was started by a bunch of rebels in
Maryland. No one seemed to know for sure where. It could have been
Prince Georges County, because that's where they first became a pain
in the ass for law enforcement. But the name Fruitland, a hick town on
the southern portion of the Eastern Shore, kept popping up. And if anyone wants to erect a commemorative billboard, either place will do. Lou
Dolkin is generally credited as the Pied Piper who hatched the idea. For
their emblem he wanted the image of an ancient god of Northern
Europe. John-John Griffith got the idea of Black Surt, the demonic
guardian of Muspell, from a comic book. They drew him up with horns
like a bull, feet like a chicken, and they sat him in an arch of fire holding a flaming sword. And the club was born.

Soon the Pagans had a half-dozen clubs terrorizing rednecks and bar
owners along the highways of Southern Maryland and Virginia. Hairy,
bearded, swastika-toting, sixties-style outlaws, born to raise hell and have

a good time. As hicksters and Southrons they had a lot of goofy rituals, like stealing your breakfast every Wednesday morning.

It wasn't long until one of the rebels got in a hassle with some punks in one of the burbs in Washington. The punks belonged to a car club called the Imperials and the car punks wanted an old-fashioned fifties style gang rumble. The parking lot of a shopping center was selected. And next to the parking lot was a field with high weeds.

About dark cars began pulling into the parking lot. There were guys from the Imperials. There were friends. There were kids who had heard about it and wanted to get a piece of the action. All together there about a hundred guys in the parking lot brandishing chains and whips made from car antennas. Everyone knew the local Pagan club only had about a dozen members. And unlike the car club, the Pagans didn't have any friends. There was no way the outlaws would show.

Then gunshots rang out from the weeds. One of the car club guys fell to the ground, holding his bloody leg and screaming. Windshields shattered. Shotgun pellets dented fenders. People screamed, engines roared, tires squeeled. And the whole parking lot cleared out in less than two minutes.

Nobody ever heard from the suburban car club again. But the Pagans were all over the *Washington Post* for a week, and the whole town was talking about them. "Suburban Washington was getting worse than Southeast Asia," the Beltway pundits were claiming.

The Pagans learned from this incident that one righteous brother willing to go down for the club was worth ten hangers-on who were only looking for loose women and cheap thrills. Whenever a prospective member came along the first question a Pagan asked was "Is he good people?" That meant if he got in a jam would he go to jail or would he talk and send a brother to jail in his place. They also learned that while a hundred people flying colors on a highway might impress motorists, you were better off with a small club of about twelve righteous people. You didn't want people who would show up for a party and then split when the shit hit the fan.

These two lessons provided the foundation on which Pagan clubs were built. Grab the twelve most righteous people in the town and let the other clubs have the rest. Let them claim to have a hundred members, let them hand out colors like candy on Halloween. When the shit came down, the Pagans would come up clean.

In the mid-sixties the Pagans came under the leadership of Fred "Dutch" Burhans, an imperialist who had visions of ruling an outlaw empire spanning the East Coast from the frozen parishes of French

Canada to the Rebel trailer parks on the sandy beaches of Florida. He established a half-dozen clubs in Southern Maryland and Virginia. Then he crossed the Mason-Dixon Line to the Amish farmlands of Lancaster County, Pennsylvania.

Here he went after a well-established and respected club, The Sons of Satan. The leader was John "Satan" Marron, a man who listened to Dutch's imperial dreams and liked what he heard. The Pagans soon had their first club in Pennsylvania.

Dutch was the empire builder, the Caesar, but Satan became the ambassador, his Mark Antony. Satan could show up at a clubhouse on Friday night and talk nonstop until Sunday afternoon. And by the time he left, everyone's sides hurt from laughter and half your club would be ready to join his new outlaw empire.

Satan also brought something else to the Pagans.

Satan's own roots were in the Dutch countryside. He had deep blue eyes and hair as black as shoe polish that he swept back in a thick mane like a lion. His jaw, his nose, his cheeks were square. Take away the swastikas and leather jacket. Put him in a black hat and pastel blue shirt with suspenders, and he could be hawking shoofly pies from the back of an Amish buggy in rural Lancaster County.

The Amish are the strictest of the Pennsylvania-Dutch religious groups that go by the name Mennonites.

Historians, journalists, and law enforcement officials have learned a great deal about the Sicilian Mafia by placing it firmly in the context of Italian historical and cultural traditions. It's tradition of silence and honor can be traced back to a 14th Century rebellion known as the Sicilian Vespers. Its ritual pomp and ceremony are seen as the dark mirror image of Roman Catholicism.

In the same manner, any journalist or cop who spent time investigating the early Pagan clubs of Pennsylvania was shocked by their strong—if somewhat perverted—similarity to the Amish and Mennonite communities. The sense of secrecy and brotherhood. The suspicion of outsiders and the whole outside world in general. The rigid codes of dress that distinguish the brethren from outsiders. The rigid distinctions in the type of behavior expected from male and female members of the community. The manner in which both communities believed in taking care of all the needs of its brethren. The fanatical devotion of the brethren to the community and its style of life. The manner in which both are expected to shun members who were thrown out of the community. The 18th Century, medieval, mystical and thoroughly Teutonic outlook on the world.

However, the Mennonites are pacifists, and here the similarity stops.

It was Satan's own Dutch roots that gave him an invaluable asset in forming new clubs. When sizing up a prospective member, Satan was unimpressed by how big the guy was, how righteous he looked, or how loud he talked. Satan was looking for something more important, and he had an uncanny ability to spot it in a guy who was ready to bring to the club the fanatical commitment of a religious martyr.

If a group of guys wanted to start a Pagan club, Satan could pull into town and he knew immediately whether they were righteous or not. It was Satan who recruited the Pennsylvania clubs and who was responsible for the shift of the club's power base from Maryland and Virginia to Pennsylvania.

I had drifted into the Pagans earlier that Spring. I had sold my car and bought a motorcycle. A 650 cubic centimeter Triumph. Harley-Davidson is forever associated with the outlaw image. And for good reason. When you saw a pack of outlaws most of them were riding Hogs. But the truth is that if you rode a Harley you needed a car. Hogs broke down a lot, and they were hell on wet ground or snow.

The Triumph and BSA (that's pronounced Beeser) started in all weather. The front ends were the best ever made. You could even ride them on snow and ice. Just put your feet down and glide along slow. If the rear wheel went sideways, you could catch your balance with your feet and straighten the bike out. Try this with a hog, and you broke your leg. But best of all the Triumph and BSA were also designed for off-road use. If a cop was chasing you down the back roads of Berks County, you could take off through a cornfield. You could never get away with that on a hog.

I rode through the winter. And I froze. On weekends my Triumph was the only bike parked outside the Gaslight East on Hempstead Turnpike. In the summer the place was a motorcycle hangout with fifty bikes lined up in the street. But in the winter these guys traveled by car. They weren't outlaws.

Occasionally on those cold winter nights another solitary rider pulled up on a BSA and parked it next to mine. Over his black leather jacket he wore a sawed-off denim vest with a 1% patch on the front. His name was Richie Gavin, and the patches on the back of his jacket identified him as a member of the Nassau Aliens.

He was impressed by the fact that like him I rode through the winter. It was the sort of thing that the old outlaws called "true class." Something you either had or did not. And you simply could not make it up like a lot of guys tried to do later. On the nights he showed up, we ended up sitting off in a corner talking by ourselves. We were different then the rest of the crowd. Like I said, real outlaws manage to find each other.

Finally one night he picked up his shot glass, clicked it against mine and said, "In the Spring you gotta come around and ride with us." We drank to it.

This meant that I had found someone to sponsor me as a prospective member. If they were all like Richie, I figured I would be an Alien by Memorial Day.

Then one of the regulars at the Gaslight East, a guy from Levittown called Billy Koharik, told me to hold off on the Aliens. He told me that the guy who ran the Nassau Aliens, the Mortician, was a pain in the ass. He said that he had a better idea.

He had his bike torn down for the winter. But he said that it would be back together in a couple of weeks. In the meantime he was having patches made up to start his own outlaw club.

"I figure we got about a dozen guys in here that would make outlaw material," he said. "The rest can go piss on themselves."

I didn't like the idea of passing up the Number One 1% club in the Number One City in the world for some Mickey Mouse start-up operation.

With clubs in most of the New York boroughs and Long Island, the Aliens had established themselves a year earlier as the only 1% club in the metropolitan New York area. On a weekend they could ride to Rockaway or Coney Island with a pack of about fifty.

The Brooklyn Aliens were the most colorful club, and that's where it all started with Johnny Pinstripe and Frankie Wheelchair. Pinstripe owned a shop in Bay Ridge where he did the best custom paint jobs in New York, and that's how he got his name.

Wheelchair is another story. He ripped his bike apart one winter in the back of Pinstripe's shop where he found welding torches. Then he bought some steel and began making his own custom seat and sissy bar. All winter he talked about this project and what a "drop-dead good-looking" piece of equipment it was going to be. Finally Spring came and the big night arrived when he had promised to show up with his new custom seat and sissy bar all chromed and polished. He pulled up to a bar in Coney Island and everyone went out to have a gander at this drop-dead custom seat and sissy bar that by now had been played up like the Eiffel Tower on wheels.

But this was Brooklyn, the wiseacre capital of the world. When they got outside somebody said "It looks like a fuckin' wheelchair ta me." And that was that.

The Bronx was the biggest Alien club and it was also the baddest. The guys had been together for twenty years. They played handball in the park together when they were kids. As teenagers they formed a street gang and stole hubcaps. The street gang became a car club. And the final incarnation was the Bronx Aliens outlaw motorcycle gang.

The Queens and Nassau Aliens were relatively new. But they were solid. Partially because they thought they had something to prove to Brooklyn and the Bronx, but also because Nassau and eastern Queens really had better material because the communities lacked the tightness of the old ethnic neighborhoods and the guys found it in the outlaw gang.

Manhattan was a joke. Like everything in Manhattan it was all fad and showmanship. The Manhattan Aliens wore outlandish clothing and hung out in Saint Mark's Place where they hoped they could get laid. In fact it was the little flower girls who first made up the word "biker" to distinguish these guys from the hippies and the heads.

I hung with Richie and Billy throughout the winter. Richie introduced me to some of the other Aliens. But I also kept my ears open, and the word I got was that the Mortician could be a pain in the ass, and I also heard that Nassau and Queens had some membership problems and were no longer the force that they used to be. There were even rumors that some of them were talking about starting a new club.

I asked Billy what was happening with his new club and told him that we might be able to pick up some of the Aliens and put something good together. It was then that he told me that he had something that was even better. He said there was a new club in New York called the Pagans.

"A bunch of hillbillies and Rebels from Virginia," I told him. "Why would anybody want to ride with guys like that?"

But he insisted that wasn't the case anymore. They had new clubs in New York, Jersey and Pennsylvania. By the summer they were going to be the biggest outlaw club on the East Coast. They were looking for members. He had been down in Elmont partying with them and he liked the guys that he saw.

I still didn't like the idea of turning down a bunch of New Yorkers like the Aliens for an upstart hillbilly club from Dixie, but I agreed to go along with him.

We met them at a hole in the wall on Jericho turnpike, where the party was going on in the back room. When we walked in the front door we were greeted by the squat little man with the walk of a slow-moving gas station attendant. He had hair like Dean Martin and he was wearing sunglasses. He liked to call himself Little Caesar, but everyone else called him Sleepy.

He pushed his sunglasses up over his forehead.

"This is bullshit," he said. "You're late. If you guys wanna ride with us, you gotta learn how to show up on time."

This is even worse than hillbillies I thought. Tomorrow I get Richie to sponsor me with the Aliens.

We went in the back room, and I got my first look at the Pagans.

There sitting on a stool was Sweet William Parker. Sweet William was big, real big, with mischievous blue eyes, a mop of curly blonde hair, and a perpetual smirk tattooed across his face. He was the only Marine, as opposed to what seemed like a whole company of paratroopers, that I ever met in the Pagans.

I had gotten to know him from the bars along Hempstead Turnpike, where I had watched him bust up furniture and throw people through windows. The guy was a one-man wrecking crew. I was impressed.

He had a big lumbering awkward hillbilly gait, and he always seemed to be spilling beer or knocking over furniture. Someone would say something about it to Sweet William, and the guy would end up getting carried out the door feet first and covered with blood, that is if he didn't end up flying through a plate glass window head-first. Sweet William was one of those guys that would rather get in a fight than get laid.

He told me that his father was part Irish and part Indian and that his mother was part Irish and part Indian. I guess that made him a barroom version of Jim Thorpe. And I told him that it was because of guys like him that the government passed laws against selling liquor to the Indians.

Sooner or later he seemed to show up everywhere. I later figured out that this was because he was constantly getting banned from every place he tried to hang out in. He seemed to be steadily working his way down the entire length of Hempstead Turnpike. A couple of times I had helped him out in a fight, and he had gotten to like me.

When he saw me, he jumped off the bar stool and picked me up and spun me around in a big bear hug. Then he planted a big kiss on my lips. This was the outlaw greeting back in the sixties, a big sloppy French kiss on the lips, not some goofy thumb hand shake or high-five. It was originally designed to blow citizens' minds, which it did. As for the outlaws, they didn't have hang-ups about things like normal people did.

The Pagans had recruited Sweet William that winter. I never even knew that he had a motorcycle, and he never told me that he was a Pagan. But then the old outlaws were secretive. As it turned out, he had a BSA, which he had wrecked the summer before and the Pagans were rebuilding for him. The Pagans never let Sweet William work on his own bike, because he could damage a motorcycle by working on it as easily as he could damage a bar by drinking in it.

Sweet William also brought his kid brother, Stretch, into the club. The kid was as tall as Sweet William. But he was a lot leaner, and also a lot nastier. And Sweet William had done a good job teaching him how to fight. At eighteen Stretch was a lot younger than most of the guys. In fact the Pagans had a rule that you had to be twenty-one to join. But like all the other rules they waived them when they had a good reason. I myself wouldn't be twenty until July.

With Sweet William in the Pagans and my buddy Billy about to join, I didn't have much choice. By Memorial Day I was on my way to Reading with the Pagans.

It was a smart choice. After Memorial Day the Pagans' star was rising over New York, and the Aliens' was about to plunge.

The week after the big Memorial Day show in Reading we were having a meeting in the cellar of a clubhouse in Uniondale, when there was a knock on the door upstairs. Sweet William went to see who it was and returned with a big grin on his face.

"Wait'll you see this" he said.

Tommy Gannon tripped and fell down the stairs behind him and rolled into the room. Les the Rabbi walked in behind him, laughing at Gannon sprawled on the floor. They were both Nassau Aliens, or had been. Their jackets were now bare where the club patches had been ripped off.

They said they both quit and wanted to become Pagan prospects. Other guys had quit too, they said, and in another week there would be no more Nassau Aliens. It was because the Mortician was a pain in the ass, they said. But that line was starting to get old. There was more too it than that. The big show in Reading had made its point. The Aliens had avoided the Reading Races. They didn't want to confront the Pagans on their own turf one hundred and fifty miles from New York. But the word had gotten back, and it was going around the motorcycle hangouts. The Pagans were now the only outlaw show in the East.

Tommy and the Rabbi became Pagan prospects, and what they said turned out to be true. A week later Richie Gavin was the only person in the world riding around with Nassau Aliens on his back. Even the Mortician was gone.

Richie soon became a joke. Everyone laughed at the Alien patches on his back and said "That ain't no club no more." But Richie promised them that the Nassau Aliens would be back. He wore the colors everywhere, and soon the jokes stopped because they began to admire his stubborn determination. The joke soon became a legend: the "Lone Rider" they called him. Even the Pagans didn't fuck with him when he showed up by himself at our parties, because he was showing what the old outlaws meant by true class.

Every time I saw him he asked me to throw down my Pagan colors and ride with him. He said he needed just one righteous person to make a new start. As soon as he had that person they were going to have weekly meetings and start paying dues. Then they would find a third person, and as soon as they could afford it they were going to rent a store-front clubhouse, because he said that not having a clubhouse was one of the things that brought the old club down. By next year, he said, the Nassau Aliens would be back.

I told him that I couldn't throw down my colors, but I also asked him to join us. I told him that the Pagans would have him in a minute. But he told me that he would fly Alien colors until he died.

And he did.

One night he stopped to see his ex-wife at a hospital on Jericho Turn-pike where she worked as a nurse. When he pulled out onto Jericho Turn-pike, a car clipped him and left him sprawled face down in a pool of blood with the words Nassau Aliens on his back staring up into the night sky.

Now there were no more Nassau Aliens.

The funeral was in Williston Park. The parents were solid middle-class, middle-aged Irish with gray hair and red faces. In three genera-tions the family had worked themselves up from the bogs and the docks to a house in the burbs with lace curtains and cut crystal. They couldn't understand why their kid had chosen the life of an outlaw over the life of an engineer or accountant.

In New York we did not do outlaw funerals like they did in the rest of the country. We gave the guy back to his parents. This was New York where family ties were stronger. Kids lived with their parents, even out-laws did. When you went to the guy's house you respected his parents because they were family. And the family respected you because you were the kid's friend. All of us had grown up in Irish, German, Polack or Italian homes. We could sit at the table, eat a lot, and praise the hell out of the food. A lot of the guys were veterans and could drink beer with the old man and talk about how the flower faggots, war protesters and civil rights niggers were going to ruin the country if they didn't start shooting them soon.

When we showed up at Richie's wake he was laid out in a blue suit. We said "Sorry for your troubles," and Mrs. Gavin said "Thank you boys for coming." She told us that she had placed Richie's colors in the coffin with him. Then she introduced us to the family. There were a couple of nuns there, and they seemed especially impressed to meet these friends of Richie's who until then they only read about in the newspapers. Sweet William wasn't raised a Catholic, and he was especially turned on by the reception he got from the nuns. He was playing up the role of the chromed cavalier and exuding as much charm as a gigolo. He even stayed to talk to the nuns while some of Richie's cousins took us across the street to a bar and bought us drinks. The priest was there and he seemed as impressed as the nuns to meet Richie's infamous brethren.

Pagans, former Aliens, clergy and citizens were all drinking together, and we all took our turns buying drinks and toasting Richie. In the end it was a grand wake. No one was about to let either a club or a religion stand in the way of two thousand years of Irish tradition.

In other parts of the country outlaws were not so tight with their families, and families were not so tolerant of the outlaw lifestyle. Many outlaws were estranged from their families, or they were orphans. When they died they had outlaw funerals, where the guy was laid out in his colors with a swastika flag over the coffin. Most of the other clubs had a guy they called Preacher who officiated at these affairs. The Preacher would also propose toasts and say some appropriate words on New Year's Eve or Thanksgiving Day.

This caused a problem for the New Yorkers and some of the Jersey people who had been raised Catholic. They may not have had any more use for the church, but the idea of a "preacher" was just too *Protestant* for them to digest. We got around this by having our Rabbi, who had actually gone to shul and learned how to chant Hebrew. He could always be relied upon to chant some Torah when the occasion called for it. Of course when the guys from Virginia came up and saw this, they howled and pissed themselves at the idea that "the New York club ain't got no Preacher, they got a Rabbi instead."

After Richie's funeral the truce between the Aliens and Pagans began to disintegrate.

Richie may have been the last of the Nassau Aliens, but there was still Brooklyn and the Bronx. And even some of the guys from Queens and Nassau were hanging around with them again and talking about reorganizing. The Aliens were hurting, but not gone. Only the Mortician seemed to be missing. It was like he just disappeared. By now the Aliens considered the Pagans not just a bunch of upstarts but a real threat. And they were determined to hold on to the city and remain the undisputed lords of Cross Bay Boulevard and Ocean Parkway. The word was that they were willing to give Nassau and Suffolk County to the Pagans. The

Bronx went to the Aliens without saying, and nobody gave a damn any-more about Manhattan. The Pagans from Maspeth and Greenpoint didn't like this arrangement of leaving Brooklyn and Queens to the Aliens, but the club had other problems it was working out. The Pagans were hav-ing growing pains.

The club operated under the *fuhrer* principal. A strong leader who ruled with an iron fist and intimidated the shit out of everyone. At first some of the new clubs had tried to run their meetings under democratic principales with elections and presidents and vice presidents and sec-retaries and sergeants-at-arms. They discussed business and decided things by votes. This didn't work. Trying to run a gang of outlaws accord-ing to *Roberts' Rules of Order* was like trying to start a motorcycle by whispering sweet words into the carburetor.

Finally the Mother Club sent all the other clubs a one-page consti-tution that was pretty straightforward:

> I. The Mother Club is the arbiter of all disputes.
> II. The leader of each club is a dictator.
> III. All clubs must accept members from other clubs as equals.
> IV. When one Pagan swings, all Pagans swing.
> V. No Ying-Yangs. (*This was slang for a Japanese motorcycle.*)
> VI. No garbage wagons. (Full dress Harleys complete with windshields, saddlebags, etc.)
> VI. No flying colors to candyass events. (*The supermarket, the doctor, PTA meetings*)
> VIII. No flying colors in cages (*cars*) unless it's on club busi-ness.
> IX. Any problems, refer back to Article I.

Sleepy was one of the leaders that had been elected. As it turned out he wasn't a bad guy. But he did not provide the kind of hardass leader-ship the Pagans were looking for. One night while he was asleep they cut the patches off his vest. When he woke up they told him he was out of the club.

At the next meeting we were told by the number two man, Danny, that Sweet William was running the club. I had grown to like Sleepy a lot, and I argued that whatever his shortcomings as a leader might have been that didn't make him a bad member and he should be given a shot a being a regular member. Sweet William would have none of it. This was a palace coup and they didn't want the old leader around. They obviously had the blessing of the Mother Club. And most of the guys just seemed confused.

The Pagan style of leadership was emerging in the new clubs. With guys like Sweet William in New York, Updegraff in Jersey and the Whiteknight in Bethlehem the leader was a guy who was physically big, and mean enough to wrestle on TV and intimidate King Kong. The leader ran the club like Chuck ruled the City of Reading. Once a week he made a phone call to Washington and reported to the Mother Club. The leader had a number two man, like Rayels in Reading or Bucky in Jersey. They were selected for diplomatic skills. They served as an advisor to the leader, enabling him to bounce ideas off them. That way most problems were already resolved and most decisions made before the leader walked into a meeting. The number two man also conveyed orders, implemented the leader's decisions, and more important, he articulated the leader's decisions for the rest of the club and explained why things had been done the way they were.

The club also had two sergeants-at-arms or enforcers. They were big and they supplied muscle. If the leader said, "We got to get everybody out of this place now," one sergeant-at-arms would run around throwing the guys out, the other would wait in the parking lot counting heads as people came out and making sure nobody went back in. The leader also brought the sergeants-at-arms along to make an impression if he had to sit down and talk to someone. In addition to brute size, the sergeants-at-arms were chosen for their cool, the abilities to think clearly in a crisis and keep their mouths shut.

In New York we had the guy we called Gypsy, the tattoo artist from Polack Alley. We also had Irish "Big Jim" Fagan. Both of these guys were over six-two and two hundred and fifty pounds. What's more they could keep cool in a crisis and had a lot of common sense.

In addition to sergeants-at-arms each club needed a couple of crazies. Guys like Skip and Righteous Fuckin' Elroy in Reading, Domino in Maryland, Rocky in Pittsburgh, Dizzy and Crazy Joey over in Jersey, and Flipout and later Bobo in New York. These guys didn't show any common sense at all. Instead they brought a sense of religious fanaticism to the club. They were always on a mission. They were willing to do whatever they had to for the club, even kill, or better yet get themselves killed, if necessary. These were the guys who really protected the leader and the whole club for that matter. No matter what the problem, the leader always knew they were behind him 100%.

Pagans were not immortal. You could kill one, or even run one down in the street like the guy in South Philly tried to do. But everyone knew that if you killed a Pagan, there was no telling how the others might retaliate. Everyone also knew that there would be no way to reason with them, or intimidate them, or even buy them off. The sixties outlaws were not in it for the money. They were like religious martyrs in their convictions, and they struck fear into everyone. This was especially important when dealing with mobsters, wiseguys and other normal criminals, who were motivated by simple greed, and therefore could never understand what made these guys tick.

After assuming the leadership of the club, Sweet William quickly resumed his policy of getting run out of every police precinct and every town from St. Albans in Queens to Lindenhurst in Suffolk County. New York soon developed a reputation for wrecking more bars than all the other clubs combined. A lot of this had to do with Sweet William's personality, but a lot of it also had to do with the fact that you could get away with it in New York.

As long as you got out the door before the cops came and got away you were okay. Just hang out in another town for a couple of weeks and you would never hear about it again. It seemed that every two weeks the guys in New York wrecked a bar. Either spontaneously or by design, with Sweet William leading the charge through the front door swinging a chain.

As I said Sweet William was the only Marine I ever met in the Pagans, and this might have had something to do with his style of wrecking bars. A paratrooper would be inclined to ask "Can't we burn the place down, or at least wait outside and get the guys we want in the parking lot?" But for Sweet William this was out of the question, he only had one play in his gameplan: Come through the front door like you're hitting the beach at Iwo Jima, beat the crap out of the whole place, and let God sort them out.

Usually the Pagans did not start trouble. They simply retaliated. But because of the *All for One, One for All* policy, this retaliation was out of all proportion to the offense. Some guy said something to a Pagan about spilling beer or being too loud, and the whole place was trashed in less than four minutes.

Four minutes, that was the key. You had four minutes to utterly destroy the place and beat everyone unconscious. Then the sergeants-at-arms began clearing everybody out, because four minutes is about how long it took for the cops to begin pulling up. As long as you got away, the cops never seemed to come looking for you.

Actually I have to believe now that the cops back then kind of got a kick out of us. Most of the cops were Irish, Italian or German back then, and since they didn't go to college, they thought all college kids were wiseasses. So when they heard some college kids started a fight and got their asses beat, they figured good for the bastards. If the place was owned by some Italian mob wannabe that was even better. The German and Irish cops hated Italian macho swagger because of the way they grew up, and Italian cops tended to hate wiseguys worse than anyone. I have to think that sometimes when the cops arrived they only thought that we had done what they would like to have done themselves, and therefore they conducted the whole investigation tongue-in-cheek and walked away with the usual report: No one was able to identify anyone.

Actually the Pagans tended to get along real good with off-duty cops. Back in those days cops were hardasses too, not like the punks with toilet plungers today. There were a bunch of New York City cops who lived in Suffolk County and owned motorcycles. They came around to hang out and made it clear that they worked in New York. What went on in Suffolk County was none of their business. But on the other hand they respected the way we never talked about anything that they could get in trouble for not reporting to the Suffolk County Police.

As New York cops they worked rotating shifts, and there was a bar in Lake Ronkonkoma where the Pagans started hanging out with the off-duty cops on autumn afternoons. After a couple of hours of drinking someone would get out a football and we all went out in the parking lot to play touch football. We were smart enough to split up sides so the Pagans would not end up playing the NYPD. So there we were under the bright autumn foliage, the Pagans and the cops, running around in knee-high boots, drunk and on asphalt, playing a friendly game of touch football like we were the Kennedys.

The cops wised us up too. They taught us what cops could do and what they could not do. What we had to say and how to say it. In other words, don't say "I know my fuckin' rights and wanna talk to my lawyer." That was wrong. The right thing was "Look I'm sorry officer, I would help you if I could, but like I said I wasn't even there, so I don't know anything about it." The cops knew you were handing them a bunch of shit, but at least you were being polite about it. And in an age when everyone was starting to hand cops shit, they appreciated a little professional courtesy and reciprocated with courtesy. I can't even remember how many times I was picked up by the cops, but I was never smacked, roughed up, or pushed around inside a police station. Part of this no doubt had to do with the reputation of the Pagans and my size, but a lot of it had to do with professionalism. If you want to be a criminal act like a pro when the cops pick you up and the cops will act like pros too. Act like a wiseass and the cops will act like wiseasses too.

It was also the cops that taught us the four minute rule. "Whatever you do, just make sure you get out of there in less than four minutes," they said. "Because that's how long it takes cops to respond to a call, and that's how professional bank robbers do it." So the Pagans were now wrecking bars with the same timing and precision that Willie Sutton used to rob banks.

It seemed to work too. One time we wrecked a bar in East Meadow and I didn't get away in four minutes. There was a guy with us from the Chicago Outlaws. He was a French Canadian named Richie. His brother was called Cal and was a member of the SoCal (Southern California: Gardenia) chapter of the Hell's Angels. The two of them just blew into town with Richie's wife and two kids that day. The guy didn't know where he was staying or even the real names of the people his wife and kids were with. I had a Triumph, he had a Harley-Davidson.

When we ran out of the bar that we had just wrecked, I leaped over the back of my seat cavalry-style. I flicked the switch, gave the starter one kick and I was ready to go. Meanwhile he was fingering his carburetor to prime it with gasoline. Then he jumped on the starter. Nothing. He jumped again, and the engine sputtered. He jumped again, and it sputtered again. Then he had to reach down and finger the carburetor again. He jumped, and again it sputtered. Only this time it nearly threw him over the handle bars. I could only sit there with my Triumph revved up, waiting for the cops to show up and arrest us.

Which they did.

They impounded our bikes, and threw us in the tank with the drunks and the pisspants. The next morning they hauled us into court. It was Saturday, it was summertime, and it was obvious that the judge wanted to play golf.

It was a barroom brawl. The judge noted that the cops who arrested us weren't in the bar at the time, and didn't even catch us inside. The judge wanted to know if the cop had a witness who could identify us. The cop said no, but he told them that there were a couple of people in the hospital who maybe could identify us when they got out. The judge said he couldn't run a court like that. Case dismissed.

This was the glorious Summer of '67, when you could still have an Angel, an Outlaw and Pagans all living in the same house. There were also no helmet laws. And there were no sexually transmitted diseases that a five dollar trip to the doctor couldn't cure. Nobody cared about drunk driving as long as you didn't have an accident. And barroom brawling was a way of life. We worked our way clear down Hempstead Turnpike from Jamaica Avenue in Queens Village all the way out to Sunrise Highway in Lindenhurst. Sometimes we wrecked two or three places in one night. Bam, smash, boom. Four minutes and we'd be on our bikes racing for the county line before the cops even found out who it was.

And we always had a quiet place where we could regroup after a fight and drink quietly the rest of the night. We split up, pulled over and slipped our colors under our leather jackets, then leisurely made our way to the rendezvous point like solitary citizen bikers. Once there we put are colors back on and yipped it up. If we were hanging out in Queens and wrecking bars, the place was over the Nassau County line. If we were hanging out in Nassau, we had a place like this in Queens or Suffolk. And the rule was no trouble in these places, because as long as we crossed the county line, they practically needed the FBI to come after us in those days.

So under Sweet William the New York club practically built single-handedly the reputation of the chain-wielding, bar-wrecking barbarians. The guys from other clubs used to come to New York just so they could wreck a bar on weekends. They got a big kick out of this because in other parts of the country cops had a lot less to do and tended to take matters like this more seriously. Besides in other parts of the country bars tended to be owned by normal people who the cops liked. In New York the Pagans had an innate knack for targeting bars that were owned by wiscass Italian mob wannabees, and the cops usually seemed glad to see these guys get there asses beat.

Contrary to what Hollywood likes to project, Italian wiseguys are not bad. Sure they kill people and they beat people with chains, but they like to do it when it presents no danger to themselves. In other words when they outnumber their victims ten to one. They do not have the Pagans All-for-One, One-for-All ethic. They hang out in the kind of places where wiseguys get respect without having to earn it. By staying in their own neighborhoods, their own clubs, and their own bars, they are not exposed to situations where someone says: "Yea you, I'm talking ta you, put up your hands and let's see you swing."

But there are not even that many real wiseguys. It's like bikers swaggering around with their chains and Harley-Davidson insignias and calling each other "Bro." They're not outlaws, they're just outlaw wannabees.

It's the same with the mob. Most of the guys you saw strutting around with their cardboard-soled patent leather shoes, expensive pants with the creases, and the Neapolitan pompadour hairdos were not wiseguys, they were just wannabees. Occasionally their fantasies went to their heads and they needed to be taught a lesson, and sometimes that lesson took the whole establishment down with them.

There was a place on Hempstead Turnpike that was owned by a guy of about forty who made it a point to let everybody think he was connected. He talked the part, he wore the clothes. And since it was his bar, it was like his sandbox, and he could play any way that he wanted. As part of the game, he always had about a half-dozen bouncers on duty, even if he only had a half-dozen customers. It was simply his way of indulging himself. With some men it's horses, some men it's boats, others it's women. With this guy it was bouncers. He kept them around like an Italian Renaissance faggot bishop kept pageboys. They stuck out their pasta-stuffed chests, rolled up their sleeves, and wore religious medals around their necks that were big enough to take down Dracula from across the street. There were usually two at the door, one or two walking around the floor, and two sitting at his table, nodding in agreement at everything the boss said, and staring menacingly at anyone who approached his table.

We were always having problems with guys like this. The Pagans with their swastikas and these guys with the giant crucifixes around their neck, it was like the Vandals and the Romans all over again. They stared menacingly at us, and we spilled beer on the crotches of their creased pants and dared them to do something about it.

But this time it was different, it really did come about by accident. It was kind of a nice place and didn't really attract the kind of ass-kicking blue collar clientele where the Pagans felt at home. But Sweet William was in love.

He had met this girl who was afraid of the Pagans. So Sweet William agreed to go out with her to a nice place where there were no outlaws. He got out a decent pair of pants and a sport shirt. He even wore his old Marine shoes instead of boots. And he let the girl drive her car to this nice place.

Now Sweet William was the kind of guy who could pull this off. He didn't wear an earring or any jewelry because he was a Marine, and his hair was cut short by Pagan standards, so he could pass for a citizen. And because he was half Indian he couldn't grow a beard, or hair anywhere on his body for that matter, other than his head.

So in walked Sweet William with his date, like any other twenty-three-year-old kid on Long Island.

But just because you could dress Sweet William up, it didn't mean that you could take him out. He had a way of moving around in a bar like some kind of large animal. Everyone in the place knew where he was at all times and what he was doing. You could not ignore him, any more than you could ignore a bull moose in a bar. Meanwhile, the legion of pompadoured Neapolitans just faded into the crowd, like mere spectators in Sweet William's circus. This would never do.

This is not how you play in the sandbox of an Italian mob wannabe. If Sweet William could ignore the legion of bouncers and disrespect the place like this, you would have the whole Hofstra football team in the next week doing the same thing.

Finally the owner turned to one of his bouncers and said "Do something about this asshole." And they did.

They hit him in the head with a club, kicked the shit out of him with their patent leather shoes, and threw him out in the street.

The girl felt so sorry for him that she drove him home and screwed him all night.

The next day the Pagans were furious.

In a couple of years, a time would come when this would be called "personal business." In other words if you got in trouble when you were not on club business, or if you managed to get your ass beat when you were not flying colors, it was your own problem and not the club's. But back in '67 there was no personal business or life outside the club. Attacking a Pagan was like attacking a member of the Order of Teutonic Knights in the middle ages. The whole order did not rest until the insult was avenged.

What made matters even worse in this case was that word quickly got around that the guy was a Pagan, and people were saying that the bouncers in this place were so bad that they threw the Pagans out.

Sweet William's brother wanted to go in with shotguns the next morning and take out the owner. But someone pointed out that it would be better to wait until Saturday night when we could be sure of getting the whole crew that had attacked him. Then somebody said something about it while he was in Jersey, and Updegraff was on the phone pleading with us to wait a week because the Jersey people couldn't make it that weekend but they were coming down the next weekend for a party.

We waited two weeks and according to the *Long Island Daily Press*:

> Between 50 and 60 leather-jacketed, black-booted members of a motorcycle group wrecked a Hempstead bar yesterday in apparent revenge for an incident in which several members were ordered out of the tavern a few weeks ago.
>
> When the two-minute melee was over, the group had demolished furniture and glassware, robbed the cash register

of approximately $200, stabbed the owner and injured five others.

Meanwhile *Newsday* claimed that we attacked the bar in *"commando fashion:"*

> *The gang members wearing dungaree jackets, motorcycle boots and helmets* (he meant Nazi, not motorcycle, helmets), *with swastikas around their necks, wielded baseball bats, tire chains, and lead pipes.*
>
> *The whole business took less than five minutes* (according to the bartender).
>
> *It was so well-planned it was ridiculous. They just came in and started swinging and stabbing.*
>
> *It was like a scene right out of a Hollywood gangster movie.*
>
> *It was like snapping your fingers, that's how fast it happened.*

Both papers reported that the incident was in retaliation for an incident *"a couple of weeks earlier when several members had been asked to leave in a gentlemanly fashion."* Of course the investigative reporters never interviewed the Pagans for their side of the story.

All the newspaper articles about us were beginning to contain the same ingredients. Black leather boots and jackets, Levi's, chrome chains and wrenches. Long hair, beards and earrings. And of course the sinister and omnipresent swastika. No story on the Pagans ever seemed to be done right unless the word swastika appeared at least twice in every paragraph. It was like the reporters were writing a new kind of softcore porn to titillate their readers.

The Legend had found its troubadours.

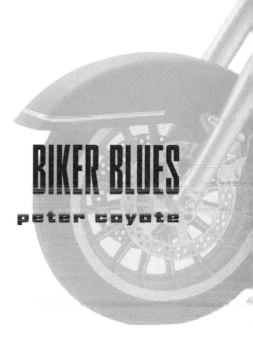

BIKER BLUES

peter coyote

at the end of that summer of 1968, Emmett and I returned to San Francisco. Sam and I had separated during one of our innumerable spats, perhaps because I refused to take her with me to New York. She had moved out of our small cabin overlooking Dolores Park and was staying at Paula McCoy's classy Victorian across the street from the Grateful Dead house on Clayton Street. She had taken our nine cats with her, which bizarrely died of distemper one after another soon after she moved into Paula's. On each visit there, part of my time was spent poking through the garage (where the cats always seemed to prefer to die), seeking the source of a stench.

Emmett and I had been using large quantities of hard drugs in New York and I was in bad shape, passing out often and unexpectedly, finding myself suddenly on the floor looking up at the bottom of a sink. One night, on a visit to Paula's, I was flirting with a woman there, much to Sam's displeasure. Sam was stalking me (which of course made this pursuit extremely difficult), emanating murderous vibes. I don't know if it was the vibes or my weakened state, but at one moment I was on top of a long stairway and in the next moment I was lying at the bottom, looking up at Sam towering above me, with her hands on her hips and backlit as a glowing silhouette. She regarded me long enough to see that I was still living, then turned and walked off without a word.

I was drifting, with no fixed abode or relationship, and if I disregarded being loaded or drug-sick, I was having a wonderful time. Our reputation and family were expanding. There were places to visit, people to see, comrades to assist, music to make, and women to love. I decided that a motorcycle would be a dashing addition to my life.

Pete Knell of the Hell's Angels lived in the bottom half of a dilapidated two-family house. Billy "Batman" Jahrmarkt lived upstairs, with his wife Joanie and children, Jade, Hassan, Digger, and Caledonia (referred to collectively as the Bat People). It was an unlikely but highly workable arrangement. Pete respected authenticity, even Billy's all-consuming dedication to heroin, and the arrangement suited the Bat People too, because Pete had a gigantic dog named Eckloff who guarded the house unremittingly. Eckloff was a monster. He appeared to me about the size of a lion and Pete's downstairs dwelling, always cool and shadowy, made a suitable cave for him.

Pete's living room featured a high-backed thronelike chair, a small bar, and a bed in one corner suspended from the ceiling by heavy chains. The decorative motif was strictly functional, since most of the functions held there would have played havoc with furniture and decorations anyway. Steel mesh over the windows protected against retaliatory bombings from rival bike gangs and gave the interior an otherworldly feel. A short corridor led past the bathroom to a small, unfinished back room attached to his garage shop. It was furnished with several mattresses, which Pete offered to let me use while I built my bike. I accepted.

Pete was an impeccable worker. He built chopped-down Harleys that were light, fast, unobtrusive, and reliable. He was also a very patient teacher. I had recently inherited three thousand dollars from a grandmother's will. I had given Sweet William a thousand dollars toward his bike, Freeman House and David Simpson something toward building *The Bare Minimum*, the Diggers' free fishing boat, and with the remainder, I bought a brand-new 1969 Harley Davidson FLH engine. While we waited for it to arrive, Pete and I located an old but sound 1937 Harley "rigid-frame," so called because it had no shock absorbers. I spent days sanding it smooth, and Pete showed me how to prime and paint it expertly with spray cans. "Watch the surface," he said. "Make it shiny and wet, but don't let it orange-peel or run." I practiced and soon possessed an electric-blue frame gleaming with kinetic energy.

Pete showed me how to disassemble the heavy-duty Harley transmission and grind and bevel the locking lugs on the gears so that they *clicked* rather than *clunked* into place when shifting. We rebuilt a clutch and bought new discs and a chain for it, then took the clutch cover, the "grasshopper" (a spring-loaded assist for a manual clutch), the tool kit, the headlight, and a few more odds and ends to be chromed. Such errands led me to the fascinating industrial section of the city, south of Market, where replaters took dingy bumpers, valve covers, fuel pumps, and pulleys and resurrected them as the gleaming fantasies of hot-rodders and bikers. Out of these grimy places with oil dirt yards, wormy dogs, and filthy facades the sorriest-looking parts emerged pristine as museum sculptures.

The San Francisco Harley dealership was managed by a terse, bald fire-plug of a man named Dave. Pete described him as "a guy who don't *like* to fight, but if he does, you know that he'll take care of business." Pete's guarantee was enough to establish my credit for the purchase of taillights, foot pedals, brake and clutch clamps, and the myriad pieces of hardware necessary to build a working "putt," as Pete referred to his bikes. This extension of Pete's credit was nothing to be taken lightly. Though an "outlaw," Pete was strict about obligations that the Diggers often dismissed casually. He paid his bills to the penny, while—to name one example—we took advantage of substantial traffic in telephone credit cards. For us, it was a victory to "liberate" a famous politician's or a corporate telephone card for "free" calls. Ditto for gasoline and bank credit cards, which often underwrote our long journeys and deliveries of supplies to the growing number of Digger family houses. Scruples about such behavior were anesthetized by our image of ourselves as guerrilla warriors living off the enemy. This was not a position that would bear overmuch scrutiny, and it was definitely not shared by Pete Knell. He was an outlaw, but his life outside the law was marked by a fixed, though contrary, relationship to it.

Like most people, I consider myself an honorable person. What strikes me in hindsight about my ethical transgressions at this time is not the revelation of a flaw in my character but the ease with which anyone can sweep away ethical concerns in pursuit of a noble goal. The facility with which I performed these sleights of mind informs my caution today when I review the noble utterances of politicians and reformers. If I was able to justify personal misconduct as a way of redressing systemic wrongs, I suppose anyone can, so it no longer surprises me when prevalently high-sounding goals become transformed into justifications for malfeasance.

Pete identified with the country, its goals, and its institutions. While he thought that much of its behavior was rife with self-serving bullshit, he did not consider these critiques to be excuses for *personal* dishonesty, and I was chastened by his example. The irony of being tutored on civic responsibility by an outlaw was not lost on me.

The time I spent at Pete Knell's was unnerving and stressful. Having to be preternaturally alert all the time around the Angels was exhausting and required even more self-medication. Freedom from the responsibilities of the Mime Troupe and a stable relationship left me ample opportunity to use heroin and methedrine whenever I wanted (which was often), and consequently my health was suffering. Signs of liver trouble appeared, and I chewed 90 percent protein tablets all day long as a junkie's tonic for avoiding cirrhosis.

My status at Pete's house was curious. Because I was not a "prospect" seeking admission to the Hell's Angels, there was much club business that I was not privy to. When three or four Angels congregated in his living room and the wooden soup bowl of pills was passed around, it was never long before someone wheeled around demanding to know just "what the fuck" I was doing there. I learned to discern pretty accurately when to get lost.

There was some dissension among club members about Emmett's intimate access as well. He had his own relationship with Pete and we were friends, so he was around often. For him, like me, the Angels were a kind of test to pass, a way of measuring our courage as well as forging an alliance that supported our social agenda. One night several members decided to give Emmett a beating as a warning to the rest of us about getting too close. They invited him to ride with them to Santa Cruz, and were drinking in a bar there when something triggered Emmett's receptors to danger. Excusing himself to get something from his bike, he walked outside, rode back to San Francisco without hesitating, and lay low until things cooled down.

Pete liked me and trusted me to keep my lip buttoned. When some members inquired whether or not they could steal the parts of my bike being stored in his garage, Pete stood up for me. One of the reasons he liked me, I think, was because of our free-ranging discussions. While not formally educated, Pete was razor sharp, well informed, and very curious. He liked to test his ideas against mine. We had many discussions about politics and he could never understand what he perceived as the "carelessness" of the Diggers. He felt that we were reckless in assuming that our *intention* to construct a counterculture would protect us from failures of strategy in dealing with the majority culture. He discounted all leftist revolutionary rhetoric, pointing out that most people calling for the revolution failed to live alertly and cautiously as warriors and consequently were no threat to anyone. He did not understand how we could be unconcerned with organization and structure, though he had to agree that it was the Diggers' lack of structure that made infiltration by government programs like COINTELPRO impossible. He appreciated my interest in his life and in motorcycles but was ambivalent about Bryden Bullington's painting on my gas tank: a voluptuous bare-breasted blonde angel with flowing white wings, creating a pentangle at the tip of her index finger. The image sparked Pete's proprietary concerns about the club's identity.

"It's an *earth* angel, Pete," I assured him, but he was never totally satisfied, uneasy that it was an infringement on the motif of his blood brotherhood. This issue of our intentions continued to reside below the surface of our relationship. Poet Michael McClure was riding a yellow and black chopper that Pete had made for him, and Emmett had one as well. Pete must have wondered whether we represented friends, pretenders, or potential adversaries.

The issue was not enough to create a breach between us. He encouraged me to participate openly in his living-room discussions and to challenge his fellow Angels intellectually and philosophically—not a particularly easy thing to do when they were loaded. The Angels were not given to dialectical subtlety and were often happy to resolve dialectical tension with a quick punch. Later, Pete encouraged younger Angels to stay at the Diggers' Olema commune periodically, though I was never certain whether he wanted them to study us, report on us, or learn from us. Still, it was always clear that they enjoyed being treated as intelligent men whose ideas mattered, and they understood such treatment as a mark of respect.

Anyone who comforts himself with easy clichés about "bikers" is deluded. During the years that I had access to the club, I met sculptors, master chemists, machinists, economists, physicists, and poets. I met individuals in the Hell's Angels who were as brilliant and incisive as anyone I have met since. Generally, they held themselves to a higher standard of honesty and commitment than most civilians I knew. Like the Diggers, they lived life as they imagined it possible. Unlike the Diggers, however, their aspirations and hopes for success extended no further than themselves.

The Hell's Angels were a conundrum and a challenge, and to none of the Diggers more so than to Bill Fritsch, our brother known as Sweet Willie Tumbleweed. He perceived in the Angels a standing rebuke to his integrity, because he loved and admired their fearlessness and lack of compromise. He confronted the issue for himself by joining them. What follows is his story, which is once again also mine.

SWEET WILLIAM'S STORY

Sweet William, born Bill Fritsch, came by his passionate, poetic, inflexibly self-confident spirit genetically. His father was a sullen Hungarian house-painter for whom family life was purgatory, and his mother was a devout Russian Communist who had once refused to sell breast milk to the aging J. D. Rockefeller, who, according to Fritsch family legend, spent his days lounging in a motorized chair that tracked the sun in his penthouse atrium, sipping breast milk because he believed it would keep him healthy and vigorous.

Bill's parents divorced when he was three, and his mother married a merchant marine left-winger who shaped Bill's political instincts and class antagonisms quite early. The remainder of Bill's early education was contributed by children of the Philadelphia Mafia. It was one of them who crystallized the dynamics of capitalism for Bill when he said, "Free enterprise is as far as your father rules."

At New Town High School, an all-boys school in Philadelphia, Bill remembers himself as "an average kid with middling talents." He tells me this with unembellished honesty as he struggles to get a Camel out of a flattened pack with his good hand. I am uncomfortable watching his difficulty, but Bill handles the moment with aplomb. A few minutes ago I watched him approach, on his way to our meeting in a little San Francisco hamburger joint, a solitary figure framed against a white wall, one arm and one leg flapping uselessly as he placed each foot and his cane with fixity. Despite this physical infirmity, his face still bore the commanding, determined expression I remember from the days when he could have stopped a mob on his own personal authority.

In the early fifties, Bill left home at sixteen to join the merchant marines and worked his way into the role of union delegate for his ship. When he shipped out, he met Richard Marley, a man who would weave in and out of both of our lives in years to come. Richard was born in England, the son of a famous militant Communist mother. On Bill's maiden merchant marine voyage, Richard delivered long lectures to him about boycotting the whorehouses in ports. Richard explained how the girls were exploited by the capitalist class and how workers, in solidarity with them, could not participate in their degradation. This was depressing to Bill, whose libido seemed to orchestrate most of his decisions. He is an extraordinarily sincere man, however, and when the boat docked in Manila, he gave up his liberty and remained on the boat for three days and nights, tormented by the tension between his conscience and his body's desires. He broke on the fourth night, sneaking off the ship like a guilty dog, streaking into the closest whorehouse. There he found Richard Marley in bed with *three* whores, laughing uproariously as they serviced him with thoroughness and imagination. This was perhaps the last time Bill was susceptible to ideological manipulation.

He was cooking in the ship's galley the day the captain sent his eggs back for the third time. Bill heaved the plate of food in the captain's face and was fired on the spot. He took his hundred-dollar discharge pay and flew to California.

Bill gravitated to the bohemian haven of San Francisco's North Beach in the late 1950s. He was parking cars for twenty-four dollars a week, so broke that he was picking cigarettes off the sidewalk. In a bar one day, a guy named Roy Miller noticed his pack with all the different brands of butts in it and asked, "You into making some money?" Bill answered affirmatively, and Roy asked if he could get a gun. Bill could not but managed a butcher knife and with it the two robbed a Safeway for $3,400. Bill was exhilarated by the experience, "hooked on the rush," as he put it. Walking down Market Street afterward, the wind kept whipping his long hair into his face, so he bought a celebratory Panama hat. That hat became his trademark, Roy followed suit, and before long, he and Roy became known as the Panama Hat Bandits.

High style was a pronounced trait of Bill's personality, which was generously endowed with charisma. He resembled the actor-director John Cassavetes, but his face was, if anything, more masculine, less softened by conflicting sensibilities. He was cocksure and apparently fearless. His fidelity to his impulses was so absolute that for people like myself, awash in ambiguities, he was a beacon of certainty and personal power.

"We'd dress up on weekends," Bill remembers, "and rob those Tahitian Hut tonga-wonga bars. It was a great life." Until one day four guys entered the motorcycle shop where he worked. Bill looked up, read the vibes, and thought to himself, "Flash, I'm dead." He assumed that the men were Italians who owned the tonga-wonga bars. Luckily, he was wrong. They were cops.

Because Bill was only twenty at the time, he was sent to the Youth Authority at Tracy while Roy did time at San Quentin. While Bill was incarcerated he took an aircraft mechanics course and became certified. When friends inquired about prison, he shrugged it off. "I did a hundred sit-ups a night, a hundred push-ups, and jerked off the rest of the time."

When he was tripping on speed, Bill could keep you spellbound, examining the cosmic potentialities of a small stone he'd found somewhere or reviewing his last act of lovemaking in staggering detail, explaining precisely what had occurred in the minds and bodies of both participants. His was egotism at its most innocent, assuming that his personal explorations had universal resonances. He regarded these explorations as his work.

When he was released from Tracy, Bill went to work in the prop shop at Pan Am. By 1962, he had married Richard Marley's sister and had two boys. His life appeared stable and normal, but this was an illusion. His family and personal plans were about to be disrupted by the social seizures and generational conflict of the decade.

East-West House was a San Francisco writer's cooperative hangout. Marley brought Bill there one day and introduced him to poet Lenore Kandel. Bill fell in love immediately, went home, got his clothes, said good-bye to his wife and children, and left.

"It was the only honest thing to do," he says flatly. I ask him if he has seen his children since, and he just shrugs. It makes me sad to think of that broken family. I wonder how different Bill's life might have been if he had stayed with them. Where he lives now, in a tiny room in a decrepit old boarding-house, there are no children's drawings, no photographs of him with a woman and children, no tarnished trophies and yellowed high school year-books. If he misses such things or regrets his choices, he will never say. Like a wolf who has chewed off a paw to escape a trap, only he knows how much the paw is missed.

It was fitting that Bill and Lenore Kandel should have fallen in love. They were extraordinarily beautiful people intimately tuned to their bodies. Their skin looked as if it would taste delicious. Bill was fire and lava, given to volcanic explosions and sudden insights that rocked him like seismic tremors. Lenore was a giggling dakini (one of the feminine consorts of the Buddha). Her psychic center of gravity appeared to be located in the earth's core; nothing perturbed her rock-steady equilibrium. Already an established poet, she was also an accomplished belly dancer who earned pocket money making beaded jewelry for a foreign import store.

Their bed filled almost a whole room and was an epicurean marvel. Both sides were lined with boxes of cookies: Oreos, pecan sandies, and various whipped-cream and chocolate confections. There were dirty books, scented oils, and things to drink. It was a bed you could live in for days, and they often did. Their coupling seemed like a universal principle, a melding of dark and light forces. They moved into a flat on Chestnut Street that they inherited from a friend. Bill went to work on the waterfront, Lenore modeled for the Art Institute, and the world appeared to be in order.

In 1966, Ronald Reagan was elected governor of California, promising to punish the mouthy students acting up in Berkeley and to fry the inmates on San Quentin's death row. His victory signaled a sea change in the social climate, and about a week later, the Psychedelic Shop was raided by the police, who seized copies of Lenore's erotic poems, *The Love Book*. These graphic paeans to monogamous love and sex had been published before, and since you could walk to any street corner and buy hard-core pornography or open a men's magazine for steamier stuff, our community perceived this as Reagan's attack on the psychedelic culture.

Lenore and her book became the center of a very public pornography trial. I had not yet met her, but I felt that she should be invited to attend the initial Artists' Liberation Front meeting, so I found her phone number and invited her. When she and Bill appeared, they galvanized everyone's attention in the packed room. They were dressed, respectively, in bright red and cobalt-blue leather Levis, radiating the charisma and self-assurance of natural leaders. Their style was effortless, authentic, royal. You could imagine them at ease in a French café or at an embassy ball; they would know people who were never bored or plagued with self-doubts. You felt yourself sinking a bit in your own estimation by comparison.

They certainly raised the mark by which I measured myself, and I was not the only one to notice them. "Emmett and I pinned each other right away," Bill laughs, "recognized each other as rivals, right off." They began to hang around together, and through Emmett, Bill and Lenore gravitated into the Digger orbit.

Sweet William loved the Diggers. "They were a challenge. It was somethin' I didn't understand," he says. "Everybody was winging it." He rose to the challenge, assuming roles with the Free Food deliveries, the truck repairs, and guarding our treasury and its record, the Free Bank book, with characteristic dedication. The Diggers respected Bill's fearlessness and dignity similarly. He was too proud to lie. He was indisputably *somebody*. I felt that way about many of my friends then; though their fame was strictly local, they had an authority that rested on character and ability rather than on wealth or social status. One of the defining attributes of the sixties was the collective impulse to reveal yourself candidly and publicly, confessing your inner visions as your daily life. It was as if the participants at a costume ball suddenly found the event too silly and simultaneously dropped their masks. Farm boys from Nebraska were writing poems, preppy girls from Grosse Point were throwing the Tarot and studying herbs. Kids with no idea of who they wanted to become could idle on the teeming streets among people who would not judge them for their confusion. Personal style counted more than a pedigree, and even within this community of dedicated life actors, Bill was a star.

In retrospect, it appears inevitable that Bill would have joined the Hell's Angels. His masculinity was so pronounced and his sense of honor so demanding as to require constant testing. One day he and Emmett were leaving an event at the University of California extension on Laguna Street and they noticed a chopped Harley Davidson parked by the curb. Emmett and Bill said, "That's my bike" simultaneously.

"I just kept saying, 'Bike, bike, bike,' everywhere—everywhere," Bill remembers. "Everywhere I went, whoever I ran into. Lenore did some kind of spell. Took some blood out of my finger. I don't know what the fuck she did with it, but the next day, you had some inheritance for me, and Jon and Sarah Glazer had an aunt who died, and they gave me money."

The bike that Emmett and Bill saw belonged to Pete Knell. During negotiations, they liked each other, and Pete offered to be Bill's sponsor if he wanted to join the Angels. When Bill returned to Peter Berg's and announced his decision to do that, Emmett spat, "What a waste!" dismissively. At the time I thought he was jealous. I did not realize that he had made a prophecy.

Bill "prospected" with the Angels for seven months, a period of apprenticeship during which he spent time with each member of the San Francisco chapter in order to win approval. He was tested in every way imaginable. Two votes against him were enough to keep him out of the club, and every member had his own criteria for passing or failing a prospect. Failure could be costly. Shortly after being turned down for the third time, Gordon Westerfelt, a dapper, handsome man with the cocky swagger of a World War II ace pilot, was slipping the key into his apartment lock one night when someone stepped from the shadows and punched his brains into jelly with a small-caliber bullet. His bike and personal possessions, including his girlfriend, subsequently circulated through the club.

My mentor at that time, an Angel named Moose who had "adopted" me as a personal friend, told me shortly afterward that he was putting out a reward for the killer. Since I was not an Angel and he did not have to tell me the truth, and since he knew that I knew this, I have no way of knowing whether this was a rumor he wanted disseminated.

Twenty-odd years later, when I ask Bill about Gordon's death, he shrugs and asks me who I thought might have done it. I tell him that I suspected that perhaps he or Moose might have had something to do with it. He looks away, and I remind him that *something* changed his fate dramatically, *something* had unaccountably punctured his impenetrable good fortune, and that I had never understood how he had moved so abruptly from the realms of the charmed to the luckless. By way of explanation to myself, I had imagined an act with terrible karmic consequences.

He looks at me levelly, without blinking, and I feel as if I am in an empty room in an abandoned house. A door creaks open and then closes. I can almost hear the rustle of something moving behind the walls. Bill takes a drag on his Camel and changes the subject.

"Everyone had their fears and fantasies about the Angels," he says, referring again to his probation period years ago. "But as long as you approached individuals and were all the way honest, you were okay. The testing is about honesty—what you are and what you're really about."

One night, during his prospecting, Bill and some friends were drinking in a bar when an Angel commanded Bill to punch a guy at the end of the bar for no reason. Bill turned to him and said, "Anybody who tells me to go punch somebody gets punched in the face." This was the candor and intuitiveness that ushered him, member by member, through the portals that closed civilian life behind him forever. Bill entered the realms of hell, and Lenore followed willingly. Their bright jeans were replaced by blackleathers now, and they raced together through the streets on Bill's barking machine like two close-coupled feral dogs.

The Angels' scene made no allowances for females or poets. One night Lenore was accidentally smashed in the face by a thrown glass beer pitcher. Another time, she crashed on the bike, injuring some vertebrae and leaving her in chronic pain. Walking was almost impossible for her, her hands and feet trembled, and she became nearly a total recluse. Eventually she bailed out.

"Lenore was a good, loyal woman with me. She did the best she could," Bill says gravely. Our community was shocked when they broke up. When I heard the news, I had an eerie presentiment that the balance in Bill's life had tipped into darkness.

There was a gathering dusk in the streets as well. By the early seventies, the Haight was tattered and worn, the original careless exuberance shadowed. The perfect expression of the change was a murderous rock-and-roll concert remembered by the name of the site at which it took place: Altamont.

The Rolling Stones were coming to town, and the Grateful Dead management wanted to throw a party in honor of their high-status rock star friends. Emissaries from the Dead requested the Diggers' help in creating the event. Both Peter Berg and I suggested events framed by multiple bonfires, each of which would be the locus of music and activity, rather than a central stage. This would ensure a collaborative frame of reference and minimize divisions between the community and its entertainers, a point we both stressed. Before the hype and marketing concerns of the music business dominated the culture, bands understood that they were of the community in which they performed and responded appropriately to that reality, rather than as objects of veneration acting out for faceless nobodies.

Our ideas did not seem elevated enough for Sam Cutler, the neurasthenic Englishman working in some managerial capacity for the Dead, so he approached Pete Knell and the Hell's Angels and told him that the Stones "wanted to do something for the people."

Sweet William was in the room when this conversation occurred, and he remembers Pete's response: "Tell 'em to come. We'll pick 'em up at the airport, bring 'em to the Panhandle, and let 'em do a free concert." Pete went on to guarantee that the equipment would be set up and ready for them and that all they would have to bring would be their guitars. The Hell's Angels knew what "free" meant too.

Sam asked Pete how much the club would want to serve as "security" at the event, and Pete told him, "We don't police things. We're not a security force. We go to concerts to enjoy ourselves and have fun."

"Well, what about helping people out—you know, giving directions and things?" Cutler queried, angling to have the Angels attached to the event in some official capacity. When Pete agreed that they could do that, Cutler returned to the question of price, and Pete said, "We like beer."

"How does a hundred cases sound?" Cutler responded, and a deal was struck. The Angels intended to give the beer away and felt that this would be good for their club's image.

Weeks went by while site after site was investigated and rejected before they settled on Altamont, farm country in the rolling hills between Oakland and the Central Valley. In Bill's words, it was "a goddamn, fucking, bereft pasture. In the middle of nothin'. Couple of barbed-wire fences.

Cow shit. Not even a barn." This was the environment in which the Rolling Stones' "gift" would be tendered and received.

Bill remembers his shock on arriving at the site on the day of the concert. A stage with three stories of scaffolding had been erected, festooned with mammoth speakers, lights, and equipment. The place was teeming with people from the lip of the stage to the horizon, a churning, roiling sea. "With my misguided sense of responsibility," Bill says, "I was crazy trying to look after people . . . see that this one didn't get crushed or that that one knew where to go."

He looked down from the stage to check his bike and was amazed to see someone sitting on it. "I couldn't believe it," Bill says. "I told him to get off the bike, and he wouldn't. I said it again, and he wouldn't. I grabbed him so hard I heard every bone in his body snap. I was so angry I would've ripped his fuckin' head off and thrown it in the pasture. The bike fell over and I went crazy. I started stompin' him. I didn't even want his ghost around." This was how the party began.

From the beginning of the event, people insisted on "crashing" the stage. They were not used to "free" events being hierarchical and proprietary and could not understand why there were off-limits at a free concert or why guards were required, and it rankled them. The event so resembled a massive commercial concert that perhaps the audience became confused and felt as if they had been demoted to nonentities and wanted to get closer to the heat and glow of the luminaries. They had, in fact, been unwittingly enlisted as extras in a commercial film and should have been paid. The concert was not free at all but had merely waived admission. Its real organizing principle was a merchandising event to create a live album and film—and a dynastic marriage between the Grateful Dead and Rolling Stones' families.

Whatever the reason, the crowd was whipping itself into froth; somehow it fell to the Angels to protect the stage and keep it clear enough so that the concert could continue. "We did it 'cause it had to be done," says Bill. The Oakland Angels arrived. Unlike their party-hard San Francisco brothers, this chapter had the reputation of heavyweight gangsters with a penchant for violence. Moving slowly and precariously through the crowd on their roaring, spitting bikes, creating a cacophony that overwhelmed the music, they edged up to the stage. Bill pulled the Angels' national president Sonny Barger up next to him. A warm-up band was playing. "I feel this shudder next to me," Bill says. "I look over and it's Sonny. He turns to me and says, 'We're keeping this stage? Do you realize that if all these people had their minds together they could crush this whole thing?' "

Sonny's perception of reality broke through Bill's preoccupations, and he too realized that their pitifully small cadre of Angels had been slicked into the role of defending the stage against hundreds of thousands of unruly people.

The crowd was impatient for the Stones, and its surges forward were becoming wilder and harder to control. Even from among so many, Bill singled out Meredith Hunter. "I shoved Meredith Hunter off that stage *myself* three times," he says. "Big tall fucker. Three times I had my hands on that guy. I shoved his fucking ass back. I *told* him. I tumbled him off the stage three times. How clear do I have to be?"

Sweet William was desperate. He went backstage for the Stones, fearful that delaying their appearance would unleash a maelstrom. "They were tuning up," Bill recalls. "Chatting. Their *little* band. I recognized Mick Jagger. I didn't realize he was just a little fart. I told him, 'You better get the fuck out there before the place blows beyond sanity. You've tuned up enough.' "

Jagger told him that they were "preparing" and would go when they were good and ready. "I'm getting really pissed at this little fuck now," Bill says. "I want to slap his face. I told him, 'I'm tellin' you, people are gonna *die* out there. Get out there! You been told.' "

Bill returned to the stage and was standing there when Hunter's murder took place, recorded for all to see in the Maysles brothers' film *Gimme Shelter*. "All of a sudden there's scuffle off to my left," Bill says. "I saw a flash, the gun going off, but it [the music] was so loud you couldn't hear it." Meredith Hunter was standing there with a pistol, stark naked, loaded out of his mind, when Allen Pizzaro made his move.

Allen was a strange guy from San Jose. He had been a member of a club called the Gypsy Jokers that had been obliterated by the Angels. He had prospected as an Angel with the San Francisco chapter for eight months, but never owned a bike. On the night he was to be voted in, he answered an ad in the paper for a Harley Davidson, beat the owner senseless, and took the bike to his initiation. "He was a wild guy," Bill says. "He'd do anything." Not too many years later, his dead body was fished out of a reservoir, where he'd been dumped for some "anything." This day, however, he was the star, center stage, on film.

Allen grabbed Meredith's arm. "He fired one shot with Allen holding him," Bill says. "It's what saved Allen from the death penalty." Allen twisted the arm away, at the same time reaching back with his free hand and drawing his hunting knife from a belt scabbard. He swung Meredith around—"a classic street move," Bill calls it—and stabbed him.

The music stopped for a moment. A girl screamed, "a forlorn, wailing scream, like a rabbit dying," Bill remembers. "You never forget it. Then they were passing his body over the crowd. It was bobbing and floating like a body going downstream in a riptide. It was like a Greek play. Everything was classical. The hunger of the people for somethin' that didn't exist. Why come on the stage? Why!?"

In the ensuing melee, my friend Denise Kaufman, a local musician with the all-girl Ace of Cups band, was hit in the temple by a thrown bottle, fracturing bone and causing a severe concussion. Denise was eight-and-a-half months pregnant at the time, and the Stones were approached for permission to use their helicopter to carry her to a hospital. They refused. Denise was ferried on a long grueling trip by car, after which, due to her advanced pregnancy, she was operated on without anesthetic. Both she and her daughter survived undamaged, but for those who know and love her, the same could not be said of the local reputation of the Rolling Stones.

The Angels took the heat for Hunter's murder in the press, but they felt betrayed by Cutler. Word circulated for a while that Cutler's life was to be forfeited and he moved to Texas abruptly. The bizarre, appropriately show-business finish to events occurred a few days later when the Maysles brothers visited Paula McCoy's house, where Bill happened to be staying at the time, to see what "piece" of *Gimme Shelter* the club wanted. They obviously had no idea of the organization's mood when they described the film enthusiastically. "We knew the Angels were a draw," one of the brothers said breathlessly, "but we didn't know that we'd get *lucky*." At that point, Angel Jerry Genly rose and kicked him square in the balls. "I think that was the end of the meeting," Bill says, laughing.

If you were forced to select an event that "ended" the optimistic promise of the Haight-Ashbury era, Altamont would be as good as any. After that, the party was definitely over, and what ensued, in the streets, in the Hell's Angels, and across America, was harder, colder, and all business.

Pete Knell used to say, "If you wanna know anything about America, look at the club. It's a reflection of America on all levels: high idealism and murder." The club was a cross section of blue-collar values and neuroses, and something murderous was afoot in both nations.

Janis Joplin and Jimmy Hendrix were dead of overdoses. Hell's Angels Terry the Tramp and Harry the Horse were murdered. Vietnam veterans were returning from the atrocities of jungle warfare, some with psyches ablaze with what they'd seen and had to do there to survive. A new element had risen to prominence in the club. A San Francisco homeboy, back from Nam crazy-dangerous, had opened a bike shop, prospected into the club, and climbed the ladder of power there with murderous ruthlessness. Little Bill, a physically sweet and beautiful club member, an amateur magician, got into a fracas in a Mission District bar one night. As he was leaving, three guys followed him to the street, bent him over his bike, and summarily executed him. The Angels retaliated by blowing away one of his killers in nearby Precita Park. Members stopped wearing their colors in the streets and affected jean jackets and hooded sweatshirts. Things got closer, tighter, more dangerous. "It was a cut-dog rotten bunch of shit" is all Sweet William will offer about that period. Murders became endemic. Expediency became the law.

Sweet William was running around with a girl from Fresno and biked down there one day to sell some cocaine. Pete Knell warned him not to go alone, but Bill was fearless. He and the girl ended up at a house party organized to raise money for the African Student Movement. Bill must have felt bulletproof to enter the all-black party alone in full Angels' colors, for the Angels were an unabashedly "white" organization that would not even allow black people who were personal friends of members to sit with them in public. He was led through a gauntlet of curious stares in the suddenly silent room and down to the cellar. He remembers a table and a drug scale and about a dozen men crowded together watching the count. After weighing out the cocaine, one of the black men said, "We're taking you off, white boy."

"No, you're not," Bill answered, and the fight started. "I wrecked that fucking room," Bill says, "fighting twelve niggers by myself. Then one of them reached over the top of the crowd that was piled on me and 'boom,' it was like a white flash. When I woke up I was in the Fresno County Hospital."

The "students" had shot him and left him for dead. Someone upstairs heard the ruckus and called the cops, and the cops discovered a pulse in Bill and called an ambulance. The bullet had entered his brain, ripping a path to a nest where it remains today. It was an expensive ticket for a trip of just a few inches: it paralyzed half his body.

When I visited him in the hospital shortly afterward, he was a wraith. His hair had been shaved off. He was blue-white, his face as taut and translucent as the skin of a drum. He was suffering terrifying hallucinations and felt that he was on the verge of comprehending secret profundities that evaporated just before he could own them.

He left the hospital a hero to the Angels, bought a three-wheeled motorcycle, and continued to party with them, but his life was shrouded in darkness. He moved in with Dee, a crazy, Faye Dunaway-lookalike witch from Georgia, and they grew so psychosexually drug entwined as to be indistinguishable. Bill began shooting heroin again, in direct contravention of Angel law.

In late October of 1980, Bill crossed the path of Pussy Paul, who owed him money. Bill held him prisoner in his apartment all night, and when he released him the next day, Paul "dropped a dime" and turned Bill in to the cops. Several nights later, on Halloween, the cops broke into Bill's place and beat him so badly that they fractured his hand and shoulder. The cops were just punctuating a lesson to Bill, but it makes you wonder what kind of men would kick in the door to pummel a cripple.

He was recovering from these wounds when a fellow Angel, Flash, called to inform him that Moose had rolled over for the police and was testifying against the club. The Angels needed Bill at the trial to verify a piece of information for the defense.

Bill refused to believe that Moose, an archetypal Angel, had rolled over. Everyone loved and admired Moose. He was fearless and roly-poly, with flaxen hair and a wispy blond mustache; when he arrived in his white Cadillac or on his white Harley with the red cross on the tank, it invariably signaled festive occasions. Moose was married at our Olema commune in a ceremony performed by poet Gregory Corso. My conversations with him had sometimes continued for days. He would often arrive at night and kidnap me with no warning. Once we left so quickly that I had no shoes, so he stopped at Tattoo Larry's house and commandeered a fine pair of Chippewa work boots that I still use.

Moose (real name Lorenzo) had been running an amphetamine laboratory, manufacturing white-crossed tablets from his home where his mother, his hillbilly Uncle Charlie, and Moose's slightly retarded son lived. One story he circulated about his arrest was that the police had discovered his laboratory. Another was that the cops had learned his mother had soaked the stamps on letters she sent him in LSD. He said the cops had threatened to put his mom and Uncle Charlie away, so he rolled over and gave her evidence against his brothers in more than a hundred cases.

When Bill heard Moose say it with his own ears—"I rolled over in February"—he was shattered. "I couldn't fuckin' believe it!" he stammers. "It was like the blackness of the sky opened up and swallowed me. I wept for that. Really. I wept and thought, if that could happen to Moose, to *Moose*, there but for the grace of God . . ." As in all matters like these, only Moose knows what really happened. Those who had observed Moose's lethal side, including myself, suspect that the police must have had a much heavier beef over his head than a simple dope bust—big-time heavier.

I got a sense of the fear Moose could inspire some time later, about 1970. Our part of the Free Family was organizing a caravan, and I was forced to sell my bike to raise the funds to ready my truck. A couple of San Rafael bikers came out to Forest Knolls in Western Marin County to appraise it. They were tough rummies, but rummies. One fellow's pistol fell out of his pocket when he squatted down to inspect my oil pan It fell in the soft dirt of a flower bed and he didn't notice it, so I retrieved it and stashed it in my pocket until the negotiations were over. I had been asking $1,200 for the bike, a fair price, but these guys were disparaging it as a prelude to bargaining. One of them walked over to me threatening and then noticed my earrings with little fox toe bones dangling from them. Few people wore more than one in those days, and three in each ear were distinctive.

He stopped short and asked, "Ain't you that guy that runs around with Moose?" I nodded. The two looked at each other, something wordless passed between them, and they pulled out a wad of hundreds, peeling off twelve without another sound. We signed the papers, and I kicked the bike into life one last time. Just before the one fellow rode off, I handed him back his pistol. It was a nice moment, but orchestrated by Moose's power, not mine.

WE ARE AT the boardinghouse. Bill is sitting on the fetid bed in his undershirt. Tattoos on his chest of the Hell's Angel's winged skull and the Tibetan *dorje* thunderbolt on his chest have blurred with time. Under the Angels' death's-head are two words, too small to read, and next to them, slightly larger, "Out 8/23." "Protocol," Bill says, referring to his ouster from the club after fourteen years. I question him about it, and he looks away. "It was on me," he says, "I was tied up with a woman with a bad reputation for drugs and shit. They told me to drop her and I said I did. But we were tied together economically and in some other crazy fucking ways and I didn't. When they found out, they booted me out. I gave my word and broke it. It's as simple as that."

Whatever life is, it isn't simple. I look at him, grim and grizzled, surrounded by obscure mementos, one arm lying useless on his lap. He used to laugh often and easily, with a smile so luminous it felt like a reward. Now when I manage to slip through his defenses and catch him off guard with a funny memory or remark, his face lights up again, shedding its haggard mien, splitting into creases and an engaging, shiny-toothed, Cheshire-cat grin. All his old power resides in that smile, just below the surface. It is hoarded now, no longer spent exuberantly. We have both changed that way, have both learned that errors have costs and that nothing is replenished forever. There are limits. Bill's are simply more obvious because he wears them on the surface of his body.

I know deep in my heart that had the Angels not changed, Bill would never have broken his word to them. His action sounds to me like one of those things we do when we desire a certain result but are not prepared to take responsibility for it. The Angels took Bill's voracious hunger for truth and manliness, his health and wholeness, and he offered them willingly to a vision of camaraderie and autonomy in which he wholeheartedly believed. When that vision soured, I believe it was too much to face, and drugs supplied the necessary anesthetic. On my lap lies a book of Bill's poems, and I am rereading one I'd first read nearly twenty-five years ago when he was still hale and whole.

THE IMAGE ROLE
(Thinking of All My Digger Friends)

Lookee where you put me up on an image of myself gaping in the yawn of your
lazy afternoon.
Lookee where you found me up on a pedestal
drowning in the fog
of your own blind eyes.
Lookee here, I'm a hero now
I got it made
I even remember panty raids
    coolin' it behind my Hollywood shades
    Yeah, I'm a jelly bean, sweet and mean
    I'm a hero, famous—a myth in my own time
    A father mother figure outta line
    A swingin' singin' holy man set afire
    The gun in my pocket ain't for hire.
I've got this image of myself pasted up on all the walls
I'm a gypsy a tramp a healer and a vamp
Everywhere I go people stop and stare

I'm known everywhere.
I was invented by MEDIA
a name that's pretty trippy
Even my friends ain't sure
who they are anymore.
They've all got a hundred
million faces
just like me.
Whose brand name are you?
Or do you see
I've got this image built on solid air
of no name and fame and tricky business games.
But I'm going, the child is getting old
and everything it ever was
is all getting sold.
The tumble is to! astonish! Oneself!

from

TEX

s.e. hinton

i got out to the gravel pits with Roger Genet. Roger wasn't real popular with a lot of people, seeing how he was given to stealing things and beating up on kids he knew he could whip. But me and him always got along okay. Anyway, I needed a ride out to the gravel pits, and he had a cycle.

There were five or six cycles out there, roaring up and down the hills, seeing how high they could jump, or who could do the longest wheelie.

Johnny was there but didn't give any indication that he saw me. That bugged me for a second, but then, I knew it wasn't going to be easy.

After a while everybody got together and talked over an old subject, doing an Evel Knievel jump over the creek. Last year a high school senior had tried it, missed, and broke his back. Since then, a lot of people talked about jumping the creek, but nobody really tried it. A couple of people, including Roger Genet, said they had tried it and made it, but unfortunately nobody had been around to witness it. I had always wanted to try it myself, but since I didn't have a bike, I didn't want to take a chance on wrecking Johnny's.

Johnny was saying something about giving it a go, except he was low on gas.

"Hell," said Roger, "that little bitty thing couldn't make it across the creek if it was pumped full."

He had a big old Honda, the kind you couldn't ride legal till you were sixteen. You'd think he wouldn't want to keep reminding everybody he was sixteen and still in the ninth grade, but somehow I don't think Roger ever saw it like that.

"Sure it could," Johnny said. He looked at his fuel gauge. "Maybe I have got enough to try it."

I swung off the back of Roger's cycle. "I don't know," I said, looking at Johnny's fuel gauge. "You look awful low on gas, to me."

I was trying to give Johnny a way to get out of a try, but he looked at me like I was razzing him.

"It's enough," he said curtly, then started up the hill. I took two long strides and hopped on behind him. He didn't say anything. On top of the hill we stopped. The trail led straight down, right to the edge of the creek, then made a sharp left. On the other side the bank was grassy— there weren't any tire tracks there. The creek sides were steep and it was a twenty-foot drop to the creek bed, at least.

"You can get off now," Johnny said.

"Hey, come on," I said. "You don't want to kill yourself."

We looked down to where everybody was grouped, watching. Roger hollered something, we couldn't hear what.

"Off," Johnny said. I got off reluctantly. "Johnny . . ."

He revved up the engine and took off. I watched him, so antsy I couldn't stand still. Geez, Johnny, faster! I was twisting my fists around like I could change the gears for him. He should have had it wide open by now, full throttle, unless he wanted to be able to stop, unless he thought he'd change his mind . . . he's going right off the cliff, dammit! I thought. He's going to be dead and I could have stopped him, I should have stopped him . . . I started running.

Johnny realized he didn't have enough speed, not enough to make the jump, but too much to stop. I felt like I was running in a nightmare; I was going as fast as I could but not covering any ground. Everything was happening in slow motion. Johnny slammed on the brakes and the cycle skidded, turning, but moving right toward the creek. Johnny laid the cycle on its side and they both slid to the edge.

I didn't stop running, even when I saw he wasn't going over.

Johnny was looking at his leg. Most of his jeans and part of his leg was in shreds from the gravel. His jacket had protected his arm, but his knuckles were skinned up, too.

Everybody else buzzed up. Roger had the decency to pause, making sure Johnny wasn't really hurt, before he said, "Run out of gas?"

Johnny didn't look up from picking the rocks out of his leg. I could tell he was wishing he had gone over the bank rather than have to face everybody.

I went over and picked up Johnny's cycle. "Shoot," I said, catching my breath. "He just hit a bump. Anybody could hit a bump. But seeing how he can't give it another chance, I will."

I started up the cycle. I wasn't worried about wrecking it. If that cycle didn't go across that creek bed, for everybody to see, Johnny'd never ride it again anyway. I drove back up the hill, turned, and paused. Everybody was standing to one side, even Johnny had limped out of the way. I saw them for a few seconds, then I didn't see anything but the creek.

When I used to ride in junior rodeos, before money was such a problem, I had the same thing happen to me. You think the crowd is so loud you can't hear yourself think, then you climb in the chute and everything disappears except you and what you're up against. I wouldn't have cared if there were five guys down there, or five hundred, or nobody. I was going across that creek.

I started down the hill, changing gears fast. I didn't even hear the roar of the engine. I kept my eyes on where I wanted to land. A motorcycle needs speed to jump, where it's mostly impulsion with a horse. A horse can tell where you're looking, and head that way, and care if he makes the jump. A horse is a partner, but on a cycle you're all by yourself. Still I leaned and steadied that hunk of machinery like I would a horse coming to a scary jump. When I left the bank and the air whistled around me, and the rocky creek bed floated out behind me, I thought, "Good boy!" and I wasn't talking to myself.

I came down where I'd planned to, but harder than I thought I would. The cycle bounced hard, and we parted company—the cycle going in one direction and me in another. I've had a lot of practice at being thrown from horses, so I know how to relax and roll. And I still got the wind knocked out of me. That sure is a sickening feeling, waiting for air and not really sure you'll get it again.

Somebody came scrambling up the creek bank. I got a mild shock when I looked in that direction. I hadn't cleared the creek by as much as I thought. In fact I'd barely made it.

"Tex?" Johnny crawled over the edge and sat down on his heels beside me. "You okay?"

I nodded, still needing all my air for breathing. Then I tried sitting up. Everything spun around, then settled into place. I waved at everybody watching from the other side. They all cheered and waved back.

"Well, I did it." I felt like I'd won a war, singlehanded. "Me and this little bitty thing."

Johnny was getting some color back in his face. He'd been white as a sheet a few minutes before.

"I thought you didn't have any competitive spirit," he said finally.

"I just wanted to see if I could do it," I said.

"It was really great. You looked like a stunt rider or something. I guess . . ." He looked away. "I shouldn't have let Roger psych me out like that. But he thinks that Honda is so cool—"

"Shoot," I said, "I don't see him jumping over here."

Sure enough the others were all driving off in different directions.

"Johnny, there are people who go places and people who stay, and I think we stayers ought to stick together."

He grinned at me. Then he said, "Your jacket's ripped."

I took it off to look at it. It was an old sheep-herder jacket of Mason's, but the only coat I had. Ripped was an understatement. It looked like somebody had rubbed a giant piece of sandpaper across the back. Then I looked at the cycle. It lay like a turtle on its back, the wheels still spinning.

"I hope the cycle's okay." I started to get up, then caught my breath. My back was really sore. Johnny got up and gave me a hand up. I was tottering around like an old man, holding my hand on my lower back.

"Are *you* okay, that's the question. I can get a new cycle," Johnny said.

"I'm okay."

We got the cycle upright and Johnny tried to get it started, but it'd just splutter and then die. We took turns pushing it home. Johnny limped a lot, and my back ached terrible. We both felt fine.

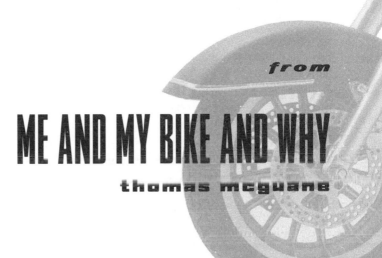

from

ME AND MY BIKE AND WHY

thomas mcguane

as with many who buy a motorcycle, there had been for me the problem of getting over the rather harrowing insurance statistics as to just what it is that is liable to happen to you. Two years in California—a familiar prelude to acts of excess—had made of me an active motorcycle spectator. I watched and identified, finally resorting to bikers' magazines; and evolved a series of foundationless prejudices.

Following the war, motorcycling left a peculiar image in the national consciousness: porcine individuals wearing a sort of yachting cap with a white vinyl bill, the decorative braid pulled up over the hat, their motorcycles plated monsters, white rubber mud flaps studded with ruby stars hung from both fenders. Where are those machines now? Surely Andy Warhol didn't buy them all. Not every one of them is a decorative planter in a Michigan truck garden. But wherever they are, it is certain that the ghosts of cretinism collect close around the strenuously baroque plumbing of those inefficient engines and speak to us of an America that has gone.

It was easy for me initially to deplore the big road bikes, the motor-cycles of the police and Hell's Angels. But finally even these "hogs" and show bikes had their appeal, and sometimes I had dark fantasies of myself on El Camino Real, hands hung overhead from the big chopper bars, feet in front on weirdly automotive pedals, making all the decent people say: "There goes one."

I did it myself. Heading into San Francisco with my wife, our Land Rover blaring wide open at fifty-two miles per, holding up a quarter mile of good people behind us, people who didn't see why anybody needed four-wheel drive on the Bayshore Freeway, we ourselves would from time to time see a lonesome Angel or Coffin Cheater or Satan's Slave or Gypsy Joker on his big chopper and say (either my wife or myself, together sometimes): "There goes one."

Anyway, it was somewhere along in here that I saw I was not that type, and began to think of sporting machines, even racing machines, big ones, because I had no interest in starting small and working my way up as I had been urged to do. I remember that I told the writer Wallace Stegner what I intended, and he asked, "Why do you people do this when you come to California?"

"It's like skiing," I said, purely on speculation.

"Oh, yeah? What about the noise?"

But no one could stop me.

There was the dire question of money that ruled out many I saw. The English-built Triumph Metisse road racer was out of the question, for example. Some of the classics I found and admired—Ariel Square Fours, Vincent Black Shadows, BSA Gold Stars, Velocette Venoms or Phantom Clubmen, Norton Manxes—had to be eliminated on grounds of cost or outlandish maintenance problems.

Some of the stranger Japanese machinery, two-cycle, rotary-valved engines, I dismissed because they sounded funny. The Kawasaki Samurai actually seemed refined, but I refused to consider it. I had a corrupt Western ideal of a bike's exhaust rap, and the tuned mega-phone exhausts of the Japanese motorcycles sounded like something out of the next century, weird loon cries of Oriental speed tuning. There is a blurred moment in my head, a scenario of compulsion. I am in a motorcycle shop that is going out of business. I am writing a check that challenges the contents of my bank account. I am given ownership papers substantiated by the State of California, a crash helmet, and five gallons of fuel. Some minutes later I am standing beside my new motorcycle, sick all over. The man who sold it to me stares palely through the Thermopane window covered with the decals of the noble marques of "performance." He wonders why I have not moved.

I have not moved because I do not know what to do. I wish to advance upon the machine with authority but cannot. He would not believe I could have bought a motorcycle of this power without knowing so much as how to start its engine. Presently he loses interest.

Unwatched, I can really examine the bike. Since I have no notion of how to operate it, it is purely an *objet*. I think of a friend with a road racer on a simple mahogany block in front of his fireplace, except that he rides his very well.

The bike was rather beautiful. I suppose it still is. The designation, which now seems too cryptic for my taste, was "Matchless 500," and it was the motorcycle I believed I had thought up myself. It is a trifle hard to describe the thing to the uninitiated, but, briefly, it had a 500 cc., one-cylinder engine—a "big single" in the patois of bike freaks—and an eloquently simple maroon teardrop-shaped tank that is as much the identifying mark on a Matchless, often otherwise unrecognizable through modification, as the chevron of a redwing blackbird. The front wheel, delicate as a bicycle's, carried a Dunlop K70 tire (said to "cling") and had no fender; a single cable led to the pale machined brake drum. Over the knobby rear wheel curved an extremely brief magnesium fender with, instead of the lush buddy-seat of the fat motorcycles, a minute pillion of leather. The impression was of performance and of complete disregard for comfort. The equivalent in automobiles would be, perhaps, the Morgan, in sailboats the Finn.

I saw all these things at once (I remember the magazines I had been reading, the Floyd Clymer books I had checked out of the library), and in that sense my apprehension of the motorcycle was perfectly literary. I still didn't know how to start it.

I didn't want to experiment on El Camino Real, and moreover, it had begun to rain heavily. I had made up my mind to wheel it home, and there to peruse the operation manual, whose infuriating British locutions the Land Rover manual had prepared me for.

I was surprised at the sheer inertial weight of the thing; it leaned toward me and pressed against my hip insistently all the way to the house. I was disturbed that a machine whose place in history seemed so familiar should look utterly foreign at close range. The fact that the last number on the speedometer was 140 seemed irresponsible.

It was dark by the time I got home. I wheeled it through the back gate and down the sidewalk through a yard turned largely to mud. About halfway to the kitchen door, I somehow got the thing tilted away from

myself, and it slowly but quite determinedly toppled over in the mud,
with me, gnashing, on top of it.

My wife came to the door and peered into the darkness. "Tom?" I
refused to vouchsafe an answer. I lay there in the mud, no longer strug-
gling, as the spring rains of the San Francisco peninsula singled me out
for special treatment. I was already composing the ad in the *Chronicle*
that motorcycle people dream of finding: "Big savings on Matchless
500. Never started by present owner. A real cream puff." My wife threw
on the porch light and perceived my discomfiture.

The contretemps had the effect of quickly getting us over the surprise
that I had bought the motorcycle, questions of authorization, and so on.
I headed for the showers. Scraped and muddy, I had excited a certain
amount of pity. "I'll be all right."

NO ONE TOLD me to retard the spark. True enough, it was in the manual, but I had been unable to read that attentively. It had no plot, no
characters. So my punishment was this: when I jumped on the kick
starter, it backfired and more or less threw me off the bike. I was limping all through the first week from vicious blowbacks. I later learned it
was a classic way to get a spinal fracture. I tried jumping lightly on the
kick starter and, unfairly, it would blast back as viciously as with a sharp
kick. Eventually it started, and sitting on it, I felt the torque tilt the bike
under me. I was afraid to take my hands off the handlebars. My wife lowered the helmet onto my head; I compared it to the barber's basin Don
Quixote had worn into battle, the Helmet of Mambrino.

I slipped my toe up under the gearshift lever, lifted it into first,
released the clutch, and magically glided away and made all my shifts
through fourth, at which time I was on Sand Hill Road and going fifty,
my shirt in a soft air bubble at my back, my Levi's wrapped tight to my
shins, my knuckles whitening under the giddy surge of pure undetained
motion as I climbed gently into the foothills toward Los Altos. The road
got more and more winding as I ascended, briskly but conservatively.
Nothing in the air was lost on me as I passed through zones of smell and
temperature as palpable transitions, running through sudden warm
spots on the road where a single redwood a hundred feet away had fallen
and let in a shaft of sunlight. The road seemed tremendously spacious.
The sound was behind me, so that when I came spiraling down out of
the mountains and saw some farm boy had walked out to the side of the
road to watch me go by, I realized he had heard me coming for a long
time. And I wondered a little about the racket.

These rides became habitual and presumably more competent. I often rode up past La Honda for a view of the sea at the far edge of a declining cascade of manzanita-covered hills, empty and foggy. The smell of ocean was so perfectly evocative in a landscape divided among ranches and truck gardens whose pumpkins in the foggy air seemed to have an uncanny brilliance. A Japanese nursery stood along the road in clouds of tended vines on silver redwood lattice. I went past it to the sea and before riding home took a long walk on the ribbed, immense beach.

A FASCINATING ASPECT of the pursuit, not in the least bucolic, was the bike shop where one went for mechanical service, and which was a meeting place for the bike people, whose machines were poised out front in carefully conceived rest positions. At first, of course, no one would talk to me, but my motorcycle ideas were theirs; I was not riding one of the silly mechanisms that purred down the highways in a parody of the equipment these people lived for.

One day an admired racing mechanic — "a good wrench" — came out front and gave my admittedly well-cared-for Matchless the once-over. He announced that it was "very sanitary." I was relieved. The fear, of course, is that he will tell you, "The bike is wrong."

"Thank you," I said modestly. He professed himself an admirer of the "Matchbox," saying it was "fairly rapid" and had enough torque to "pull stumps." Ultimately, I was taken in, treated kindly, and given the opportunity to ride some of the machinery that so excited me: the "truly potent" Triumph Metisse, an almost uncontrollable supercharged Norton Atlas from New Mexico, and a couple of road-racing machines with foot pegs way back by the rear sprocket and stubby six-inch handlebars — so that you lie out on the bike and divide a sea of wind with the point of your chin.

One day I "got off on the pavement," that is, crashed. It was not much of a crash. I went into a turn too fast and ran off the shoulder and got a little "road burn" requiring symbolic bandages at knees and elbows. I took the usual needling from the crew at the bike shop, and with secret pleasure accepted the temporary appellation "Crash Cargo." I began taking dawn trips over the mountains to Santa Cruz, sometimes with others, sometimes alone, wearing a wool hunting shirt against the chill and often carrying binoculars and an Audubon field guide.

Then one day I was riding in my own neighborhood when a man made a U-turn in front of me and stopped, blocking the road. It was too late to brake and I had to put the bike down, riding it like a sled as it screeched across the pavement. It ran into the side of the car and I slid halfway under, the seat and knees torn out of my pants, scraped and bruised but without serious injury. I had heard the sharp clicking of my helmet against the pavement and later saw the depressions that might have been in my skull.

The man got out, accusing me of going a hundred miles an hour, accusing me of laying for a chance to create an accident, accusing me of being a Hell's Angel, and finally admitting he had been daydreaming and had not looked up the street before making his illegal maneuver. The motorcycle was a mess. He pleaded with me not to have physical injuries. He said he had very little insurance. And a family. "Have a heart."

"You ask this of a Hell's Angel?"

At the motorcycle shop I was urged to develop nonspecific spinal trouble. A special doctor was named. But I had the motorcycle minimally repaired and sent the man the bill. When the settlement came, his name was at the top of the stationery. He was the owner of the insurance agency.

Perhaps it was the point-blank view from below of rocker panels and shock absorbers and the specious concern of the insurance man for my health that gave my mortality its little twinge. I suddenly did not want to get off on the pavement anymore or bring my road burn to the shop under secret bandages. I no longer cared if my bike was rapid and sanitary. I wanted to sell it, and I wanted to get out of California.

I did both those things, and in that order. But sometimes, in the midst of more tasteful activities, I miss the mournful howl of that big single engine as it came up on the cam, dropped revs, and started over on a new ratio; the long banking turns with the foot pegs sparking against the pavement and the great crocodile's tears the wind caused to trickle out from under my flying glasses. I'm behind a sensible windshield now, and the soaring curve of acceleration does not come up through the seat of my pants. I have an FM radio, and the car doesn't get bad mileage.

from

ZEN AND THE ART OF MOTORCYCLE MAINTENANCE

robert m. pirsig

my watch says nine o'clock. And it's already too hot to sleep. Outside the sleeping bag, the sun is already high into the sky. The air around is clear and dry.

I get up puffy-eyed and arthritic from the ground.

My mouth is already dry and cracked and my face and hands are covered with mosquito bites. Some sunburn from yesterday morning is hurting.

Beyond the pines are burned grass and clumps of earth and sand so bright they are hard to look at. The heat, silence, and barren hills and blank sky give a feeling of great, intense space.

Not a bit of moisture in the sky. Today's going to be a scorcher.

I walk out of the pines onto a stretch of barren sand between some grass and watch for a long time, meditatively. . . .

I'VE DECIDED TODAY'S Chautauqua will begin to explore Phaedrus' world. It was intended earlier simply to restate some of his ideas that relate to technology and human values and make no reference to him personally but the pattern of thought and memory that occurred last night has indicated this is not the way to go. To omit now would be to run from something that should not be run from.

In the first grey of the morning what Chris said about his Indian friend's grandmother came back to me, clearing something up. She said ghosts appear when someone has not been buried right. That's true. He never *was* buried right, and that's exactly the source of the trouble.

Later I turn and see John is up and looking at me uncomprehendingly. He is still not really awake, and walks aimlessly in circles to clear his head. Soon Sylvia is up too and her left eye is all puffed up. I ask her what happened. She says it is from mosquito bites. I begin to collect gear to repack the cycle. John does the same.

When this is done we get a fire started while Sylvia opens up packages of bacon and eggs and bread for breakfast.

When the food is ready, I go over and wake Chris. He doesn't want to get up. I tell him again. He says no. I grab the bottom of the sleeping bag, give it a mighty tablecloth jerk, and he is out of it, blinking in the pine needles. It takes him a while to figure out what has happened, while I roll up the sleeping bag.

He comes to breakfast looking insulted, eats one bite, says he isn't hungry, his stomach hurts. I point to lake down below us, so strange in the middle of the semidesert, but he doesn't show any interest. He repeats his complaint. I just let it go by and John and Sylvia disregard it too. I'm glad they were told what the situation is with him. It might have created real friction otherwise.

We finish breakfast silently, and I'm oddly tranquil. The decision about Phaedrus may have something to do with it. But we are also perhaps a hundred feet above the reservoir, looking across it into a kind of Western spaciousness. Barren hills, no one anywhere, not a sound; and there is something about places like this that raises your spirits a little and makes you think that things will probably get better.

While loading the remaining gear on the luggage rack I see with surprise that the rear tire is worn way down. All that speed and heavy load and heat on the road yesterday must have caused it. The chain is also sagging and I get out the tools to adjust it and then groan.

"What's the matter," John says.

"Thread's stripped in the chain adjustment."

I remove the adjusting bolt and examine the threads. "It's my own fault for trying to adjust it once without loosening the axle nut. The bolt is good." I show it to him. "It looks like the internal threading in the frame that's stripped."

John stares at the wheel for a long time. "Think you can make it into town?"

"Oh, yeah, sure. You can run it forever. It just makes the chain difficult to adjust."

He watches carefully as I take up the rear axle nut until it's barely snug, tap it sideways with a hammer until the chain slack is right, then tighten up the axle nut with all my might to keep the axle from slipping forward later on, and replace the cotter pin. Unlike the axle nuts on a car, this one doesn't affect bearing tightness.

"How did you know how to do that?" he asks.

"You just have to figure it out."

"I wouldn't know where to start," he says.

I think to myself, That's the problem, all right, where to start. To reach him you have to back up and back up, and the further back you go, the further back you see you have to go, until what looked like a small problem of communication turns into a major philosophic enquiry. That I suppose, is why the Chautauqua.

I repack the tool kit and close the side cover plates and think to myself. He's worth reaching though.

On the road again the dry air cools off the slight sweat from that chain job and I'm feeling good for a while. As soon as the sweat dries off though, it's hot. Must be in the eighties already.

There's no traffic on this road, and we're moving right along. It's a traveling day.

NOW I WANT to begin to fulfill a certain obligation by stating that there was one person, no longer here, who had something to say, and who said it, but whom no one believed or really understood. Forgotten. For reasons that will become apparent I'd prefer that he remain forgotten, but there's no choice other than to reopen his case.

I don't know his whole story. No one ever will, except Phaedrus himself, and he can no longer speak. But from his writings and from what others have said and from fragments of my own recall it should be possible to piece together some kind of approximation of what he was talking about. Since the basic ideas for this Chautauqua were taken from him there will be no real deviation, only an enlargement that may make the Chautauqua more understandable than if it were presented in a purely abstract way. The purpose of the enlargement is not to argue

for him, certainly not to praise him. The purpose is to bury him—
forever.

Back in Minnesota when we were traveling through some marshland
I did some talking about the "shapes" of technology, the "death force"
that the Sutherlands seem to be running from. I want to move now in
the opposite direction from the Sutherlands, *toward* that force and into
its center. In doing so we will be entering Phaedrus' world, the only
world he ever knew, in which all understanding is in terms of underlying form.

The world of underlying form is an unusual object of discussion
because it is actually a *mode* of discussion itself. You discuss things in
terms of their immediate appearance or you discuss them in terms of their
underlying form, and when you try to discuss these modes of discussion
you get involved in what could be called a platform problem. You have
no platform from which to discuss them other than the modes themselves.

Previously I was discussing his world of underlying form, or at least
the aspect of it called technology, from an external view. Now I think it's
right to talk about that world of underlying form from its own point of
view. I want to talk about the underlying form of the world of underlying form itself.

To do this, first of all, a dichotomy is necessary, but before I can use
it honestly I have to back up and say what *it* is and means, and that is a
long story in itself. Part of this back-up problem. But right now I just
want to use a dichotomy and explain it later. I want to divide human
understanding into two kinds—classical understanding and romantic
understanding. In terms of ultimate truth a dichotomy of this sort has little meaning but it is quite legitimate when one is operating within the
classic mode used to discover or create a world of underlying form. The
terms *classic* and *romantic*, as Phaedrus used them, mean the following:

A classical understanding sees the world primarily as underlying form
itself. A romantic understanding sees it primarily in terms of immediate
appearance. If you were to show an engine or a mechanical drawing or
electronic schematic to a romantic it is unlikely he would see much of
interest in it. It has no appeal because the reality he sees is its surface.
Dull, complex lists of names, lines and numbers. Nothing interesting.
But if you were to show the same blueprint or schematic or give the
same description to a classical person he might look at it and then
become fascinated by it because he sees that within the lines and shapes
and symbols is a tremendous richness of underlying form.

The romantic mode is primarily inspirational, imaginative, creative,
intuitive. Feelings rather than facts predominate. "Art" when it is

opposed to "Science" is often romantic. It does not proceed by reason or by laws. It proceeds by feeling, intuition and esthetic conscience. In the nothern European cultures the romantic mode is usually associated with femininity, but this is certainly not a necessary association.

The classic mode, by contrast, proceeds by reason and by laws—which are themselves underlying forms of thought and behavior. In the European cultures it is primarily a masculine mode and the fields of science, law and medicine are unattractive to women largely for this reason. Although motorcycle riding is romantic, motorcycle maintenance is purely classic. The dirt, the grease, the mastery of underlying form required all give it such a negative romantic appeal that women never go near it.

Although surface ugliness is often found in the classic mode of understanding it is not inherent in it. There is a classic esthetic which romantics often miss because of its subtlety. The classic style is straight-forward, unadorned, unemotional, economical and carefully propor-tioned. Its purpose is not to inspire emotionally, but to bring order out of chaos and make the unknown known. It is not an esthetically free and natural style. It is esthetically restrained. Everything is made under con-trol. Its value is measured in terms of the skill with which this control is maintained.

To a romantic this classic mode often appears dull, awkward and ugly, like mechanical maintenance itself. Everything is in terms of pieces and parts and components and relationships. Nothing is figured out until it's run through the computer a dozen times. Everything's got to be meas-ured and proved. Oppressive. Heavy. Endlessly grey. The death force.

Within the classic mode, however, the romantic has some appear-ances of his own. Frivolous, irrational, erratic, untrustworthy, interested primarily in pleasure-seeking. Shallow. Of no substance. Often a para-site who cannot or will not carry his own weight. A real drag on society. By now these battle lines should sound a little familiar.

This is the source of the trouble. Persons tend to think and feel exclu-sively in one mode or the other and in doing so tend to misunderstand and underestimate what the other mode is all about. But no one is will-ing to give up the truth as he sees it, and as far as I know, no one now living has any real reconciliation of these truths or modes. There is no point at which these visions of reality are unified.

And so in recent times we have seen a huge split develop between a classic culture and a romantic counter-culture—two worlds growingly alienated and hateful toward each other with everyone wondering if it will always be this way, a house divided against itself. No one wants it really—despite what his antagonists in the other dimension might think.

It is within this context that what Phaedrus thought and said is significant. But *no* one was listening at that time and they only thought him eccentric at first, then undesirable, then slightly mad, and then genuinely insane. There seems little doubt that he was insane, but much of his writing at the time indicates that what was driving him insane was this hostile opinion of him. Unusual behavior tends to produce estrangement in others which tends to further the unusual behavior and thus the estrangement in self-stroking cycles until some sort of climax is reached. In Phaedrus' case there was a court-ordered police arrest and permanent removal from society.

I SEE WE are at the left turn onto US 12 and John has pulled up for gas. I pull up beside him.

The thermometer by the door of the station reads 92 degrees. "Going to be another rough one today," I say.

When the tanks are filled we head across the street into a restaurant for coffee. Chris, of course, is hungry.

I tell him I've been waiting for that. I tell him he eats with the rest of us or not at all. Not angrily. Just matter-of-factly. He's reproachful but sees how it's going to be.

I catch a fleeting look of relief from Sylvia. Evidently she thought this was going to be a continuous problem.

When we have finished the coffee and are outside again the heat is so ferocious we move off on the cycles as fast as possible. Again there is that momentary coolness, but it disappears. The sun makes the burned grass and sand so bright I have to squint to cut down glare. This US 12 is an old, bad highway. The broken concrete is tar-patched and bumpy. Road signs indicate detours ahead. On either side of the road are occasional worn sheds and shacks and roadside stands that have accumulated through the years. The traffic is heavy now. I'm just as happy to be thinking about the rational, analytical, classical world of Phaedrus.

His kind of rationality has been used since antiquity to remove oneself from the tedium and depression of one's immediate surroundings. What makes it hard to see is that where once it was used to get away from it all, the escape has been so successful that now it is the "it all" that the romantics are trying to escape. What makes his world so hard to see clearly is not its strangeness but its usualness. Familiarity can blind you too.

His way of looking at things produces a kind of description that can be called an "analytic" description. That is another name of the classic platform from which one discusses things in terms of their underlying

form. He was a totally classic person. And to give a fuller description of
what this is I want now to turn his analytic approach back upon itself—
to analyze analysis itself. I want to do this first of all by giving an exten-
sive example of it and then by dissecting what it is. The motorcycle is a
perfect subject for it since the motorcycle itself was invented by classic
minds. So listen:

A motorcycle may be divided for purposes of classical rational analysis by means of its component assemblies and by means of its functions.

If divided by means of its component assemblies, its most basic division is into a power assembly and a running assembly.

The power assembly may be divided into the engine and the power-
delivery system. The engines will be taken up first.

The engine consists of a housing containing a power train, a fuel-air
system, an ignition system, a feedback system and a lubrication system.

The power train consists of cylinders, pistons, connecting rods, a
crankshaft and a flywheel.

The fuel-air system components, which are part of the engine, consist of a gas tank and filter, an air cleaner, a carburetor, valves and
exhaust pipes.

The ignition system consists of an alternator, a rectifier, a battery, a
high-voltage coil and spark plugs.

The feedback system consists of a cam chain, a camshaft, tappets and
a distributor.

The lubrication system consists of an oil pump and channels
throughout the housing for distribution of the oil.

The power-delivery system accompanying the engine consists of a
clutch, a transmission and a chain.

The supporting assembly accompanying the power assembly consists
of a frame, including foot pegs, seat and fenders; a steering assembly;
front and rear shock absorbers; wheels; control levers and cables; lights
and horn; and speed and mileage indicators.

That's a motorcycle divided according to its components. To know what
the components are for, a division according to functions is necessary:

A motorcycle may be divided into normal running functions and special, operator-controlled functions.

Normal running functions may be divided into functions during the
intake cycle, functions during the compression cycle, functions during
the power cycle and functions during the exhaust cycle.

And so on. I could go on about which functions occur in their proper
sequence during each of the four cycles, then go on the operator-
controlled functions and that would be a very summary description of the

underlying form of a motorcycle. It would be extremely short and rudi-
mentary, as descriptions of this sort go. Almost any one of the components
mentioned can be expanded on indefinitely. I've read an entire engineering volume on contact points alone, which are just a small but vital part
of the distributor. There are other types of engines than the single-cylinder
Otto engine described here: two-cycle engines, multiple-cylinder engines,
diesel engines, Wankel engines—but this example is enough.

This description would cover the "what" of the motorcycle in terms
of components, and the "how" of the engine in terms of functions. It
would badly need a "where" analysis in the form of an illustration, and
also a "why" analysis in the form of engineering principles that led to
this particular conformation of parts. But the purpose here isn't exhaus-
tively to analyze the motorcycle. It's to provide a starting point, an
example of a mode of understanding of things which will itself become
an object of analysis.

There's certainly nothing strange about this description at first hearing. It sounds like something from a beginning textbook on the subject,
or perhaps a first lesson in a vocational course. What is unusual about
it is seen when it ceases to be a mode of discourse and becomes an
object of discourse. Then certain things can be pointed to.

The first thing to be observed about this description is so obvious you
have to hold it down or it will drown out every other observation. This
is: It is just duller than ditchwater. Yah-da, yah-da, yah-da, yah-da, yah,
carburetor, gear ratio, compression, yah-da-yah, piston, plugs, intake,
yah-da-yah, on and on and on. That is the romantic face of the classic
mode. Dull, awkward and ugly. Few romantics get beyond that point.

But if you can hold down that most obvious observation, some other
things can be noticed that do not at first appear.

The first is that the motorcycle, so described, is almost impossible to
understand unless you already know how one works. The immediate
surface impressions that are essential for primary understanding are
gone. Only the underlying form is left.

The second is that the observer is missing. The description doesn't
say that to see the piston you must remove the cylinder head. "You"
aren't anywhere in the picture. Even the "operator" is a kind of per-
sonalityless robot whose performance of a function on the machine is
completely mechanical. There are no real subjects in this description.
Only objects exist that are independent of any observer.

The third is that the words *"good"* and *"bad"* and all their synonyms
are completely absent. No value judgments have been expressed anywhere, only facts.

The fourth is that there is a knife moving here. A very deadly one; an intellectual scalpel so swift and so sharp you sometimes don't see it moving. You get the illusion that all those parts are just there and are being named as they exist. But they can be named quite differently and organized quite differently depending on how the knife moves.

For example, the feedback mechanism which includes the camshaft and cam chain and tappets and distributor exists only because of an unusual cut of this analytic knife. If you were to go to a motorcycle-parts department and ask them for a feedback assembly they wouldn't know what the hell you were talking about. They don't split it up that way. No two manufacturers ever split it up quite the same way and every mechanic is familiar with the problem of the part you can't buy because you can't find it because the manufacturer considers it a part of something else.

It is important to see this knife for what it is and not to be fooled into thinking that motorcycles or anything else are the way they are just because the knife happened to cut it up that way. It is important to concentrate on the knife itself. Later I will want to show how an ability to use this knife creatively and effectively can result in solutions to the classic and romantic split.

Phaedrus was a master with this knife, and used it with dexterity and a sense of power. With a single stroke of analytic thought he split the whole world into parts of his own choosing, split the parts and split the fragments of the parts, finer and finer and finer until he had reduced it to what he wanted it to be. Even the special use of the terms *"classic"* and *"romantic"* are examples of his knifemanship.

But if this were all there were to him, analytic skill, I would be more than willing to shut up about him. What makes it important not to shut up about him was that he used this skill in such a bizarre and yet meaningful way. No one ever saw this, I don't think he even saw it himself, and it may be an illusion of my own, but the knife he used was less that of an assassin than that of a poor surgeon. Perhaps there is no difference. But he saw a sick and ailing thing happening and he started cutting deep, deeper and deeper to get at the root of it. He was after something. That is important. He was after something and he used the knife because that was the only tool he had. But he took on so much and went so far in the end his real victim was himself.

from

JUPITER'S TRAVELS

ted simon

I first thought of becoming a god as I was riding north from Madurai. The fever was gone. I felt more than just healthy, I was bursting with life and joy, floating as you do when you have put down a heavy load. Without exhaustion or discomfort to blunt my senses, without the distorting effect of fever, I saw myself to be in a paradise.

First there were the trees. Paradise would be unthinkable without trees. The neem, the peepul, the tamarind, countless others, stood at stately intervals alongside the roads and fields like giant witnesses from another age. By their presence they transform everything, framing the landscape, giving it depth, variety and freshness, making green-glowing caverns under the sun and casting pools of dappled shade where people and animals can feel at peace.

The ox's creamy hide is made to reflect this flickering light. Under a shade tree a pair of pale oxen passed, yoked to their rumbling cart. The oxen tossed their heads, brandishing their high crescent horns painted in red and blue bands and tipped with glittering brass. The slack, velvety hide beneath their throats rippled in the sun, and the image was printed on my memory for life. Only on *my* memory? So intense was the image, is still, that I could not believe it was meant only for me. I felt it burning into some larger consciousness than my own.

Small groups of women walked the roads carrying vast but apparently weightless burdens of fodder, produce, pottery or household furniture. The breeze swirled the hems of their saris into the classic mould of nymphs and goddesses. Wrapped in those gauzy layers of lime green and rose red their bodies were so poised and supple, all of them, that it was sometimes a shock to see close up the deep wrinkles and grey hair of age.

From the road I saw fields of grain and paddy. Women worked in lines, advancing across the mud, stooping and rising easily, brilliantly coloured against the green rice shoots. The men worked almost naked, with just a triangle of cloth between their long powerful thighs, black-skinned and gleaming. A team of six oxen harnessed together and guided by one man was churning up a paddy field, flying around at a tremendous rate. Everywhere people moved briskly and with confidence. They and the land were part of each other and had shaped each other. The harmony was so complete that it seemed to promise utter tranquility. As I rode through it I felt it reaching for me, as if I had only to stop and let myself slide into it like a pebble into a lake.

I knew those Indians were most unlikely to share my vision. How could they, since they were in it? How could a fish describe water? And when I stopped the bike and stood idle by the roadside it faded for me too under the remorseless glare of so-called reality. I would have to strip naked, go hungry, live with the mosquitoes and the parasites in the paddy squelch and shed a large part of what I liked to call my personality. The very part of me that could envisage such a life would prevent me from living it. Did that make it an illusion?

Throughout the journey, as I rode through so many landscapes, passed through so many lives, forming impressions, holding them and developing them, had I just been wallowing in illusions? It seemed very extraordinary to me that, riding through southern India, observing this life around me, I could at the same time summon up vivid mental images of Africans working with sisal and sugar cane, of Americans working among corn, cattle, bananas and oil palms, of Thais and Malays working with rice, sago and pineapples. I could create living pictures of people and places as remote from these Indians as they had once been from me. If my head could only be wired to a coloured print-out terminal I could have trailed a blizzard of picture postcards from the four corners of the earth.

Just to be carrying the consciousness of so much at the same time seemed to me to be miraculous, as though I were observing the earth from some far-off point, Mount Olympus, perhaps, or a planet. Riding a motorcycle at thirty miles an hour on the road to Dundigal, among people deeply involved in manual skills, so close to the earth and each other and so different from me, I could imagine myself as a mythical being, a god in disguise that might pass their way only once in a lifetime.

Memories of Madras, of ashes and honey, gods and temples, were strong in me. In India it is quite plain that there is more to life than what the senses can perceive. I was thinking about my plan to meet Sai Baba, the holy man, wondering how it could happen.

'There is no cause to bother,' a devotee advised me. 'He will know. Just go there. He knows everything. If he wants to see you it will happen.'

Apparently he had a headquarters at a building called Whitelands, near Bangalore. At certain times of day he appeared before his followers. I would go there, but I would make no other attempt to get in touch with him. I had heard and read about his miracles, but I knew that such things could, in certain circumstances, be 'arranged.' It seemed very important not to go there expecting magic.

If he 'knows' then let him call me out. That will be miracle enough for me.

I smiled at the idea of it happening.

Just imagine that he does know, that he knows I am riding towards him now, still several days away but coming closer all the time, until finally I ride up to this Whitelands place and Sai Baba falls to his knees beside the motorcycle and says: 'My God. You have come at last.'

That was how the notion of being a god came to me originally. As a joke. After all, there were so many gods in India already, in such wild and wonderful guises, why not a god on a motorcycle?

The southern hills were a great surprise, rising to nearly nine thousand feet and demolishing my notion that India south of the Himalayas was a flat hot triangle. I rode up to Kodaikanal, the more southerly hill station where log fires roar in the grates at night as they did in the White Highlands of Kenya, and then over the Cardamom Hills to Cochin to enjoy the splendour of the west coast and the green tidiness of Kerala. Then up again to Ootacamund, which the British nicknamed 'Ooty.'

At the foot of the last big climb to Ooty were groves of areca palms, quite improbably graceful and slender for their great height. It seemed incredible that they could support the weight of the men who clambered up them to reap the betel crop from below their feathery crowns, swinging from one to another like monkeys. There were monkeys too, silvery

grey ones with long furry limbs. Halfway up the hill I stopped to contemplate them, my head light with thought, recalling all the other times
I had watched them in Africa, America, Malaysia and most recently at
the rest house in Mannar where I had played with one for hours.

They seemed so close to enlightenment, as though at any moment
they might stumble over it and explode into consciousness. Their curios-
ity is extreme. They experiment with any unfamiliar object, a coin, a
hat, a piece of paper, just as a human baby does, pulling it, rubbing it,
sticking it in their ears, hitting it against other things. And nothing
comes of it. To be so close, yet never to pierce the veil!

I looked at myself in the same light, as a monkey given my life to play
with, prodding it, trying to stretch it into different shapes, dropping it
and picking it up again, suspecting always that it must have some use
and meaning, tantalized and frustrated by it but always unable to make
sense of it.

'If I were a god that is how I would view myself,' I thought. At times
I felt myself coming very close to that understanding, as though I might
rise above myself and see, at last, what it was all about. The feelings that
had begun to form in Sudan, in the Karoo and on the Zoe G and at
other times seemed to be coming to fruition in India. A latent power of
perception was stirring in me.

I was astonished by my confidence with strangers. Often I was able
to talk to them immediately as though we had always known each other.
For a long time I had been training myself to want nothing from others;
to accept what was offered but to avoid expectation. I was far from perfect, but even the beginnings I had made were richly rewarding. I could
feel that people appreciated my presence and even drew some strength
from it, and in turn that feeling strengthened me. There were the beginnings of a growth of power and I was determined to pursue it.

The journey continued, as it always had, with this close interweaving
of action and reflection. I ate, slept, cursed, smiled, rode, stopped for
petrol, argued, bargained, wrote and took pictures. I made friends with
some Germans, and some English, and some Indians. I learned about
mushrooms, potatoes, cabbages, golden nematodes, Indian farmers and
elephants.

The thread connecting these random events was The Journey. For
me it had a separate meaning and existence; it was the warp on which
the experiences of each successive day were laid. For three years I had
been weaving this single tapestry. I could still recall where I had been
and slept and what I had done on every single day of travelling since
The Journey began. There was an intensity and a luminosity about my

life during those years which sometimes shocked me. I wondered whether it might be beyond my capacity to hold so much experience in conscious awareness at one time and I was seriously afraid that I would see the fabric of the tapestry beginning to rot before I had finished it. I thought I might be guilty of some offence against nature for which I would be made to pay a terrible price. Was it improper for a mere human to attempt to comprehend the world in this way? For that was my intention. The circle I was describing around the earth might be erratic but the fact remained, it was a real circle. The ends would meet and it would enclose the earth. I would have laid my tracks around the surface of this globe and at the end it would belong to me, in a way that it could never belong to anyone else. I trembled a bit at the fates I might be tempting.

People who thought of my journey as a physical ordeal or an act of courage, like single-handed yachting, missed the point. Courage and physical endurance were no more than useful items of equipment for me, like facility with languages or immunity to hepatitis. The goal was comprehension, and the only way to comprehend the world was by making myself vulnerable to it so that it could change me. The challenge was to lay myself open to everybody and everything that came my way. The prize was to change and grow big enough to feel one with the whole world. The real danger was death by exposure.

In India I was on the last and most significant leg, and during the long hours of solitary riding my brain shuttled back and forth, delving into the past for new connections and meanings, synthesizing, analysing, fantasizing, refining and revising my ideas and observations. The pattern on the tapestry still eluded me, though it shimmered somewhere on the edge of recognition. What must I do to see it clearly? Must I, like Icarus, strap on wax wings and fly to the sun? Whatever it was I felt ready to try because I had finally to admit it, I was in search of immortality.

The vital instrument of change is detachment and travelling alone was an immense advantage. At a time of change the two aspects of a person exist simultaneously; as with a caterpillar turning into a butterfly there is the image of what you were and the image of what you are about to be, but those who know you well see you only as you were. They are unwilling to recognize change. By their actions they try to draw you back into your familiar ways.

It would be hopeless to try to become a god among friends and relations, any more than a man can become a hero to his valet. It was chilling to realize that the sentimental qualities most valued between people, like loyalty, constancy and affection, are the ones most likely to impede change. They are so obviously designed to compensate for mortality. The old gods never had any truck with them.

Kronos, the king of the ancient Greek gods, began his career by cutting off his father's penis with a sickle and tossing it into the ocean. He went on to swallow his own children to make sure they did not unseat him. Zeus, the son that got away, put his father in chains and had him guarded in exile by monsters. There are endless tales of betrayal, bloody vengeance and fearful dismemberment. Zeus, who became Jupiter in Roman times, adopted deceitful disguises and committed rape as a cuckoo, a swan and a bull, and he reigned over Olympus more by cunning than virtue.

The Indian gods seemed little different in their own behaviour but, reading the *Mahabharata*, I saw that in Indian mythology they became more closely involved with mankind than did the Greek gods. They allied themselves to various warring factions and offered advice. The best-known example was when Lord Krishna became the warrior Arjuna's charioteer, drove him to battle and encouraged him in words that have become known as the Bhagavad-Gita.

Arjuna, of course, was fighting for good against evil, but many good men had found themselves compromised and were on the wrong side. It sickened Arjuna to have to kill his own kith and kin, and he lost heart, thinking that it must be wrong to do so. What Krishna told him was that his primary duty lay in being true to what he was, a warrior, and not to be crippled by sentimental attachments to his family. There is an elemental brutality about this advice which I found as thrilling as it seemed cruel. When I read it every line struck home, and I relived episodes of the journey vividly, recalling my own fears and confusions.

> Heat, cold, pain, pleasure-
> these spring from sensual contact, Arjuna,
> They begin and they end.
> They exist for the time being,
> you must learn to put up with them.
> The man whom these cannot distract,
> the man who is steady in pain and pleasure,
> is the man who achieves serenity.
>
> The untrue never is,
> the True never isn't.
> The knowers of Truth know this.
> And the Self that pervades all things is imperishable.
> Nothing corrupts this imperishable self.

Lucky are soldiers who strive in a just war;
for them it is an easy entrance into heaven.

Equate pain and pleasure, profit and loss,
victory and defeat.
And fight.
There is no blame this way.

There is no waste of half-done work in this,
no inconsistent results.
An iota of this removes a world of fear.
In this there is only single-minded consistency;
while the efforts of confused people
are many-branching and full of contradiction.

Your duty is to work, not to reap the fruits of work...

Wanting things breeds attachment,
from attachment springs covetousness,
and covetousness breeds anger.
Anger leads to confusion
and confusion kills the power of memory.
With the destruction of memory, choice is rendered
    impossible
and when moral choice fails, man is doomed.

The mind is the ape of the wayward senses;
they destroy discrimination as a storm scatters boats on a
    lake.

The concept of the Self seemed to connect with my own thought in South Africa, of being made of the stuff of the universe, all-pervading and imperishable. The Truth was in the stuff itself, revealed in the natural order of things. You have only to merge with the world to know the Truth and find your Self.

There are shapes and forms which rise out of this natural order. Trees, caves and animal architecture lead naturally to thatched roofs, stone houses and mud walls. If you knew this you would not choose to put up a roof in corrugated iron. Nor would you think of throwing a plastic bag in a stream, not because of what you have been told about pollution, but because the idea of a plastic bag in a stream is offensive in itself. Without this sense of what is naturally fitting you can be cleaning up the world with one hand and spreading poison with the other.

It surprised me to discover that this sense of rightness does not appear naturally in people, even though they live in the heart of nature. In my own village in France the same people who fished the streams shoved every possible kind of refuse and sewerage into them, even when offered convenient alternatives. In Nepal, where not a single engine or power line disturbs the mediaeval rusticity of the Himalayan valleys, people shit in their rivers with a dogmatic persistence ensuring that every village is infected by what the people upstream have got.

The Truth obviously does not reveal itself unaided to humans. It has to be uncovered by an effort of consciousness. Or, more likely, it exists only in human consciousness. Without man around to recognize it, there is no Truth, no God.

Yet it is not consciousness that governs the world, nor even ideology, nor religious principle nor national temperament. It is custom that rules the roost. In Colombia it was the custom to do murder and violence. In a period of ten years some 200,000 people were said to have been killed by acts of more or less private violence. Yet I found the Colombians at least as hospitable, honourable and humane as the Argentines, whose custom is merely to cheat. Arabs have the custom of showing their emotions and hiding their women. Australians show their women and hide their emotions. In Sudan it is customary to be honest. In Thailand dishonesty is virtually a custom, but so is giving gifts to strangers.

Every possible variation of nudity and prudishness is the custom somewhere as with eating habits, toilet practices, to spit or not to spit; and almost all of these customs have become entirely arbitrary and self-perpetuating. Above all it is customary to suspect and despise people in the next valley, or state, or country, particularly if their colour or religion is different. And there are places where it is customary to be at war, like Kurdistan or Vietnam.

Speaking of the more vicious customs, and of men who should have known better, St. Francis Xavier said a long time ago: 'Custom is to them in the place of law, and what they see done before them every day they persuade themselves may be done without sin. For customs bad in themselves seem to these men to acquire authority and prescription from the fact that they are commonly practised.'

Custom is the enemy of awareness, in individuals as much as in societies. It regularizes the fears and cravings of everyday life. I wanted to shake them off. I wanted to use this journey to see things whole and clear, for I would never pass this way again. I wanted to be rid of the conditioning of habit and custom. To be the slave of custom, at any level, is much like being a monkey, an 'ape of the wayward senses'. To rise above it is already something like becoming a god.

With these elevating thoughts forming in my mind I rode along narrow country roads among trees in a state bordering on ecstasy, and there did come a moment when I was actually prepared to take seriously the possibility of some semidivine status. At that very moment, which I recognized only in retrospect, I turned a corner and came upon a travelling holy man, a *saddhu*, his forehead smeared with the colours of his profession, dragging his bundles on to the next shrine. He looked up at me as though he had expected me, and his face showed pure distaste. Then he spat vigorously in my path as I passed him by.

The comment could not have been more appropriate.

Really, I told myself, you could hardly ask for a more convincing demonstration, and I took the hint.

Even so I did go to see Sai Baba at Whitelands. There was a walled compound the size of a football field, with a rain shelter in the middle that could house a lot of people. The holy man apparently lived in an opulent villa at one end of the garden, accessible by a flight of broad stone steps. Scattered around near the villa were several keenly nonchalant young men of the kind you see working for progressive candidates at American conventions. There was a new building going up too, hand-made in the Asian tradition with women doing most of the work. When you have seen women working a coal mine in saris, nothing in the field of human labour seems improbable.

I sat on the ground among a mixed crowd of Indians and Europeans, and one of the guru's staff men asked me to take off my shoes. Eventually Sai Baba came down the steps with a small group and inspected the building operations. Later he came to look the rest of us over. He looked much as he had in the pictures, in his ankle-length robe of crimson, and his great head of frizzy black hair, but he seemed anxious and preoccupied. A thin red line of betel juice stained his lips. There were no miracles, and he did not even smile. He looked at us in the way a worried farmer might examine his crops for blight, and then he departed. I did not form the impression that he was God, and he seems to have been equally disappointed in me.

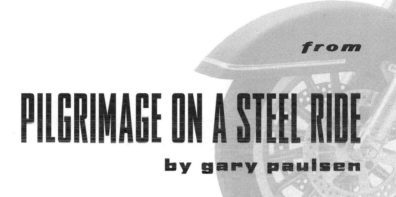

PILGRIMAGE ON A STEEL RIDE

from

by gary paulsen

I am a man, in a time when it has become anachronistic to be masculine.

It's my fifty-seventh birthday and I have heart disease.

It had not and has not yet killed me and to my great surprise I am somehow two years older than Columbus was when he died. Twenty-two years older than Mozart.

I have accomplished more than I ever thought I would. Certainly more – considering the rough edges of my life – than I deserve to have accomplished. My children are through college and launched, my wife is set for life, and yet…

And yet.

Just that. An unsettling thought, like a burr under a saddle, rubbing incessantly until at last it galls and still it was and is there…

There had been a time when I was content. Not completely, and only briefly, but at least enough to settle, to accept, to live – shudder – within an accepted parameter. Then it changed and in the change I learned a fundamental truth about myself; I saw a weakness that was a strength at the same time.

It is very strange what saves a man.

I had a friend caught in the blind throes of bottom-drinking alcoholism who was going to kill himself, had the barrel of the .357 in his mouth and the hammer back and pressure on the trigger, ready to go out when he saw a spider weaving a web and became interested in it and forgot why he wanted to kill himself. Another friend, a soldier, was saved on a night patrol in Korea because Chinese soldiers ate raw garlic and he smelled them coming and hid.

As I drove into Mankato, there was a Harley dealer, and that dealer saved me as sure as if it had been a spider or garlic.

I pulled over and parked, killed the motor on the Chevette, and sat looking at them. He had two outside—a red Dresser with a sidecar and a Softail, and I watched the bikes and let myself go.

Away.

That's what they meant to me then. Not to a place, not from a place, but just away. Gone. In and out of myself, away from what I was in danger of becoming, and I got out of the car and went to the Softail and sat on it and let it talk to me.

"You like her?" The dealer came outside.

I nodded. "What's not to like? It's a Harley."

"It's used," he said. "Just four months. Man had a heart attack and his old lady wants to get rid of the bike. I can make you a good deal on it . . ."

For a second, then another, I let it run in my head. Start the bike, the thought said. Start the bike and let it run. Just go. Leave the Chevette, leave it all. Ride.

For a second. Clean thought. Clear thought. Start it and go. Never look back. Never see the same place twice. Just the wind and the sun and the motor between your legs. Cliché. Clean, clear cliché.

Ride.

Then I shook my head. "I have a wife, a son. I have to work."

He smiled. "You can still have a bike."

"No." I thought of where my mind had been. The lonesome and lonely roads, the sun out ahead, nothing behind. "No, I can't. Not now."

"Ahh," he said. "I see . . ."

And I think he did. There was pity in his eyes and I let it wash over me for a moment, and had I known then, known then how long it would be before I at last rode and knew about Harleys, I would have done it. I would have run. But I was young then and very narrow thinking and did not see the nature of the trap, did not know that my bondage—confining, crippling, and total—was entirely self-inflicted and that I could have stopped the jaws of the trap from closing then, right *then,* that instant and I would have been free.

But the thought was there, the dream. I turned away from it, from the freedom, and would not see it again until I was fifty-six years old and it was almost too late. Or perhaps is too late. But the lust was there and I am running now, coursing now, and will not know if it is too late until I die and still—please God—have not found the grail.

Then more life. The son grew, the marriage grew, the trap grew. I built a house and found that—why was I surprised?—Thoreau was right. If a man builds a barn, the barn becomes his prison.

I closed the prison doors on myself. Made the house and the family, and lest it is misunderstood, I have had perhaps the best family a man could. A wife who understands me and does not complain, a son who did not do drugs or run crazy and has become all that I could have hoped a son to be.

But I made a house and then had to service the house, and made a family and then had to support the family, and made a career and then had to furnish my career, the way a house is furnished, a piece here and a piece there, and thought and still think it was good and right to do these things.

Nor was my prison as onerous as many. I did not sit in a windowless office or have to listen to what I did not want to hear. I worked at home, doing what I loved to do—what Michener has called following "the loops and whorls of words on paper"—and not one part of it is possible to complain about and to my utter and complete and continuing amazement—and it *still* is unbelievable—I had a measure of success.

And I am grateful.

And more, still more, I have not been as confined as most men in their prisons. I have lived and trapped in the bush and have twice run the Iditarod sled dog race—indeed I have over twenty thousand miles on sleds—and have hunted when I wanted and fished when I wanted and played poker when I wanted and taken horses on long pack trips when I wanted and been able on several occasions to actually say no to some things and people when it was not prudent to say no; when all around me have counseled me to say yes because, they said, it would be for my own good—then I said no. *Then.*

I have had a life of such good fortune and seeming looseness that many who know me or of me envy what they term my "freedom."

True, I have not had to work in a bank nor become a lawyer and god knows I came to have some external trappings of what many term liberation.

And yet.

And yet . . .

I was never really loose. I lunged on the chain and stretched it, slammed against the pull of it but never could break it. Always it jerked me back until I would pace and walk the end like a cat in a cage—my own chain, my own cage—until I had rested enough or gathered enough strength or courage or desperation, *whatever* it was I needed and then out again. Running, pulling until I hit the end again, and again, and again . . .

But never loose.

Never the run.

Always the feeling of it, always the taste of it, but only imitation.

Only freedom lite.

Never the clean run.

Never the Harley.

YEARS LATER ANOTHER Harley salesman, not like other salesmen. There was no glib phoniness about him, no checkered pants or white belt or lacquered hair or manicured hands. He was dirty with grease under his nails, had a full beard and almost no hair on top, calluses on his hands and scars from road rash on one arm, a face burned by wind and sun and a couple of teeth gone. There were tattoos on his arms and backs of his hands and probably on his body as well, though it was all covered by a black tee shirt with the orange emblem and HARLEY DAVIDSON written across it in large white letters.

He had ridden.

The display room was filled with Harleys. There must have been eight or nine new ones and perhaps another seven or eight used.

"I want," I said, "to buy a bike."

He perhaps knew what it had taken for me to come to this point in my life. All the living, the wrongs, the rights, the scars and the unhealed wounds; the near-divorce that it caused now. Many, perhaps most, men who came in had gone through the same thing to come to this point. He looked at me evenly, smiling slightly, understanding, waiting.

"I want," I amended it, "to buy a Harley." Stupid and simple and straightforward all at once. I had of course "wanted" to buy a Harley for years, decades. What I really meant was that I was "going" to buy a Harley. I had come to it in my life, had reached it.

The salesman nodded. He'd been sitting at a metal desk that looked like it came from army surplus. One of those gray things with the soft blotter top. He stood, smiled a flash of teeth, except for the missing ones. "You've come to the right place."

Here my ignorance kicked in. There were many different models—Softails, Softail Customs, Dressers, Sportsters, Heritages, Strokers, Shovelheads, Fat Boys, Springers, to name a few. Walking in and saying I wanted to buy a bike without a word as to what bike I wanted was like pointing at a menu and simply saying: Give me something.

I pointed at a red bike, glistening chrome and so beautiful it made me catch my breath. "How about that one?"

He nodded again. "Beautiful bike," he said. "It's a Fat Boy. Brand-new."

"How much is it?"

"It's sold."

"Oh." I pointed at a turquoise-green one with white trim, black saddlebags. "How about that?"

Another nod. "Great bike. Softail Custom."

"How much?"

"It's sold, too."

"Oh. The black one next to it?"

"Sold."

I stopped looking at the room and turned to face him. "Let's do it this way. Which new bikes haven't been sold?"

He shook his head. "None of them. All the new bikes are sold, waiting for the owners to pick them up. If you want a *new* bike you have to order it ahead of time and wait for delivery."

Well, I thought, what the hell. A couple of weeks, a month. I'd been waiting my whole life—what was a month more? "So. Let's order one like that green one."

He nodded. "Good choice. The Softail Custom. Sit down and I'll write it up while you pick a color out of brochures."

He handed me some pamphlets with beautiful color illustrations and I pointed at one of the pictures. "This color."

He nodded and kept writing. "You have ID?"

I gave him my driver's license and he took information from it and put it on the form.

"How are you paying?"

"How much is it?"

"Sixteen thousand five hundred dollars."

I winced internally but I had known they would be higher than other bikes and I had spoken to a bank ahead of time. "Cash," I said. "A bank loan."

"Good. Good. All right, with taxes and delivery it comes to just over seventeen thousand two hundred dollars."

I told him the name of the bank and he scribbled it down on a piece of paper. "How long," I asked, "will it take to get the bike?"

He squinted at the ceiling, thinking. "It takes a few days to set it up with the bank and OK the payment, then I'll send the order in. Of course, we can fax that so that won't take any time . . . say just at three years."

"Three *years?*"

"Well, maybe a bit more or less. It seems to be running that now. Of course, in a year or so things might change. But new bikes are spoken for between two and three years ahead. Sure. Why, is that too long?"

I thought he was joking but he wasn't smiling and he had stopped writing on the order form.

"I am fifty-six years old."

He nodded. "Most of us are that old. Almost no young people can afford to buy Harleys. I just passed fifty-five myself . . ."

"I have heart disease. There is at least a chance I won't be *around* for three more years."

He laid his pen down and without batting an eye said, "Then you'll want a used bike."

I studied him for a moment but he still wasn't joking. "All right—do you have any *used* bikes for sale?"

"Oh, sure." He stood from the desk and looked around the room at all the bikes, then shook his head. "No, I take that back. There aren't any . . ."

"No bikes at all?"

He looked again. "No. Sorry. Oh, wait a minute. We took one in this morning. It's back in the shop being tricked up but I think it's sold."

He walked to a door in the rear of the display room marked EMPLOY-EES ONLY and motioned me to follow him. "It's back here."

I passed through the door into the back and found myself in a small garage area. Gutted, wheel-less Harleys stood on stands around the room in various stages of repair. By the back door on an elevated stand

stood a blue-and-chrome Heritage Softail. It had spoked wheels front
and back, leather saddlebags covered with slide studs, foot pads and a
motor protection (crash) bar, a small windshield and the wide front end
with fog lights.

"Here, this one." The salesman stopped next to it. "But like I said, I'm
sure it's sold."

It looked new and I checked the speedometer to find it only had
eighty miles on it. "It's not even broken in."

"No. The guy bought it and his old lady made him bring it back."

"Pussy-whipped," a voice said from beneath and on the far side of the
bike. I leaned over to see a mechanic covered in grease. He looked like
a garden gnome soaked in used oil and I saw he had two fingers missing. I noticed that the two other mechanics had fingers missing and then
remembered the time I tried a brief stint at racing dirt bikes; a lot of the
pit crews were old riders who had parts missing. Occupational hazards.
"Waits three years for a bike like this and then he's so pussy-whipped he
brings it back. Jesus Christ."

"Some men like to live that way," the salesman said. "It's what makes
them move . . ."

"The bike," I said, bringing the conversation back to what was important. "Are you sure it's sold?"

"Oh—yeah, I think so."

"Deal fell through." The mechanic looked up again. "Couldn't get
the bread."

"I'll buy it." It was out before I thought. I couldn't stop it. Years of
waiting were in back of it, a frustration-powered blurt. "Now."

"I don't know how much the boss is asking for it."

"Go find out." He left but I stayed with the bike until he came back.

"Nineteen," he said. "Nineteen thousand plus tax and license."

I nodded. "Done." And then I thought of the first place we'd bought
when we went north to live in the bush and run dogs; the whole farm,
eighty acres and buildings, cost less than this bike. We lived then on two
thousand dollars a year and all the beaver and venison we could eat. We
could have lived for nearly ten years on what this Harley was costing.
"Tell him it's done. I'm buying it. When can you have it ready to go?"

"Half an hour," the mechanic said, smiling like a drunk who has met
somebody to drink with. "Just have to check her out."

"Come out front and we'll get the papers started. You'll need some
accessories as well."

"Accessories?" I followed. "What kind of accessories?"

"A helmet. We've got the helmet law here. Do you have a helmet?"

"No."

"Do you have a jacket?"

I shook my head. Part of me now rebelled. I was in for the Harley but something in me made me suddenly shy away from all the geegaws. "It's the middle of summer."

"A jacket's good if you have to lay her over. You'll lose less meat."

"Ahh." I did not know then but within a year I would "lay her over" three times and all three times I would be deeply grateful that the salesman talked me into buying and wearing a heavy horsehide jacket, even when it was warm. "I'll buy the jacket."

"And goggles."

"I need goggles?" Jesus, I thought, I'm going to look like a geek. New leather jacket, helmet, goggles. All I needed was a silk scarf. "I was going to wear sun-glasses."

He nodded. "In the day. But when you ride at night you have to have clear goggles—unless you want to wear safety glasses. I had a cousin riding at night without glasses and a bee came over the top of the windshield at about seventy and drove his fucking stinger completely *through* his eye. Like to gone out the back of his goddamn head . . ."

"I'll take the goggles."

"Gloves?"

"I'll pass on the gloves." I would sincerely regret this before I got home. At sixty miles an hour a grasshopper on the end of a knuckle was like a bullet—right before it smeared out and covered the hand with guts.

It turned out there was a hitch in the deal—something the bank called "a small ding, really only a dimple" in my credit having to do with my entire past, the fact that I'd been sued and had judgments against me and that writers in general do not make the best of borrowers.

We worked it out after I agreed that whatever happened in the *rest* of my life I would pay them first, but going back and forth took nearly three hours and it was near closing, close to eight o'clock before everything was at last signed and folded and put in envelopes and I stood looking at the bike.

My bike.

My Harley.

The mechanic had brought it around outside to the front after checking the bike out, changing the oil, and topping the tank with gas.

"You put the key here," the salesman told me, "in the ignition by the speedometer. You turn it on and the starter button is up here on the right handgrip. The choke is here." He motioned to a small button down between the cylinders on the left side. "She'll need a little choking at first, even in hot weather—just for a mile or so until she catches up"—I thought of the Whizzer—"but then she'll smooth out and you won't need it if you start her warm."

He showed me all this but he did not start the engine, nor did he sit on it. There were ethics here that I did not know yet. You didn't sit on another man's bike unless you had permission and you didn't start the engine unless told to.

"Have you ridden a motorcycle before?"

I nodded. "All my life. But never a Harley."

"No problem. You'll be in love before you clear the lot. Just remember the weight. They're low and stable but they're heavy. Let the motor do the work—motor and balance."

He then turned and left, driving away—rather prosaically, I thought in a small Honda Civic. The owner came out—he hadn't spoken to me and gave me only a nod now—and left in a Toyota pickup and now I was truly alone.

The mechanic had shown me the gas valve, how to turn it on and go to reserve if I ran out, and I turned it on now. I put papers and a tool kit I'd bought—about twelve dollars worth of tools for forty-five dollars—in the left saddlebag, punched the helmet on top of my head, and straddled the bike.

I felt strange but in some way whole. It was like an extension of my body, and I cradled down in blue steel and leather and chrome and sat that way for a time, perhaps a full minute, and let the bike become part of me. I know how that sounds but it was true. I would meet hundreds of men and four women who owned Harleys and they all said the same—that the bike became an extension, took them, held them.

This is one hell of a long way, I thought, from clothespinning playing cards on the fork of a bicycle to get the sound of a motor when the spokes clipped them, but it had all started then. The track from that first rattling-slap noise in the spokes led inevitably to here, to me sitting on this Harley, sure and straight as any law in physics.

I turned the key, reached down and pulled the choke out to half a click, made sure the bike was in neutral, took a breath and let it half out, like shooting an M1 on the range. Then I touched the starter button with my thumb.

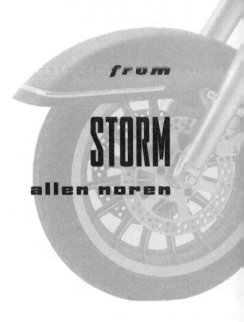

from

STORM

allen noren

we could have crossed the Arctic Circle that day. It was only another two hundred and fifty miles and everything was in our favor. Midday the rain passed as if it had been vacuumed away, leaving only occasional gray motes that drifted harmlessly overhead. The chill was replaced by a tepid stillness, and the many miles of road construction were behind us. We could have easily made Finland had we wanted to. But then, about thirty miles south of Luleå, I noticed a motorcycle parked on the side of the road. The rider was crouched on the far side of the bike inspecting the engine, and I decided to stop.

"*Hej,*" I said as I walked across the road. "Do you need any help?"

A woman pushed her head over the seat. A cigarette hung loosely from her lips and she took it with her grease-stained fingers.

"Ah!" she said. "Problem."

I walked around the bike to where she was kneeling. Her leather jacket was spread on the ground for her to kneel on, and a collection of clean steel tools were arranged on a canvas sheath beside it.

"I don't know how you call these," she said, and pointed into the engine.

"Points. What's the matter?"

"She dies. Just like that," she said, snapping her fingers. "Kaput."

"I'm Allen. That's Suzanne," I said, and waved for Suzanne to join us from across the road.

"Malin. Thanks for stopping," she said, and we shook hands.

It was difficult to keep from staring at the gentle angles of her face, her long auburn hair that hung in strands across it, her bare brown arms, and the way her thin hands moved as she pointed with a screwdriver. It wasn't just her features that attracted me, but that she was on the road alone, on a motorcycle with a duffel and sleeping bag tied to the back of the seat. She was broken down on the side of the road, and she knew how to take care of it.

"It is this thing," she said, and showed me how the screw holding the points in place had stripped, causing them to spring closed as the engine vibrated. Malin pushed at them, demonstrating how the bracket holding the assembly would slip closed with a flick of her finger. "You have a drill machine, and the other to make the road for the screw?" she asked. "I don't know how to say in English."

"A drill and tap? Afraid not."

"Hmmm. So I thought," she said, and smiled slyly.

"Do you have a longer screw?"

"I was looking," she said, and spilled a bag of parts onto her jacket.

I watched Malin's long, slender index finger sort through screws, washers, and nuts. She flipped a small container of fuses with a little kick of her nail and discovered two washers, which she moved toward the others.

"Here," I said. "How about that one?"

"The same," she said. "Same size."

I wanted to join her in her search, to move my own finger through the parts beside her own until I found the right one.

"Nice bike," Suzanne said, suddenly beside me.

Malin looked up and smiled. She wiped the hair from her eyes with the back of her hand. A strand fell back across her left eye. She pushed her lower lip out, shot a puff of air up the length of her face so she could see Suzanne clearly.

"She is an old thing," Malin said of her bike. "Swedish military machine from fifties."

Malin went back to her sorting. She pinched a screw between her nails and inspected it. She positioned the points with her left hand, set the screw, and carefully screwed it in. Her hands moved with the assurance of a mechanic's but with a woman's grace, and she held her tools with a familiarity that comes only from using them. It was all I could do to keep from reaching out and pretending to help.

"Ha!" Malin said as the screw bit into some remaining thread. The bracket holding the points flattened against the engine, and when she pushed them with her finger they remained in place. "There. Please stay," she asked the points. "About one hundred kilometers and I will be home."

"Where did you come from?" I asked.

"From Luleå," Malin said as she screwed a metal cover back over the points. "This road take you through. Not so far. Big motorcycle rally over the weekend. Crazy time."

"Oh, really? Allen and I went to a rally on Gotland. *That* was a crazy time. Is it over with?"

"Yeah. Everyone goes home," Malin said, and chuckled at a memory. She lit a cigarette, took a drag. She offered us one, and then asked where we were from.

"There is some American guy in Luleå you should visit. Really. Talk about crazy. He rides a broken Harley around the world. He comes from across Russia—alone. I think my bike goes farther," she said, and patted the engine.

"Do you remember his name?" I asked.

"No. Too much drink. But I can write my friend's telephone. He live in Luleå and will take you to him."

"You don't think it would be a problem?" I asked.

"No. Just say to him Malin sent you."

She wrote a name and number on a piece of paper and gave it to me. Then she wrapped her tools up, tied them with a leather strap, and stowed them in a metal tube below the seat.

"Okay," Malin said, and offered her hand to Suzanne and me. "I must go. Thanks for stopping. Go see that guy. I think maybe you like him."

"We will," I promised.

I watched Malin as she put on her jacket and helmet, and then kicked her engine over. It caught right away, and she waved before pulling onto the road. I waved back and listened as she shifted smoothly into second gear, then third. And then she disappeared around a bend.

"Come on," Suzanne said, and pulled at my arm. "That's enough looking."

AN HOUR LATER Suzanne and I were standing in a phone booth on the edge of Luleå. The phone at the other end rang only twice, and then a man answered.

"Sven-Erik?" I asked.

I explained who we were, that Malin said to call, that perhaps he could tell us where the American was staying.

The voice on the other end was thickly accented and methodical. Sven-Erik sounded pleased that we'd called and wanted to know all about us.

He said he'd be happy to show us where the American was staying but asked if we'd mind going the following day. He made a point of stressing the weather would be especially nice the next few days, that it had been a long, wet summer, and that he was leaving work in just a few minutes to take a motorcycle ride through the mountains. Sven-Erik said something about a waterfall and that it would make him very happy if we'd go, too.

"What about the American?" I asked.

"No problem. I take you tomorrow."

"Just a moment," I said, and covered the mouthpiece.

"He wants to take us to a waterfall," I said. "Into the mountains. He sounds like a nice guy."

"Ask him how far it is."

I relayed the question. Sven-Erik said it wasn't far. Just enough for a nice afternoon ride.

"It's up to you," Suzanne said, and shrugged.

WE HEARD SVEN-ERIK'S bike before we saw it, a deep, throaty, high-revved roar.

"I hope he's not a Hell's Angel," Suzanne said and rolled her eyes.

Sven-Erik came into view around a long, sweeping turn. He saw us and slowed, then slid to a halt beside us. He wore a worn leather riding suit, and I took it as a good sign that there were no abrasions and tears from previous wrecks. He took his helmet off and offered his hand in greeting.

The first thing I noticed about Sven-Erik was his slightly mad, pale blue eyes. In the bright sun that illuminated that afternoon they seemed especially bright, almost a source of light themselves.

"A very special day," he said anxiously, and searched the sky as if he was looking for something. "We have not so many here."

Sven-Erik led us to a youth hostel on the edge of town and helped us carry our gear into our room.

"A wonderful ride I take you on," he promised as we passed each other in the door of our room. "You will see."

He was inspecting our bike when Suzanne and I joined him. "It is right for your journey," he said. His bike, an older model BMW, looked worn and tarnished in comparison. The paint was faded and the fairing looked as if it had been scrubbed with a wire brush. The short plexiglas windscreen was cloudy and yellow from weathering.

"I made it from three bikes," Sven-Erik said of his. "I have no money for a new one, so I bought the pieces from three, and made one. A little Frankenstein," he beamed.

He seemed to forget the urgency of our leaving as he explained to Suzanne and me all the modifications he had made to it. He pointed out the dampening on the steering, the four-valve heads, the stiffened suspension, tuned exhaust, a throttle linkage he'd machined himself at the local university where he worked as an engineer designing mechanized logging equipment. He explained in great detail the interior modifications to the valves, cam, timing, carburetors, and pistons. He got down on his hands and knees to explain the faults in the original drive-train, and how he'd corrected them. Then he was ready to go.

"Okay," Sven-Erik called out over the rumble of his engine. "How fast can you go?"

"Depends," I called back, not quite sure how to respond. "Depends on the roads."

"I like one hundred-forty," he said with a crooked smile.

"Miles an hour?" Suzanne asked incredulously.

"No. Kilometers. Something like eighty, eighty-five of your miles. Okay?"

I turned around to look back at Suzanne. She looked ready to get off but didn't. "We'll do our best to keep up," I said to Sven-Erik. "But don't worry if we fall behind."

He waved and roared off.

It was a wild ride into the mountains of northern Sweden, one that took us in a drawn-out loop halfway to Norway and back. At one point early in the ride, when I was still trying to catch up with Sven-Erik for the first time, I thought of all Suzanne and I were missing by riding so fast. I was tired, and eighty-five miles an hour on mountain roads I didn't know was too fast for me after a long day. And then I started to catch him, and I was able to slow to seventy-five. We swept cleanly through a turn that opened onto a wide valley. Sven-Erik sped up and we crossed the valley in a beautifully blurred moment. The road climbed steeply out the other side into a jade sky, then crested, and for an instant it seemed as if the world had fallen away beneath us.

We sped across ridgelines, beside rivers, through meadows and pastures. We raced through forests so dark the road became illegible. A reindeer bounced from the edge of the forest and crossed in front of us. A second slipped by before I realized there would have been little or nothing I could have done had it stopped in our path. I felt impossibly alive.

Eighty-five miles an hour became a dilated state of mind, one that created its own momentum and tempo, one that I became entangled in. Eighty-five miles an hour became a lean line scribed across the earth, and it was extraordinary. Eighty-five miles an hour became something I wanted to sustain.

We crested another ridge and rode down the other side into a long valley. The road ran straight before us, and Sven-Erik slowed until we were beside him. He was trying to yell something to us but I couldn't hear over the wind. He lifted the front of his helmet as if that was the impediment between us. I stole glances of his moving lips and tried to read them, but the words caught on the wind and dropped quickly behind. Then he pointed forward and began to pull away. I kept pace and noted the needle on the speedometer sweep past 95, 100, 105. The landscape became an adrenal rush of sapphire, magenta, fire-yellow, emerald, and saffron. One hundred-ten and the wind sounded as if it would crush us. One fifteen and the bike was still surging as if this was just the beginning.

And that was enough.

I eased the throttle back and Sven-Erik rushed ahead. The needle on the speedometer fell back past eighty, seventy, sixty, and it felt as though we were barely moving at all. The world slowly regained its focus and I felt an elated sense of relief. Suzanne loosened herself from the knot she'd become behind me and uttered a giddy laugh. "My God," she said through the back of my helmet. "Why'd you do it?" She laughed again, punched me on the shoulder. She said, "My God! My God!"

SVEN-ERIK WAITED FOR us at a point where the road narrowed and the asphalt turned to gravel. He led us into a valley where a river hurried toward the sea, and we meandered beside it for several miles as we moved farther into the mountains. At some point I began to feel a percussive thrumming in my bones, a low-level vibration that could have been something in the engine of the bike.

"Do you feel that?" I asked Suzanne.

"Yes. Like a tremor."

We rode farther and the tremor became a rumble I also heard.

"It must be the waterfall," Suzanne said.

We rounded another turn, and while I was trying to avoid potholes and loose gravel, Suzanne tapped my shoulder and pointed ahead. I brought the bike to a stop.

It wasn't a waterfall in the sense of Niagara or Victoria with an abrupt cliff the water spilled over. Nor was it like the precipitous cascades famous in Yosemite and Hawaii. The fall was a wide hemorrhage in the mountain, a violent rent through which a great pressurized geyser had burst. The river thundered and roared over house-sized boulders as it fell several hundred feet toward the valley below.

"Well?" Sven-Erik yelled above the noise. He smiled at our reaction to the fall.

"Come on," he said after a minute. "We go up, to the edge."

We rode partway up the mountain and parked in a clearing of trees. The thrumming we felt on the bike was a pounding there, and the air filled with a mist of atomized water carried on swirling eddies of wind. The three of us followed a trail through the trees, and then we were on the edge of the fall. We stood just where the river broke and quickened to transparent blue mounds that slid over the cold, granite bed, just where it shattered into a churning white rapids.

A narrow path led down the side of the fall, through an area of softly rounded boulders and polished nodes as smooth as hardwood. A drizzle fell, and multiple rainbows arced over the water. We walked to a point where we could look up and down the fall, to an impossible point where it seemed the ground must be frail, in danger of being eroded and consumed by the river. The three of us stood there anyway, perched on the edge of the current as though its force was pulling us in.

On a sliver of rock Sven-Erik told us about a friend he'd brought to the same spot a year before. She was going through a long, painful divorce, and her emotions had reached a crescendo that day. They too walked to the edge of the rock and stopped, as we had, just a few feet from the water. He described the way she stood, still and pensive, and I imagined a woman ready to dive, never to be seen again.

"And then!" he yelled over the rumbling of the fall. "And then she start to scream!"

She screamed as loud and for as long as she could. The river absorbed every decibel and sent them crashing over the rapids. Sven-Erik's eyes were wide and glowed as he told the story, and he seemed to hint at some secret power the place held. When he was through, a long pause enriched his stare, and I wondered if he'd brought us on purpose, if he had sensed we were troubled and needed to cast out our own devils.

OUR RETURN TO Luleå was like a long doze in the half-light that was night. We were surrounded by an intermediary dusk our headlight did not help us through. The effect was a sense of time suspended. Each ridge revealed another in an endless series, and the rhythm of ridge, valley, ridge, valley, had a perfect tempo, a groove too good to escape.

Somewhere in the mountains, the clock on the bike pushed beyond midnight and it was sometime after that we arrived at the edge of Luleå. We said good night to Sven-Erik, and he promised to come for us around midday. Then he roared off, and we rode slowly through the night to our room.

At ten the next morning I was outside checking the bike and swatting mosquitoes when I heard the distinct sound of Sven-Erik's motorcycle through the woods. The tuned roar grew louder and I pictured him crouched over the gas tank as he swept through each turn, a knee extended for balance. I wondered what luck had brought him through so many years of riding. I could hear the quick pauses when he shifted gears, and the compressed rumblings as he slowed for turns. And then he came into sight, and because he had on the same helmet, suit, and scarf, it seemed as though he hadn't stopped all night.

"Tonight," he said after taking off his helmet. "We go to see the American. And today, I take you for something special."

"What?" I asked, hoping it wasn't another ride.

"Not a ride," he said as if he'd read my mind. "I take you sailing."

WE ONLY KNEW what Malin had told us about the American: that he was staying somewhere in Luleå, that he was riding around the world on a Harley-Davidson, and that he might enjoy seeing Suzanne and me.

"He stays at the Aurora Harley Club," Sven-Erik announced as we were putting the boat away. "Outside town."

"There's a Harley club up here?" Suzanne asked.

"Sure. Why not?"

"How many members?"

"Mmmm. Three. Maybe four."

Suzanne and I followed him out of town, through a neighborhood of low-level apartments, a cluster of homes, and into the forest. We turned down a narrow lane that skirted a swampy area where the sound of our bikes interrupted a feeding moose. The bikes cleaved through clouds of mosquitoes that became a smear on the windscreens. We turned down a lane that narrowed as the limbs of trees hung over the edge like arms trying to snag us, and I thought the lane would soon dissolve into the swamp. Then Sven-Erik slowed and turned into an overgrown yard that surrounded an old two-story house.

It was properly dilapidated for a Harley club. The entrance to the yard was decorated with the rusted sculpture of a Harley created from an assortment of ancient parts and odd pieces of pipe. A layer of white paint peeled from the high walls of the house, like dead skin. The bare wood was discolored by moss and soot. Pieces of faded fabric hung loosely inside to cover the windows. The coming and going of people and machines had formed trails through the grass and weeds, and the trails were all that kept the forest from annexing the yard completely. We parked, and nothing moved. The house appeared deserted.

We removed our helmets and the distinct hum of insects filled the air. "Mosquitoes," Sven-Erik said looking around him.

Convective clouds of them tumbled through the air searching for a place to land. A haze of them rose from the shrub-clogged swamp behind the house like boils of smoke. They covered our clothes and hair, probed our jackets, gloves, and boots. I fanned the air in front of my face to keep them from landing, and I felt their soft bodies collide against my hand with each stroke. They were tenacious, ravenous, and Sven-Erik retreated under his helmet and closed the visor to protect his balding scalp. I felt mosquitoes on my head, parting my hair with their legs as they burrowed toward my skin. I swatted them off Suzanne's scalp, and I felt the sting of several along my neck and ears.

A curtain parted, and someone looked out at us. I waved, the curtain fell back into place, and someone opened the front door.

"*Hej!*" Sven-Erik greeted, his voice muffled inside his helmet.

A man with a shaved head, and wearing an oily sleeveless denim jacket, walked into the yard. He looked at us skeptically, as if our brand of machines and dress suggested we were from the wrong side of town. Sven-Erik lifted the visor of his helmet and introduced himself. The man looked annoyed, but then visibly softened as Sven-Erik spoke to him in Swedish. The man pointed once at Suzanne and me, and then rubbed his chin as if to adjust his expression. He looked again at Sven-Erik, and back at us. Sven-Erik looked our way, gestured, explained something, and the man laughed. His arms rose as if to welcome us, and then he went back inside.

Sven-Erik cleared the air around his head with one hand before closing the visor of his helmet. He assured us the American was still there, that he was asleep, but would be out in just a few minutes.

The three of us waited and swatted mosquitoes. Suzanne snapped the collar of her jacket around her neck and I helped her wrap a scarf around her head and neck so only her eyes showed. Sven-Erik looked snug in his helmet and gloves, and I thought of doing the same when the door opened and a ragged, road-worn man limped toward the steps leading into the yard. He looked like a mechanic, complete with black grease embedded into the crevices of his skin like tattoos. He wore a ragged pair of blue pants that were patched and frayed at the bottom of the legs, a shirt of indistinguishable color, and what looked like a Mao vest.

"Hi!" he said, not sure whom he should address. He walked heavily down the stairs holding the rail, and he kicked his right leg forward as if it was shackled with a heavy weight. "One, two of you, are from California?" he asked, and moved one finger like a pointer between the three of us.

"Us," I said. "I'm Allen, and this is Suzanne. Sven-Erik is a local. He showed us how to get here."

"David Barr. Pleased to meet you," he said, and gripped my hand with what felt like a rawhide chew-toy for a big dog.

"Someone told us you're going around the world on a Harley."

"Yeah, you could say that. Traversing all the continents actually, so it's a little farther than going around the world."

I looked down at his right leg, noticed the foot was made of metal, and realized it was a prosthesis. "Isn't it a little difficult riding with that?" I asked.

"I'm missing both," he said laughing, and reached down to pull the legs of his pants around his knees. David's left leg was an ordinary skin-tone prosthesis, but the right was created from an assortment of metal parts, welded and bolted together.

"What happened to that one?" Suzanne asked.

"I fell on it so many times the plastic disintegrated. I was in Colombia when it finally gave out. I went to a doctor there who told me a new one would cost seven-hundred dollars, but I didn't have that kind of money. So, I went to a welding shop and had a guy make me this one. This part here is made from a section of hydraulic ram, and this, the foot," he said as he lifted it for us to see, "is just a piece of quarter-inch steel plate with a piece of tire bolted to the bottom. It's not great, but it gets me around."

"Apparently. Where have you been so far?"

"Well, let's see. I began two and a half years ago. That was in South Africa. I first rode the length of Africa, crossed the Mediterranean on a ferry, and then rode through Europe to Nordkapp, the northernmost point in Western Europe. That's when I met these guys from Aurora for the first time. Then I rode to England where I did some work for the Leonard Chesshire Foundation. It's a group that helps people with handicaps. After a few months I shipped the bike to New York, rode to Washington State, up the Al-Can highway to Dead Horse Camp, Alaska. Then I turned around, headed south, and didn't stop until I reached Tierra del Fuego, in Argentina."

"Jesus!" I said, and felt all the grandeur of our own trip melt away like a wax monument. The place names spawned glorious images as David ticked them off like kilometer posts—the Congo, Sahara Desert, Algiers, Mediterranean Sea, Nordkapp, Anchorage, Managua, Pan-American Highway, the Amazon, Andes Mountains. I looked over at Suzanne and her mouth was hanging slack like a shoelace she'd forgotten to tie. She barely noticed as I picked a mosquito engorged with blood from her cheek.

"Why are you in Sweden again?" I asked.

"Well, that's part of the story," David said. "I shipped the bike to Hong Kong, rode across China, Mongolia, and Russia. I just came through Murmansk a week ago, and then rode to Luleå."

"Murmansk? That's a secret Russian naval base, a closed city." I said.

"Yeah, I know. But great people. I stayed with a retired submarine captain. The bike was on her last legs, again, and this guy and his buddies put me up and used a bunch of old equipment to help me get this far. At the border the Russians just let me through, wanted me out of there like I was a liability or something."

Sven-Erik poked me in the ribs with his elbow. He shot me a look of skepticism through his visor and rolled his eyes.

I asked David where he was going next.

"Back to England, and then I'll ship the bike to Australia. I'm planning to begin in Perth, ride around the country, then island hop through Indonesia, ride through Singapore, Malaysia, Thailand, Vietnam, and back into China. Then the trip will be over, and I don't know what I'll do. I'll be broke."

"That's unbelievable," Suzanne said. "Where is your bike?"

"She's in the back, in a shed. Would you like to see her? I have to get a key from inside."

David walked toward the house, his leg making a metallic ratcheting in protest each time he kicked it in front of himself. I watched as he pulled his body up the steps and paused so he could right himself on his damaged legs before going in the door.

"He's *crazy*," Suzanne said in admiration.

"I think so, too," Sven-Erik said, believing Suzanne had been critical. "I don't think he did all those things. He is crazy in the head."

"I think he's wonderful!" I protested. "Can you imagine his journey? Across Africa, the Sahara, all the way to Argentina? China, Mongolia? That means he crossed the Gobi Desert! All the way across Russia."

"You think he did all those things?" Sven-Erik asked.

"Sure. You think he made it up?"

Sven-Erik looked bored and suggested it was time for him to go. The mosquitoes were getting worse, and he had things to do.

"You've got to at least see the bike," I said.

"Okay. We see the bike."

We followed David along a trail through the high grass, past an old wooden boat lazily concealed with a plastic tarp, to a shed behind the house. David unlocked a heavy wooden door and pushed it open. In the middle of the floor was his Harley-Davidson resting on its kickstand in the shadows. He turned on a light and we approached the bike.

The bike was as Malin had described it. It looked broken, as though someone had beaten it until the engine had stopped running. It was once a bright red Shovelhead model with a black frame and forks. There was a reminder of the chrome that had once highlighted the engine, rims, handlebars, and headlight. A greasy pillow was tied with a leather strap to where the seat had been. The area behind the rider had been transformed into a luggage rack with oilcloth bundles and leather bags tied to the frame. A wooden box, held together with wire and strapping, was set behind the pillow. The top was open and I looked inside. There was rope and wire, tools, plastic bottles of oil and tubes of grease. David explained how he tied on extra gas cans, his sleeping bag and tent, where he placed his small duffel of clothes and his rain suit. In front of the handlebars was another leather pouch that held additional tools, and below that a very small headlight the size of a bowl, which seemed inadequate for lighting David's way around the world. The gas tank was a log of his trip. On the right side was a painting of the world with an astral band surrounding it like a halo. The top of the tank revealed the true scope of the journey. The name of each country traversed had been painstakingly hand-painted in small white letters in columns that stretched from the top of the tank to the bottom.

"When the trip is over," David said, "she's supposed to go on display in the Harley-Davidson Hall of Fame. I hope that happens, so other people can see it and realize they can do a trip like this, too."

Small things on the bike attracted me: buckles and hooks, empty holes drilled into the frame, an upside-down Esso decal on the top of the air cleaner, a brass plaque fixed to the engine casing. I rubbed a coat of grease from it with my index finger and revealed a dedication from the Brazilian Policia Militaría.

"Nice boys," David said. "They helped me out of a big jam. Let me sleep on the police grounds and helped me get parts for the bike."

"But why are you doing this?" I had to ask.

"Well, that's a long story. If you'd like, we can go inside. Have some coffee, and talk."

Sven-Erik left, but Suzanne and I went inside and talked until one in the morning. Some guys in the club had bought David a big map of the world and had him trace his route. He spread it across a table and patiently retraced it for us, continent by continent, country by country, desert by desert, river by river. He told us about spending days in remote African villages, waiting for flooded roads to become dry enough to continue; of being blown off roads by gale winds and of falling off the bike twenty times in one day because of ice in the Andes; of having to wait hours in the middle of nowhere for help to lift the heavy bike from his body as precious gasoline dripped from the tank onto his clothes. He told us of crossing the Sahara, of the heat and endless sand, of getting stuck so many times he thought about walking away. He told us of his exhilaration of reaching Nordkapp in the middle of winter, of crossing the United States and reaching Anchorage exactly one year after leaving South Africa. We followed his finger around the world and listened to the long stream of words as he took us down the Americas, across China, Mongolia, Russia, and then, it finally came to rest in Luleå. "And here we are," he said.

A moment of reflective silence followed as Suzanne and I surveyed the scope of the map on the table. David took a sip of his now cold coffee and shifted his weight. The metallic ratcheting of his leg and the creaking of boards below his feet were the only sounds.

"That's incredible, David," Suzanne said. "But, once again, why are you doing this? It can't be easy for someone like you."

David explained how he was born in California, led a normal Central Valley life until the Vietnam War. "I did *time* over there," he said. "And when it was over, I just couldn't take any more of America. I've always been someone who had to act, and Vietnam was about inaction."

David said he went to Israel, worked on a kibbutz, did some work with the military, but grew weary of the factionalism that diminished the clarity of the Israeli cause. He roamed from job to job in the oil fields of the Middle East for some years, and then the desire to act lured him to South Africa, where he fought against rebel forces in Rhodesia. He lost his legs when the personnel carrier he was riding in hit a land mine. After twenty operations and four amputations, David returned to active duty servicing heavy machine guns and training recruits in their use.

A year later he completed military service and returned home to California. As a way of putting his life back together he began restoring his Harley, and then struck upon the idea of riding it around the world. He planned, dreamed, and pored over maps. Then he went back to South Africa to work and took his bike with him. He saved his money and continued to plan the trip. One day it was time to go.

When his story was told, David said he had to get up early the next morning to begin his ride to England. He walked us outside and watched as we pulled our helmets on, mounted the bike, and rode away. I turned my head for a last look at him, and even through the semi-darkness of night I saw him waving.

Suzanne and I levitated back to the hostel, floated on the tide of David's words. The roads were deserted, the night so still I imagined how the whine of our engine rolled through the quiet like the wake of a boat. We walked on tiptoe to our room, pulled our sleeping bags around us, and then whispered about our meeting with David until the sky began to brighten again.

from

SPEED TRIBES

karl taro greenfeld

from the side, front, even from above, as far as he could tell in the full-length mirror, it was perfect. Then he leaned closer and checked the three-quarter view and detected a flaw, a tiny imperfection, a lock of hair out of place above his ear, and with a sigh he started over. Tatsuhiro squeezed another palmful of Stiff hair gel from the tube and tried once again to get his hair just right.

It was 12:30 on a Friday afternoon, and Tatsuhiro Nobutani—Tats— was just starting his day. This was a personal, contemplative time for him and he made it clear to his mother that he was not to be disturbed during his morning routine: a half-hour devoted exclusively to his hair. And if it didn't come out just right he would spend another half-hour. When he was finally satisfied, having inspected the back with a hand mirror and checked the gaudy, swooping ducktail for bounce and hold, he went downstairs to where his mom was watching samurai dramas and had his usual breakfast of cigarettes and iced coffee while guys in wigs sliced each other up on TV.

He finished his own pack, then bummed a menthol from his mom and waited for Small Second Son to chop up Red Mask. Right when the hero had worked his way through about a dozen evil underlings and had the black-kimono-clad Red Mask backed up, the phone rang. Tat's mom shouted at him to get it because she didn't want to miss the ending.

He picked up the phone. "Yeah?"

"What the fuck are you doing at home?" said Yamada.

"I got caught up in something," Tats said, hoping Yamada couldn't hear the television as Small Second Son stabbed Red Mask, who let out an agonizing, ear-piercing screech, and then Red Mask ripped off his mask and turned out to be Small Second Son's long-lost older brother.

"You fucking a cat over there?"

"What?" Tats asked. "Nah, my mom's watching samurai shows."

"Listen," Yamada told him. "Go over to Kimpo's on Ameyoko and tell that faggot to give you the package, you follow?"

Tats grunted. He looked at the tattoo above his elbow of a kamikaze pilot riding a sword and flexed his skinny arm. He wondered how his hair was holding up. Yamada was talking again but Tats missed what he said.

"You follow?"

Tats didn't grunt. He heard Yamada's breath against the phone and thought maybe Yamada was getting pissed off, but so what, what was Yamada going to do from jail?

"Take the package over to Miki out in Juban, you know the place?"

"Yeah."

"Give him the package and tell him it's from me and that I'll call him and that he shouldn't do anything until he hears from me, you following me here?"

Tats grunted again. Maybe he would get another tattoo, one on his chest, maybe a hawk or a heron, some kind of bird, swooping—no—diving.

"How's it going in there?" Tats asked.

"What the fuck do you think? I'm bored. Do what I said for me."

Tats promised he would and then hung up and after checking his hair in the hallway mirror went to find his mom to bum another menthol. She refused and told him to get a job.

NINETEEN-YEAR-OLD TATS hadn't had any kind of job since he paid off his car two months ago. He used to drive a truck, but now he was unemployed and hadn't exactly been scanning the want ads. Actually, since Yamada had gotten three-to-five in Fukushima Prison for sticking a knife through the trachea of a welsher who had had about a dozen bad months at the track, Tats hadn't done much of anything but run errands for his former boss who called him every day from jail.

Yamada, now twenty-six, had headed the Tokyo chapter of the Midnight Angels motorcycle and hot-rod gang until three years ago when he rose to become an associate of the organized crime group Sumiyoshi Rengo. Now he planned and executed numerous little scams, most of them having to do with loan collecting and occasionally some drug peddling. He had worked with a few other, older guys until he was sent up when his partners testified against him to save themselves. Tats had taken over the Midnight Angels from Yamada. He didn't like running Yamada's errands for him but felt he didn't have any choice: it was Yamada who had taken him into the Midnight Angels four years ago.

Tats stepped out into the bright sunlight and removed the gray canvas cover from his white 1989 Nissan Skyline, folding it carefully before placing it in the trunk. He opened the driver's side door and climbed in to rummage around beneath the seat and in the glove compartment for a cigarette. He found one in the porch next to the seat and lit it and sat in the car, listening to the radio, some new song by Hikaru Nishida, until he had smoked the cigarette down to the butt. He opened the door, dropped the butt in the dirt, then stepped out of the car, shutting the door behind him. He was on his way back inside to get a pair of sunglasses when he realized—fuck—he'd locked his keys in the car. He wouldn't be able to drive anywhere—but it was a nice day for a walk anyway.

Tats was dressed casually in a gray zoot suit over a black T-shirt and traditional *geta* sandals. He strolled through Arakawa Ward, in the heart of east Tokyo's Low City, where shabby wooden houses and run-down ferroconcrete apartment blocks lined the narrow roads. During the U.S. occupation of Japan immediately after World War II, the Ameyoko Market streets had been where black-market goods, misdirected from the American PX, were sold to Tokyoites. Now dried fish, uncensored porn videos, and Japanese Bart Simpson T-shirts were hawked beside endless stores of "designer" clothes. Brand names such as Paris Tailor, Hi-Touch Fashun, and Running Dapper Man were Japan's answer to Members Only.

Tats walked among the tile-roofed houses, pachinko parlors, convenience marts, and liquor stores. He waved at the kid with the bad acne behind the counter at the 7-Eleven and courteously bowed to a graykimono-clad friend of his mother's, and he checked his hair in a store window.

Arakawa Ward was one of the poorest of Tokyo's twenty-three wards, and here the Japanese family values of unity, cohesion, and diligence were cracking right down the middle. This was not the land of Sony and Mitsubishi. Here, Tats would tell you, *bosozoku* ruled.

THE BOSOZOKU — SPEED TRIBES — are Japan's discontented youth. A little under half of them come from broken homes. They revel in noise and spectacle and disturbing the quiet, orderly operation of Japanese society. But they are more than gangs of delinquents. They are also proving grounds for the Yakuza. *Bosozoku* gang members perm their hair, dress like wiseguys, and drive flashy cars and motorcycles without mufflers, hoping to be noticed by the local *gumi*, or Yakuza family.

Maybe a Yakuza lieutenant needs a young tough to hold a shipment of methamphetamine, the drug of choice for Japan's half-million speed addicts, or, like Yamada, a messenger to run a hot pistol out to a fellow gangster holed up in a Juban flat. A Yakuza always needs a good *chimpira* (little prick) who's cool, tough, and can keep his mouth shut.

The *bosozoku* have been around since Japan's rebirth as an industrial power after World War II. The Tokyo Metropolitan Police Department's first record of the existence of the *bosozoku* or *kaminari* (thunder tribes), as they used to be called — dates from September 4, 1959, when fifty-five "juvenile delinquents" on motorcycles gathered at Tokyo's Meiji Shrine.

Now there are hundreds of different gangs, including Medusa, Fascist, Black Emperor, Cats, Kill Everybody, and the Devils, many loosely federated. They've adopted an eclectic array of styles and symbols, from traditional samurai to *The Wild Ones*. The Midnight Angels dress in red-and-black jackets — their colors — with gold Chinese characters on the back. Many wear tiny, almost effeminate slippers and roll *haramaki* (stomach wraps) around their chests. These last are all Yakuza affectations. A veteran police department observer estimates the percentage of *bosozoku* who go on to become Yakuza at 40 percent.

Tats was Yamada's little prick. For eighteen months before going to jail Yamada had been on a streak where he could turn shit into yen. Everything he touched, every venture he tried, was making money. He was generous with Tats and his former cronies in the Midnight Angels. Yamada remembered where he was from, and just because he was making more money in a week working with his new friends than he ever made in the motorcycle gang didn't mean he turned his back on his old posse. He still showed up at the Skylark family-style restaurant where Tats and his friends played cards and mah-jongg. Yamada picked up checks, lost a bundle on the tiles, and then slipped Tats and his friends a few big bills and maybe some new clothes or free brandy or whatever swag had come his way. He treated Tats and his friends like princes, and he reminded them of this constantly. "Remember what I do for you," he would say from behind the wheel of his Mitsubishi GTO before peeling out, "you follow?"

He asked for a few favors, which were no problem for Tats. Yamada got him the job driving the truck and arranged for Tats's tiny down payment for the Nissan Skyline that was Tats's pride and joy.

At first Tats didn't mind doing favors for his mentor, like stashing a 9-mm. Beretta pistol beneath his bed for six weeks or delivering a van loaded with pirated *Bluce* [*sic*] *Springsteen Greatest Hits* cassettes to a drop-off point in Shinjuku Ward. Tats, however, tired of the little—and not so little—favors. He had begun to dislike answering the phone every morning and getting his daily itinerary from Yamada. All this running around for Yamada was taking up too much of his time. The Midnight Angels were still his main priority and Yamada, having once been a member himself, should have known that.

Yamada had presided over perhaps the greatest era in Midnight Angels history. When Tats was fifteen, he was sniffing a lot of glue and barely attending Kokushikan High School—a high school that in its entire history had never sent anyone on to college. He was what his teachers described as learning impaired: he had a short attention span. He had shown even less aptitude in shop classes than in academic classes, and neither department wanted him anyway. He dropped out of school. He had seen the Midnight Angels around and was dazzled by their loud motorcycles, gaudy cars, and kamikaze outfits; as they rode around Arakawa Ward they reminded him of the kind of delinquents who were the heros in *Akira*, his favorite comic book. So Tats joined.

For the initiation, a few older members, Yamada included, jumped him. He emerged bloodied, with a black eye and several broken fingers, but unbowed. "That's our only rule: you have to be able to fight," Yamada told Tats after the initiation.

That summer, Tats went on his first run with the Midnight Angels, down to Shonan Beach in Kanagawa. Nearly four hundred Midnight Angels from Tokyo, Yokohama, Chiba, Ibaraki, and Kanagawa were there as the gangs took over the beach near Enoshima Island and turned the half-acre parking lot and boardwalk into a two-day debauchery reported in local newspapers as the "*Bosozoku* Nightmare." Tats had ridden down in an older member's car, waving a Rising Sun flag, drinking Ozeki One Cup sake, and sniffing glue as they crawled down the Tokaido Highway at just ten miles an hour, intentionally blocking traffic and scaring the hell out of everyone else on the road. That had been a glorious time, the hundreds of cars with after-market tail fins, airfoils, skirts, and flashing lights strewn around the parking lot terrifying the local summer vacationers as the gang made a leather-and kamikaze-jumpsuit-clad spectacle of themselves on the dirty, polluted beach.

The night after they arrived they built bonfires as the older members passed out beer and brandy and some members raced motorcycles back and forth. By then the local population had come out and was watching in awe from across the coast highway as the Midnight Angels seemed to be working themselves into a frenzy. The locals shook their heads but couldn't do anything because the police were hesitant about moving in—they didn't want a riot on their hands, and they still hoped the Midnight Angels would honor an order to disperse by morning.

That night, amid the flames and roaring engines, the stench of motor oil, the radios playing traditional *enka* music, and the frequent sound of breaking glass, Tats was utterly thrilled. He followed Yamada and watched him as he talked with other chapter heads and decided Yamada was one cool *bancho* (gang leader). Yamada was wearing a black jumpsuit zipped down to his chest to reveal a tattoo of a fiery pair of crossed swords with dragons intertwined around them. His hair was cut short and slicked back with a combination of hair gel, sweat, and axle grease, and all the guys that were there seemed to want to know him and all the girls seemed to want to fuck him.

When the sun rose over the Pacific Tats was still awake, still excited. As the beach gradually brightened—the sand turning from gray to tan to white and then to white with specks where the beach was strewn with garbage—he saw a figure dressed in black, like a TV samurai villain, riding along the wet sand near the water, and around the black human form was a white glow like a lunar eclipse as the morning sun made a silhouette of him. Tats wondered for a second if he was really seeing the guy on the motorcycle. The bike turned, spinning out a little as the rider had some trouble keeping control in the dry sand, but he made it, and just before the bike reached the boardwalk where Tats was sitting with his arms around his own knees, Tats saw it was Yamada. He had a few chicken sandwiches and deep-fried fish he had bought at some greasy shack down the beach and he gave the bag to Tats, who had forgotten how hungry he was. Tats thanked him and ate the food with his fingers and washed it down with warm beer and it all tasted so fucking good he felt like laughing.

He went to sleep on the beach, while behind him the Midnight Angels entertained local newspaper reporters by riding their motorcycles in circles standing on the seats of their bikes. The reporters, in their eagerness to give their readers the story of a motorcycle gang terrorizing a beach town, incited the Midnight Angels to more outrageous behavior, at one point even paying a Midnight Angel's girlfriend to pose topless as a few members poured beer over her breasts.

It was blazing hot by the time Tats woke up. The sun was three quarters of the way across the sky; there was no ocean breeze. A Chiba Midnight Angel handed Tats a beer and Tats wandered around the parking lot searching for Yamada. A few other *bosozoku* gangs had arrived, the Hit and Runners, a few chapters of Black Emperor. Some OBs (Old Boys, the phrase used for older, retired members) had also shown up with more beer, sake, and brandy. Their cars were like American lowriders, all shag carpeting, fuzzy dice, deep bucket seats, and graphic equalizers emitting waves of lights. In one of the OB's cars Tats saw something he had never seen before: people sticking hypodermic needles into their legs or tattooed arms. A few of the OBs had brought speed with them and were selling injections of methamphetamine for ¥2,500 which, Tats overheard, was a pretty good price. The guys who had taken the injections had faces like cartoon dogs when they're shown a big bone: eyes bulging and their tongues practically wagging.

Meanwhile, the composition of the crowd of locals milling across the highway had changed: before there had been women and children watching curiously from behind the guardrail; now there were only men in casual clothes, some carrying golf clubs and a few with baseball bats. Tats noticed they looked angry and barely budged when an empty beer bottle was hurled across the highway at them. A few squad cars lined the highway as tourists continued to drive past to have a look at the scene on the beach.

As the sun began to set Tats found some of his friends from Arakawa and drank with them. He'd drunk so much the alcohol wasn't doing anything to him anymore, just making him piss, but he kept drinking because everyone else was drinking. He climbed onto the hood of a Toyota Crown and surveyed the scene. The *bosozoku* were scattered in small groups all over the parking lot. He had either overestimated how many there were or a few hundred had already taken off; he now counted maybe a hundred and fifty. Those who remained were a sweaty, greasy mass of drunken delinquents: tattooed limbs, curvaceous pompadours, kamikaze jackets with obscenities stitched on the back, inebriated girls draped like hood ornaments across cars whose airfoils and spoilers and unmuffled engines and obscured license plates were all against the law. With the engine noise and the loud chatter and frequent amphetamine-driven shouts, it sounded as if there were a thousand kids in the lot and on the beach.

He also noticed that more police cars were arriving. Tats wondered if they were there to keep the Midnight Angels in check or to keep the agitated locals from assaulting the Midnight Angels.

Then Yamada walked up to Tats. He was holding a beer and had that wide-eyed look so many of the older guys had. The bonfires were going again and Tats could see the fire reflected in Yamada's eyes. "You gotta try this stuff," Yamada was saying.

"What?"

Yamada took him by the arm and led him over to a Toyota station wagon where a guy in a pin-striped suit and a punch perm—the short, tight curls popular with the Yakuza—was counting money and stuffing the bills into his *haramaki*. He smiled at Yamada and nodded.

"Let's get loaded," Yamada said and handed the punch-permed money-counter a five-thousand-yen note. The money-counter removed a crumpled brown paper bag from beneath the bucket seat and told Yamada and Tats to climb aboard. He shook out two syrettes of Philopon methamphetamine and then pulled the caps off the syrettes. The Philopon was pharmaceutical amphetamine, the kind of speed Japanese soldiers used to shoot during World War II and that Japanese factory workers and taxi drivers still preferred over smokable speed.

Tats cringed a little when he saw the short needles. Yamada clapped his hands together and bobbed his head up and down and slapped Tats's thigh. "In the leg," he laughed, "put it in the leg. You follow?"

He rolled up the cuffs on his black jumpsuit and threw his leg between the bucket seats, resting his calf on the emergency brake handle. The money-counter grabbed his leg and twisted it forty-five degrees so that the fleshy back of his calf was facing him and then jabbed in one syrette. Yamada flinched and sucked air through his teeth and then rocked back as the speedy rush of the skin-pop gradually circulated through his body, up his neck, to his brain. He shook his head, said, "Wow."

Tats's cuffs were too tight to roll up so he had to slip off his pants, and by the time he had been injected Yamada was out of the car and telling anyone who'd listen, "It's going to go off tonight."

As soon as the needle hit his skin Tats tasted the bitter amphetamine in the back of his throat—and pulled up his pants so fast he almost caught his dick in the fly. Then he was out of the car and trying to keep up with Yamada who was jogging from group to group, shouting greetings, bowing, back-slapping, taking swigs of brandy and sake, bumming cigarettes, showing off his tattoos. "It's going to go off, boys, it's going to go off."

Tats's heart was palpitating and his head was spinning, not in a drunken way but in a clear way that enabled him to see everything around him—360 degrees simultaneously, the world at a glance. Bonfires, bikers in black leather, unconscious girls with their tits hanging out of their tops, Yamada with a bottle of Hennessey going vertical in his mouth. And above it all a full moon shining bright and casting dull, white, vicious light over the whole scene. He felt like telling Yamada what he was seeing, how clear it all was, what a fucking great time he was having, but then he couldn't find Yamada. He had been there a moment ago, slap fighting with some guys from Yokohama, but now he was gone. On his motorcycle? With some girl? Tats was on his own, wandering around between cars and staring open-mouthed at the distorted faces that bobbed toward him out of the chaos. He didn't recognize anybody. These weren't Midnight Angels—this was some other gang: Black Emperor or the Hit and Runners.

Tats heard popping, like the sound champagne corks made in movies, and saw white plumes of smoke rising from between cars and something metallic came skittering past him along the hood of a black Mazda sedan trailing a gray gash of smoke. Someone pushed him aside and ran to the smoking canister and threw it back where it had come from. Smoke stung his eyes and a terrible burning sensation stuck in his throat; he couldn't breathe and he instinctively backed away from where the canister had been, even though there was nothing there now but a brown stain on the pavement.

"Tear gas!" someone screamed.

"They're coming!" shouted someone else. Engines were starting everywhere, guys were running to their cars and bikes and peeling out, but the police had already blocked off the parking lot. Nobody was getting out.

And the popping noises continued as more canisters were shot into the parking lot. Tats found an old T-shirt on the pavement and held it over his nose and mouth as he ran toward the parking lot exit. But traffic was stuck; police were letting out one car at a time and then pulling the drivers from the cars, making arrests, and tearing off aftermarket parts from the vehicles. The result was a huge traffic jam with screams coming from the sprawling lines of cars.

A few motorcycle riders tried to slip out by riding over the boardwalk or the beach. They were clotheslined by locals wielding bats and golf clubs. Tats watched as a fellow Midnight Angel was smacked clean off his bike when a chubby local with a bandana wrapped around his head tagged him with a graphite driver.

It came down to a choice between being arrested by cops or beaten up by locals, with tear gas in between; two hells with a hellish purgatory in the middle. Then the police stopped firing the tear gas canisters, which meant the locals could start closing in, forcing those *bosozoku* who had managed to survive the gas to choose between an arrest or a beating. Tats started looking for a ride out; he had decided on arrest over beating. The police weren't arresting everyone anyway, and Tats figured that those who didn't have criminal records, like him, would be free to go.

But the speed Tats had taken two hours ago was now making him nervous—all his confident energy had turned to anxiety and panic. He wished he were anywhere but there. He saw the locals massing in small clusters on the sand, their golf clubs and aluminum bats shining in the moonlight. A car nearby had caught fire—the tongues of a bonfire having ignited a polyurethane airfoil. Flames were now consuming the back end, and the owner desperately tried to put it out by patting it down with his leather jacket.

"Give me a ride," Tats asked him.

The guy looked at him and shook his head. "In what?" The car was now a flaming hulk.

Tats was still crying because of the gas, his tears stinging his flesh as they rolled down his cheeks. The crowd of locals was closing in, seeking stragglers and working them over. Tats ducked between cars, searching for a familiar face, looking for a way out. Where was the confidence that had intoxicated the *bosozoku* earlier? Why was everyone suddenly bolting?

He emerged from between a silver Toyota Corolla and a Nissan Fairlady and then some middle-aged, angry salaryman type with a tennis racket—a tennis racket?—took a swing at him. The strings caught him squarely on the side of the head and then bounced off; the wood of the racket had missed completely. Tats took a two-handed swing that caught the older man in the chest. He stumbled backward, pivoted, and ran.

From behind the windows of those cars nearest Tats other *bosozoku* were cheering his small victory. He smoothed back his hair, reveling in the moment before he would get his ass kicked.

A motorcycle rolled up from between two bonfires.

"Get on," Yamada ordered.

Tats climbed on the back, grabbed Yamada's sweat-soaked jumpsuit and held on as he spun a half-donut on the pavement and screamed out of the parking lot.

"Duck!" Yamada shouted back.

They did and a baseball bat whizzed over their heads, brushing the top of Tat's pompadour.

Yamada steered the bike over the sand, the weight of two people and the sand's now damp hardness giving the bike better traction than had been possible during the day. Yamada maneuvered the bike down near the water to the firmest sand where they rode for about a kilometer. They passed resorts, where piles of beach chairs were chained up, and crowded oceanfront bars and cafes where the patrons looked curiously at the motorcycle speeding by on the beach. Then they hit the highway and Yamada drove them back to Arakawa.

The next night, back at the Skylark in Arakawa, Yamada told them that eleven Midnight Angels from their chapter had been arrested and two had been hospitalized, but that two guys had lost their virginity. Six cars and five motorcycles had been impounded. Police had announced a new crackdown on the *bosozoku*.

But despite those setbacks, the mood of those who had made it through the Shonan Run, as it came to be known, was of elation at having taken part in the epic *bosozoku* event of all time.

Yamada was particularly pleased with Tats. He had seen Tats fight off the guy with the tennis racket.

"You're my *kohai*," he told Tats, using the word that implied protegé, assistant, apprentice, and sidekick all in one. "You're going to be the head when I retire. You follow?"

But now, while Yamada played mah-jongg, placed bets over the prison phone, and depended on his *kohai* to take care of illicit business, Tats had spent half the day in bed and an hour standing in front of a mirror blow-drying his hair into a shining, swooping ducktail while listening to a tape, not of Bruce Springsteen, but of car and motorcycle engines at full throttle.

IN THE STUFFY storeroom of a small shop on Ameyoko Street, Tats found his buddy Kaoru Takagi, nineteen, known in the Tokyo Midnight Angels as "The Joker." The Joker was working, unloading cheap, knock-off, made-in-Thailand Sansabelt-style slacks from a panel truck and sorting them by size and color. The job paid ¥120,000 ($180) for the day.

The Joker sat on a pile of lemon-yellow slacks and lit a cigarette. He wore sunglasses, a bright red T-shirt, and tight black pants. His hair was done in a punch perm. The Joker had attended high school for just three days. "I didn't like the teachers," he had explained to Tats, "and they didn't like me. They didn't like my clothing, my hair, nothing about me."

Tats rubbed the synthetic fabric of the citrus-colored pants between his thumb and ringed forefinger. He took pride in sussing out the crap from the real crap in the poly-blend genre. "Bangkok bullshit," he said, disgusted, and lit one of the Joker's Seven Stars with his own Zippo lighter.

"No smoking," Kimpo—a wiry, sunglasses-wearing, gold-chain-flaunting associate of Yamada—told Joker and Tats when he walked in. "Those pants are highly flammable." He himself was puffing away on a brown cigarillo.

Joker snuffed out his cigarette on the concrete floor. "Whatever you say, boss."

Tats kept on smoking. "You got something for Yamada?"

Kimpo looked him over. "Wait here."

As soon as he walked away Joker lit up again.

Tats and Joker had *bosozoku* business to discuss, something about another big run. Hell-raising needed to be organized, Tats knew, so they had to meet tonight. "Big fucking run," he told Joker, "biggest yet, like the Shonan Run. Bigger, even."

Joker smiled. He hadn't been at the legendary Shonan Run.

Kimpo came back and handed Tats a brown-paper-wrapped package that weighed about a pound. "Don't lose it," Kimpo said. Tats pretended not to hear him. Who the fuck was this guy to be treating him like a punk?

Kimpo stood chewing the plastic tip of his cigarillo, sizing Tats up. Kimpo broke into a wide grin around the cigarillo. "You want some pants?" Kimpo asked. "We've got about six hundred pairs. They go out front for a thousand each."

Tats shook his head. "I wouldn't *steal* those pants."

INSTEAD OF TAKING the package straight out to Miki in Juban, as Yamada had instructed, Tats carried it home with him. His keys were locked in his car and Tats figured he'd drive the package out to Juban once he took care of that.

In his room, surrounded by posters of motorcycles, cars, and girls; stickers advertising car parts stores; traditional wood-block prints of sword-wielding samurai; and a big Midnight Angels banner, he unwrapped the package. Inside the folds of crumpled, heavy brown paper and oily plastic bubble wrap was a Ruger P-89 9-mm, pistol with two clips and thirty loose rounds in a small cardboard box. He removed the handgun and held it by the hard graphite grip. He flipped the safety to what he thought was the "S" position and pulled the slide back and held the gun up to the light to see if a round had been chambered. It wasn't loaded. (Yamada had taught him the rudiments of how to handle a pistol, though Tats had never fired one. He'd once shot a hunting rifle.) The magazine was also empty. He slid a clip into the handgrip of the pistol and flipped the safety off; some oil from the clip rubbed off on his hands. He wiped his hands on the towel he used for cleaning up after working on his car engine.

Standing in front of a full-length mirror, he tossed the pistol from hand to hand and posed with it, looking at his reflection as he sighted down the barrel at himself. He held the pistol in various poses, from the hip, at shoulder height, at a forty-five-degree angle, pointing down at the ground as if he were being casual. He spun the gun around on his finger and it slid off, making a loud thump against the tatami-mat floor. He kneeled down to pick it up and rolled over, as if he were dodging bullets, and aimed back at the mirror. He had bumped into a stack of porn and motorcycle magazines and they came tumbling down on him; this heightened the illusion he was really being shot at. He began pulling the trigger and listening to the solid clicks of the firing pin against the empty chamber. (He knew he wasn't supposed to do that. Firing against an empty chamber is bad for the firing pin.) He unbuttoned his jacket and slipped the gun into his pants, buttoning the jacket over it and then checking to see if there was any bulge.

It felt cool to have a gun, especially a nice gun like this, not some Russian piece of crap like a Tokalef or Makharov. This was the real thing, like an American gangster would use. Tats figured Yamada would get about a ¥1 million ($9,100), maybe more, for this. (In the United States the same pistol retailed for $350.) Handguns were illegal in Japan and even hunting shotguns were strictly controlled. Only police and the military were allowed to possess handguns; no ordinary citizens were legally entitled to carry them. Yet in 1991 police had seized over a thousand guns, most of them from racketeers and gangsters. Yamada had sold plenty of Tokalefs and Makharovs, shoddy, Russian-made pistols brought over by Russian seamen and sold for bargain prices. Russian guns went for about ¥1200,000 ($1,800).

American small-caliber rifles sold for about the same while Russian rifles were the cheapest, sometimes going for less than a hundred thousand yen. Machine guns were expensive: Uzis, Mac-10s, or even Russian-made RPKs; Yamada had never had one, at least that Tats knew about, but he had once told Tats they went for up to ¥14 million ($36,400). Guns were big business, and when there was a gang war on, prices would go through the roof. Bullets alone could sell for ¥15,000 ($45) each.

The penalty for being caught with a handgun was stiff: five-year sentences were typical for Yakuza members. But for Tats, who had already done a month at Gunma Prefecture's juvenile detention center for possession of Yamada's Beretta, the penalty would be much less severe. At nineteen, he was still legally a minor.

The Ruger would have to be delivered to Miki out in Juban, and then, once he had checked it out, Yamada would call Miki and tell him to deposit a million or so into his bank account. Tats knew the system— he'd delivered everything from guns to crotchless panties all over Tokyo as Yamada wheeled and dealed from the prison canteen.

Tats drew the gun as fast as he could, like a cowboy, and pointed it at his reflection. "Bang," he said. He noticed his hair was a little messed up and tossed the gun on the bed so he could tend to his do.

"CHECK THIS OUT," Tats said, holding up the Ruger.

Chiharu Sato, seventeen, rolled her eyes. She'd seen guns before.

"This isn't some Russian-made piece of shit. This is a real American pistol." He flipped it over in his hand and held it out to her by the barrel. "Like in 'Yokohama Vice.' "

Chiharu had stopped off on her way home from Bunkyo High School. She sat on Tats's single bed and smoked one of Tats's mom's cigarettes. She blew smoke at the gun.

Tats swung around, aiming at himself in the mirror, and then swung the barrel back around so that he was pointing it at Chiharu. She still wasn't impressed.

Losing interest himself, he dropped the gun on the bed and plopped down beside her. Chiharu wore a pink dress and was heavily made up with purple eye shadow and matching lipstick. She walked and talked with exaggerated femininity, like one of the Japanese girl-idol singers on television, all curtsies, bows, and giggles. But behind all that excessive politeness was a lack of interest in anything that wasn't of immediate benefit to her. And the gun, obviously one of Tats's innumerable errands, didn't concern her. Chiharu was the head of the female auxiliary of the Tokyo Midnight Angels, a loosely federated group of girlfriends and hangers-on called the Lady Bombers. Yamada had been before her time; when she and Tats started going out Yamada was already in jail and the Shonan Run was ancient history, something that had happened in the distant past, like Pearl Harbor or astronauts walking on the moon.

"We're going on a big run," Tats said, picking up the pistol and sliding it into his pants. "Biggest run of the year."

Chiharu nodded. "Great. Let's go to the Skylark."

On their way downstairs, Tats remembered he had locked his keys in his car. He wondered if Chiharu wouldn't mind walking to the Skylark, about a mile away.

"It's a nice evening," Tats said as Chiharu fastened her high heels and he slipped on his *geta*. "Why don't we stroll there?"

Chiharu looked at him as if he was crazy.

"Okay, wait here." Tats slid off his sandals and went upstairs. He came back down with a wire coat hanger, which he undid and twisted into a tight loop. But when he went outside and tried to slide it around the window glass he realized it would never work on his car: the door locks were down around the inside handle and didn't protrude at all.

"What are you thinking?" Chiharu said, clearly annoyed.

Tats shook his head. "You're right, this won't work."

"Call someone," Chiharu said. "I don't want to stand here all night." She went back inside, took off her shoes, and sat at the kitchen table with Tats's mom. Mom gave Chiharu cigarettes, Tats noticed, but she wouldn't give him any. Tats stood in the doorway a moment and played with the useless coat hanger. He'd call Joker. Joker had one of those flat metal car-door jimmies.

He phoned Kimpo's down on Ameyoko Street.

"You drop off the package?" Kimpo asked when he heard it was Tats.

"I'm on my way," Tats said. "Car trouble."

"Car trouble?" Kimpo sounded pissed off. "Don't fuck around. That package is worth more than your whole fucking car."

"I'm not fucking around," Tats explained. "That's why I'm calling Joker, I really got car trouble."

Tats didn't want to have to explain he had locked his keys in his car.

Kimpo laughed. "You got trouble and you call this punk?" He called Joker to the phone.

Tats told Joker his problem. Joker laughed.

"Don't tell Kimpo about it," Tats begged him.

"What's in it for me?" asked Joker.

"I'll let you check out the gun."

"Russian?"

"American. Ruger."

JOKER DEMANDED TO see it as soon as he arrived on his Suzuki GXR 400. Tats lifted up his jacket and revealed the black handgrip.

"Do the car first and I'll let you check it out," Tats insisted. They were standing on the narrow street before Tats's small house.

Joker pretended to inspect the Nissan's door. He felt around the rubber molding and reaching into his black pants for the metal jimmy.

"This is a hard door to pick," he said, shaking his head. "Don't know if I can do it."

"Come on," Tats begged.

"Can we shoot the gun?" Joker asked.

"What?" Tats said. "No way. They'll know. You can tell if a gun's been fired by the way it smells."

Joker smiled. He was missing one front tooth and had a gold cap on one of his canines. "Then you better call a mechanic or someone to unlock this." He walked over to his motorcycle and threw a leg over it.

Tats sighed. "Okay, one shot."

Joker climbed off his bike. He was twisting the jimmy in his hands, bending the malleable steel back and forth. He rubbed the flat rod against his pant leg to warm it, bent it again, and slid it between the bottom window gasket and the glass. It took him just three tries to pop the lock.

"I can do it in one," Joker boasted. "Let's shoot it after the meet tonight, at the tire yard."

Tats watched Joker roar off up the street. He slipped his keys out of the ignition and closed the door.

When he went inside to get Chiharu, she was watching game shows with his mom and smoking more of his mom's cigarettes. They looked so happy sitting there on the tatami, cups of tea, small plates of sponge cake, and a carton of Caravel Menthols on the table before them.

When Tats reached for a pack his mom told him to get a job. And a haircut.

Chiharu laughed.

THE TIRE YARD was enclosed by a chain-link fence and had once been a furniture factory's dirt parking lot. Now the factory was closed and there was nothing there but thousands of old tires and abandoned household junk: worn-out couches, broken televisions, trashed refrigerators.

Tats had spelled out to everyone the details and agenda of tomorrow's run up to the Moriya Exchange, a highway rest stop in a small Ibaraki Prefecture town, so named because it was where the Joban Expressway intersected with several smaller highways. The plan, as it had been laid out to him in a phone call from the Yokohama chapter leader, was for the four main chapters of the Midnight Angels to head up the Chuo Expressway and rendezvous at 1:30 A.M. at the Minowa exit.

Around midnight, while the gang passed around a bottle of Hennessey brandy, Tats had excitedly described the run to the thirty-five members present; he told the boys that this could be another Shonan Run. (Of all the active Tokyo Midnight Angels, only one other member had taken part in that legendary event.) This was the high point of Tats's year. To him, the endless petty errands for Yamada were less important than *bosozoku* business. Yamada, of all people, should have known that.

Now Tats, Chiharu, and the Joker stood alone in front of Tat's Nissan Skyline. Tats had pulled the gun from his pants, removed the clip, and was sliding 9-mm. parabellum SWC shells into the magazine. Joker raptly watched him. Chiharu walked around the car and climbed in the passenger seat, playing with the radio.

Tats told her to keep it down; they didn't want anyone to hear them.

"You're shooting a gun," Chiharu pointed out. "Everyone's going to hear you."

"Just shut up," Tats told her. He concentrated on sliding the rounds into the spring-loaded magazine. He loaded four rounds, popped the clip, and pulled the slide.

"We'll shoot at the tires." Tats pointed to the mass of black rubber forty feet away that was taller than he was.

He pointed the gun, closed his eyes, and squeezed the trigger. Nothing happened. He lowered the gun and examined it carefully.

"Safety's on," he said.

Tats flipped the safety and fired off a round. The recoil was less than he'd expected, and when the hot, spent shell casing flew from the gun and bounced off the Nissan next to Joker, Tats began laughing hysterically. The paint on his car had been chipped, but so what? He squeezed off another round, and another and another. The shell casings nicked his car's paint job each time, but he didn't care. Even Chiharu had been excited by the noise and dump, sulphuric smell of gunpowder and cordite; she'd stepped out of the passenger door and was now standing behind Tats.

"My turn," Joker demanded.

Tats flipped the safety and released the magazine, setting the gun on the roof of his car after he did so. He only had four more bullets in his pocket; suddenly he wished he had brought the whole box with him. All thirty rounds. He hurriedly pushed the shells into the clip. He was elated to be shooting a real pistol and was looking forward to tomorrow's run. Fuck Yamada and Kimpo and all these errands. He was Tats, president of the Tokyo chapter of the Midnight Angels. He slammed the magazine back into the Ruger, flipped the safety, and fired again.

"Fuck all of you!" he shouted.

Then he gave the gun to Joker.

"You okay?" asked Joker.

Tats nodded.

Joker shrugged and gripped the pistol carefully in his right hand. He wrapped his left hand around the right and shot once, twice, three times, and then he kept pulling the trigger and saying, "Bam, bam, bam," until Tats wrestled the gun away from him.

AFTER HE DROPPED Joker off at the Skylark, Tats drove Chiharu home and she let him sneak up to her room with her. Because they had to stay silent the sex wasn't as boisterous as Tats liked but it was still a great way to wrap up an excellent evening.

At home, he removed the Ruger from his pants and smelled the barrel. It stank of powder and he could see black marks around the firing pin and some kind of brown streaking at the edge of the barrel. The gun had to be cleaned before it could be delivered anywhere. Fuck Yamada—he would drop off the gun when he was ready, clean or dirty, who cared. He slipped the gun under his bed. As he was hanging up his jacket, he changed his mind. After all Yamada had done for him, he couldn't let him down by dropping off a dirty pistol.

Sitting in his underwear, a can of spray-on metal cleaner that he used to clean his car radio antenna and a soft, metallic-fiber scrub pad arrayed beside him on a newspaper, he turned the gun over in his hands. He depressed the slide-release and pulled on it to see if it would give at all. To his surprise it pulled out without much resistance. The barrel and slide assembly then slid back easily off the frame. Tats grinned at how easy it was. The recoil spring and guide were quickly detached from the frame, and then the barrel could be removed. He held the short barrel up to the light. It was ingenious, he decided, simple yet brilliant. The whole pistol stripped down to just eight parts. He carefully rubbed the firing pin and then the barrel with cleaning solution, scrubbing them till they smelled like metal and oil. He scrubbed the rest of the gun as well and enjoyed feeling the metal parts in his hands, cool and greasy, each with a satisfying heaviness, like rolls of hundred-yen coins.

When he determined the pistol was clean, he commenced to reassemble it. But the parts that had disassembled so effortlessly suddenly didn't seem to fit together, it was like a badly designed puzzle. He found no way to manipulate the barrel, recoil spring, and guide so that the slide would fit on top. He couldn't do a thing with the slide release; fitting that piece back under the slide seemed against the laws of physics. He played with the pieces of the pistol, trying every combination of parts, forcing, pushing, sliding, and jerking; the closest he could come to a reassembled gun was if he left the recoil spring out completely. Tats gave up at three A.M.; he would try again in the morning.

HIS MOTHER WAS shouting that Yamada was on the phone. When Tats picked up the phone, Yamada was furious with his young protegé for having disrespected him.

"What the fuck are you doing, you little prick?" Yamada demanded. "Where the fuck is that package?"

Tats shuddered as he remembered the mass of pistol parts scattered on the newspaper beneath his bed. "I got it. I had car trouble."

"I don't care if you have to crawl out to Juban," Yamada growled, "you get that package to Miki, you follow?"

"Yeah, yeah," Tats said. He thought about the big run tonight; it was going to be epic — five hundred *bosozoku* all in one rest stop. They were going to rule that place.

"You do what I tell you, you little prick," Yamada shouted. "You follow?"

Tats didn't say anything. He'd had enough of being a "little prick," of being ordered around. Tats was nineteen, he was a man and Yamada should treat him like one.

"I'll do it," Tats said in a low, cool voice. "Just shut up."

Yamada shouted, "Deliver the package. You've got big problems, you little prick, bigger than you could ever imagine."

When Yamada hung up, Tats felt a rush of elation. He didn't need Yamada, he didn't need anyone but his buddies and the big run. He popped in a tape of some car engines, this a recording of his own Nissan Skyline's unmuffled 244 power plant, and did his hair.

Fuck Yamada. The pistol could wait, forever, as far as Tats was concerned. Today was the day of the Moriya Run, and it promised to be as exciting as the Shonan Run. As he did his hair and regarded himself in the mirror, he concluded this was what he was, a *bosozoku atama* (headman) not some errand boy for a washed-up, incarcerated ex-*bosozoku*. Let the pistol, Yamada, Kimpo, Miki out in Juban, let the whole fucking world wait; Tats had *bosozoku* business to attend to.

HE MET WITH the other Tokyo Midnight Angels on a deserted shopping street. Tats wore black pants and a red jacket with Chinese characters on the back that read, "We do what we want. We don't care what you say. We don't care about you."

A little after midnight he received bad news from Yokohama. Police roadblocks at the border of Kawasaki and Tokyo had stopped the Yokohama chapter. The Midnight Angels discussed the bad news and the light rain as they put the finishing touches on their cars and motorcycles. Before they pulled out of the lot, the Joker sounded his motorcycle's new customized horn. It played "La Cucaracha."

Tats's white Nissan Skyline, with its fins, airfoils, and skirts, took the lead. He and several other Midnight Angels mounted flashing purple imitation police lights in their rear windows and removed their license plates to avoid identification. They rode two or three to a car, driving slowly, a waltz of lane-changing and jockeying. The Joker's horn blared. They drove at five miles an hour down the Chuo Expressway, jubilantly shaking fists, their voices drowned out by engine noise. Tats remained at the head of the column, swinging his Nissan back and forth across four lanes of highway.

"I love the noise," shouted the Joker from his motorcycle, "I love driving people crazy. It's like yelling 'This is who we are, and if you don't like it, what the fuck are you going to do about it?' "

Over the surreal parade flew several Rising Sun flags. As the traffic piled up behind them, the Midnight Angels began smiling, beaming, and gunning their engines. Tats completely forgot about the pistol and Yamada. He wasn't even thinking about his hair. He gunned his engine, spun his car around in a 180-degree slide and stopped for a moment, watching the ragged column of Midnight Angels advance toward him. He swigged from a bottle of Hennessey. This was great, and it was only going to get better.

Elevated over northwest Tokyo, the highway wound through Adachi Ward, over the Sumida River, and then the suburbs. The expressway was bright with white light and the pavement was slick, making it easy for Tats and the rest of the Midnight Angels to spin 360s or 180s and drive in reverse. A few Midnight Angels climbed up and stood on the hoods of their cars or sat back on the roofs, smoking cigarettes, waving flags, and pumping their fists.

A flurry of excitement rose from the rear of the column as more *bosozoku* joined. A few members of the Yokohama chapter had managed to run the roadblocks and brave the elements, and they were there, gunning their motors and shouting greetings.

The Chiba chapter waited alongside the road near Misato. Ten more cars and ten more motorcycles. A pretty girl with long black hair whipping in the breeze of passing cars and exhaust raised her fist exultantly and pumped the air, cheering on the boys. She climbed onto the roof of one of the Chiba cars—a white, barbed monster of a Toyota—and the Chiba chapter got rolling, falling in behind Tokyo and Yokohama.

When the Ibaraki chapter came aboard near Kashiwa, two hours since Tats and the Tokyo chapter had massed on their home turf, the Midnight Angels were at full strength, over a hundred cars and sixty motorcycles. The highway sputtered with the sounds of combustion and a kaleidoscope of flashing red and purple lights and fluttering Rising Suns sparkled. Occasionally, the Midnight Angels came to a complete stop, halting traffic to set off fireworks or attend to car trouble. They had backed up traffic for over twenty miles, the line of cars and trucks stretching to Tokyo over the giant arc of the elevated expressway. If angry drivers leaned on their horns, Tats couldn't hear them.

Overhead a gigantic traffic advisory sign flashed four-foot high yellow letters reading, TRAFFIC JAM: FROM KIBA 10 KILOMETERS.

In front of Tats was nothing but open road. He owned the highway.

AS THE MORNING sun broke through scattered clouds and for a confusing instant it drizzled and was sunny simultaneously, the Midnight Angels rolled into the Moriya Exchange. About fifty other *bosozoku* were already gathered there, their cars and bikes parked near the curb in front of a small curry snack shop and restroom complex and an out-of-business gas station. The waitresses and cooks from the curry joint stared through the plate-glass windows as the Midnight Angels pulled to a stop amid the scorching smell of racing tires and exhaust and burning motor oil.

Tats was a little disappointed by the turnout but within minutes more motorcycles and cars rumbled in. The Edokko Racers arrived, as did the Crazies, the Kanto Warriors, and Imprisoned for Life a few minutes later. And there were more girls than Tats had ever seen at a *bosozoku* rally; good thing he'd left Chiharu at home. (She'd become angry when she found out he hadn't delivered the package. She told Tats he was irresponsible and immature, that he never did anything but play with his car and his hair.) Tats, as one of the oldest *bosozoku atama* there, was treated to deep bows by other *bosozoku* leaders.

The president of the Eddoko Racers asked Tats how Yamada was doing.

"Who cares?" Tats said and chugged the rest of his beer.

The Hit and Runners were also there, Tats noticed, leaning on their horns and accelerators. So were the Top Ladies — a gang of girl *bosozoku* who wore their purple satin uniforms seductively hanging off their pale shoulders. There was no shortage of boys leaning against their violet convertible, where two of the hottest girls sat straddling the vinyl headrests of the backseat, smoking Vogue-brand cigarettes.

One biker with a white-tanked Yamaha 400 entertained a small audience of his own. Tats briefly joined the circle around him and listened while he gunned his unmuffled engine, making it play the first notes of Beethoven's Fifth at earth-shaking volume.

The Midnight Angels, with about three hundred members present, was the largest of the gangs. Tats and his friends had brought up plenty of brandy, beer, and sake. This was going to be a fun few days, Tats figured, at least until the police broke it up.

Tats and Joker passed a bottle of brandy back and forth as the rain recommenced, drenching the boys' jackets and saturating the girls' tops.

"Is this great or what?" Tats announced as he wiped his lips with his sleeve.

Joker didn't answer. He was sitting on his motorcycle, checking out the scene. "I want to get me a girl, some country girl," he said, looking over the prospects. "Going to get me a country girl and take her back to the city." He kick-started his bike and rode off between parked cars, leaving Tats holding the pint of Hennessey.

Tats wandered among the huddles of kids, joining a clique of Ibaraki Midnight Angels and passing around his bottle of brandy. He listened as they excitedly recounted the ride up and explained why they had chosen, for example, the Hotline BMT shifter instead of the Moma, or the Tokiko suspension coil instead of the Nayaba, or why a *Zetto* (Nissan 280 Z) was better than a *Suka* G (Nissan Skyline GT).

The car talk bored Tats. He wanted to tell them all about the Shonan Run, about the tear gas and methamphetamine and newspaper reporters, about the locals wielding baseball bats and — he suddenly remembered Yamada, riding out of the rising sun on his motorcycle, and shivered. He didn't want to think about Yamada. He didn't want to think about the pistol. Instead, he yawned as some pimple-faced punk talked at length about his new Yoshimura header pipes.

Who cares? He wanted to ask. Who gives a shit? Then he remembered he used to love talking cars and car parts; just yesterday he had been listening to a cassette of his car engine.

Then the kid stopped talking cars and seemed to be listening to something. Sirens. Tats craned his neck to see six flashing squad cars and twenty cops in light-blue riot gear sweep into the rest stop. *Bosozoku* were laughing and yelling and running and clawing at the doors of their cars. Bikes were peeling out, heading toward the far side of the lot. Drivers hit their horns. Tats watched as a couple of kids were grabbed while desperately trying to kick-start their water-logged bikes. A gang who had come in a lowrider got nabbed because their leader locked his keys in the car. Two Midnight Angels were collared walking out of the men's room. Tats knew whoever got busted would be dragged into the station, grilled, fined, released in the custody of his parents, or, if he was old enough, arraigned. His car would be stripped by the cops.

"Don't go," Tats shouted as he screwed the cap back onto the brandy. "It's not over."

In the chaos, two hot-rodders spun taunting 360s around a cop. A couple of bikers feigned surrender, then high tailed it over the grassy embankment and onto the highway, leaving the cops standing there with their batons and ticket books. Everyone was pulling out, even Tats's Tokyo Midnight Angels. The early morning air was pierced by a wheezy high-pitched "La Cucaracha." Tats turned just in time to see Joker riding toward him, a fat girl in acid-washed denim perched on the bike behind him.

"I'm gone," Joker shouted.

The rain had turned torrential.

Tats couldn't believe it: they'd just gotten there, nothing had happened, and these kids were already taking off.

Tats walked to his car. The run was over.

As he looked up at the sky and let the thick rain drops pelt his face and mess up his hair, he remembered he would somehow have to put that pistol back together again.

He had a package to deliver.

BROOKLYN LOGIC

martin dixon

for many people life is just one long experience. For a biker, life is just one never-ending ride. Enjoy it while it lasts. Does this sound fatalist? Maybe. Does it smack of extremism? Possibly. Is it accurate? Well, that depends on who you call your friend. Because my friends are bikers. And if I have ever learned this fact of life, I have learned it from them. I am now a member of a very large, unconventional family, a family that loves to ride, drink, party, fuck, and fight. My brothers Larry O, East, Gun Smoke, John, Sweet Pete, Spydar, DC, Blaze, Whisper, Derek, Mean Gene, Fat Daddy, and Tayta, have taught me everything I need to know to survive fifty lives. But maybe that's just another element to Brooklyn Logic—you don't choose it, it chooses you. Now let me introduce you to the family . . .

I don't know who started the concept or what perpetuated it, but bikers are some fierce characters. It must be something about riding with your balls so close to the gas tank or the fumes that make these guys so insane. Best friends swear and curse each other. Enemies get pistol-whipped and shot at. Women have been known to pull out razors from their cleavage and fight other women and men over the most trivial things—an insult, a smack, infidelity. The language is brutal yet comical. "Welcome to the Sophisticated Gents, now get the fuck out . . ." "No, you don't have to go home, but you do have to get the hell out of here. . . ." "Sure, you can take my picture, but then I'll take your camera. . . ." "Here, drink this . . . tell me if it tastes like real Jack Daniels,'cause if it don't I'm gonna shoot somebody. . . ."

To enter this world is to leave all vestiges of your past behind. Far behind. Even if only for the hour or two you visit. There exists a Dodge City mentality that pervades many biker clubhouses; only the strong survive. Fuck the world—forever together. Police don't exist. Laws were made to be broken. No one is perfect. Brooklyn Logic again. "Get them before they get you. . . ." "If you're not sure, do it and ask questions later. . . ." "I'd rather be judged by twelve than carried by six. . . ." I've heard them all. Among biker clubs, loyalty is paramount. No one rats out. All things are handled internally. "Justice may be blind, but we're not. . . ."

All clubs maintain democratically elected hierarchies, which include a President, Vice-President, Treasurer, Sergeants-at-Arms, and Road Captain. Violate and you will be dealt with. Punishments range from stripping colors (a form of exile from the member rank and file), monetary fines, beatings, and expulsion. And as odd as these rules may seem to lay people, nobody expects anything different. These clubs have been in existence since the late sixties, and whether one agrees with their warped logic or not, the peace is kept by this allegiance to order. Day in and day out, you would never know that the man or woman doing your taxes, driving the buses, or connecting your cable television is an undercover biker who has a temper that could melt wrought iron. Hell, there are even senators and congressmen who ride.

Week after week, month after month, year after year I endured taunts and provocations from my new brothers. I was a prospect, a new recruit. Clean-cut and all green. As time went on, I came to really know and respect these people. These are men and women whose family roots grew primarily outside of New York. More often than not they were from the deep south. The remnants of segregation have conditioned them to accept that anything you want done you will have to do yourself. No one is going to help you. And this is one of the most admirable elements about these clubs. They are completely autonomous. And not unlike many successful Baptist churches, they utilize the resources of all their members and guests to help expand and promote their calendar of events, which range from social dances, road trips, and trophy parties to bikini bike washes, birthday strippers, and the like.

After dodging countless offers to officially join one of the groups, I was finally accepted as what you'd call an independent on the circuit—a loner, wearing no colors—but a kid compared to these guys. The circuit itself is enormous, comprised of nearly 50 bike and auto-van clubs throughout the five boroughs and tri-state region. A rough estimate of 1,000 – 1,500 hard-core members would be fair. I am proud to say that within these last ten years I have met and photographed nearly all of them. And they, in turn, know me—if only through my images. To these men I am just Dred, the picture man. But for practically a decade I have documented all of their tro-phy parties and socials, their Myrtle and Virginia Beach Runs, their weekly fish fries and "Crab Nights." I have finally earned their trust, and have access to their closed-door society. And that's saying something: this is a very tightly guarded association. But to this very day — all trust aside—I still remain out-side certain walls. There exists a mistrust, a nervous and deep-seated expec-tation that in some way and at some time I will do a disservice to them. Brooklyn Logic again. Never forget, never let up, never sleep.

I understand them, and perhaps they will learn to understand me. I am very different from them; I have no visible scars, no gunshot wounds, no children, no wife, no stream of women paging my cell phone, no hus-tles. I don't have any favorite near-death escapades to share on hot sum-mer nights. I've never been jailed, arrested, robbed, maimed, mauled, or jumped. I was never lucky enough to leap out of a window fleeing from some angry husband's wrath. I've never had the pleasure of inviting my parole officer out to a titty bar. For some, that makes me a punk. A small fry. To this day there are still people who swear I must be a cop or some informant, even though I have never caused the slightest scandal. It's an all-too-common fact that you can't please all the people all the time. But respect is a funny thing. The harder you try to earn it, the less likely are people to give it to you. So fuck it.

IT WAS JOE Frye who brought me into the circuit. Joe is an old jazz gui-tar man and pool shark. We played blues music at the Dean Street Cafe on Underhill every Tuesday night. We got to know each other because we both parked our bikes on the sidewalk so they wouldn't get knocked over by drunk drivers parking or leaving. It was Joe who told me about the Imperials and their parties. In hindsight, I can honestly say that I never searched them out, they found me. I was told to come to the Pythons' on Sunday; they were having a "Bike Blessing." A Bike Bless-ing? Hell, I'd give it a shot.

If you've never seen a Bike Blessing, you have no idea what to expect. We were on Saratoga Avenue in the Brownsville section of Brooklyn, a real gritty area with Mom-and-Pop stores on every corner selling Philly Blunt cigars to kids rolling weed. Walking up the street from the subway I kept hearing the roar of screaming race bikes strafing up and down the avenues. When I turned the corner, I was startled to see at least 300 chromed-out race bikes and cruisers all neatly lined up in two long rows parked opposite each other, space at a strict premium. Helmets worth $500 and better were left hanging from rearview mirrors, while men and women with smoked sausages and beers in hand made the rounds, inspecting each other's wheels. The streets were teeming with at least a thousand brothers from near and far who came for the honor of attending the first sanctioned blessing of the new riding year, beginning in April. I was shell-shocked, and in complete disbelief. If you had added up the cost of all this steel and aluminum, it would have come to well over a million five. Many of these rods were brand-spanking new, with extensive custom work done after the purchase. On this little Brooklyn street, far removed from the corporate financial world of Manhattan, separated by city buses and sprawling public housing, was yet another facet of our metropolis that reminded me, once again, that the family of man has many relatives. And I, for my part, was in paradise.

Bike Blessings are so populated that the locals who actually live on the street are often afraid to use their cars for fear of bumping a bike. Watch anybody back into a group of parked motorcycles and you will see both owners gasp in abject terror, the blood rushing out of their faces—one for the beating he must obligingly administer, and the other for the pain he will surely receive. The biggest trouble with stereotypes is the degree to which they must be reinforced and perpetuated, despite any degree of reluctance on one or both sides of a situation. Rules are rules, I'm told, and we are not at liberty to reinvent the wheel.

We are all too frequently reminded of the motorcycle rider mystique as analogous to that of the frontier cowboy, alone in his saddle, surveying uncharted plains through the sights of his rifle. Unsheltered by the elements, vulnerable to the capricious nature of fellow motorists, and romanticized by women for the erotic nature of their unbridled masculinity, bikers are seen as titans among men. They are the elite, the battle weary, the chosen few. The demarcation lines of male identity and masculinity are never better observed than when speaking of bikers. The bike as icon is deeply rooted as a masculine ideal. The quality of your ride can make you suspect. Riding a rat bike to a function is akin to pulling up beside a Shelby Cobra at a red light in your Gremlin: you start feeling gravity slowly exerting its force on your shoulders, making you want to examine your floor mats a little more closely.

All chauvinism aside, real men ride. It's what defines us, describes us, and selects us for service. We don't ride for the easiest way home. We don't ride for the hatchback Civics and the life of Riley. We don't ride because it's cheaper or because we can't afford another vehicle. We ride because we define ourselves by our wheels. And our wheels are our signature, our fingerprint.

DEFACING A MAN'S ride is akin to raping his virgin daughter. And if defacing a man's ride warrants, in its mildest manifestation, minor cosmetic surgery, what do you do to the clown who outright steals your wheels, and then crashes it running from the police? How do you make it right? Well, you call your people in and you tell them in your clearest levelheaded voice, "Brothers, we have a problem." Brooklyn Logic again. You call in a favor only for the most serious of all crimes. There is no action without reaction, and favors are very expensive; you use them wisely.

When my rainbow-colored Honda VFR was stolen one Sunday morning, I could think of only one man to call. And as is often the case when you absolutely, positively have to whip some ass right away, I called my riding partner Larry O, who's like my personal bodyguard, a friend in need and a friend indeed. He will answer to Major Pain, Button Man, or Baldy Locks (if you're me) or Shine (if you're Tayta). But at five nine and 235 lbs, Larry O, President and last man standing of the Harlem Riders, has the muscled look of a very threatening man. He's loud, quick-tempered, unforgiving, something of a tightwad, and one of the most straightforward and honest men you'll ever be lucky enough to meet. He is also without doubt one of my closest friends, and while our lives are as different as Mr. Rogers and Mike Tyson, our friendship, however stressed at times, has never been called into question. When I first met Larry he was as outlaw as the rifle that shot Martin Luther King, as quick-triggered as Colin Ferguson with hemorrhoids, and as humorous as Eddie Murphy on speed. But it is Larry I call when shit hits the fan.

Larry values friendship the way he values life, and if you are lucky enough to be really and truly called a friend, you have in him someone who will take a bullet as well as send one for someone he sincerely respects. I remember one time he called me, a little sad and dejected, after the death of his partner, Stone, from Far Rockaway. Stone was involved in a late-night driving collision, and Larry was really broken up inside, borderline tears, thinking about their friendship. Stone was clearly someone he would have gone to war for. He is neither suicidal nor mani-acal, but knows better than most that he has both the mental and phys-ical stamina to survive a direct physical assault. It is something he prepares for every single day. Larry, along with the others — Fearless One, Gun Smoke and his brother Tex, Fat Daddy, Dirty, Nytro, JR, and Quick — are men among men who live by the biker code, a code that expects you, in any situation and under any duress, to handle your affairs, trials, and disappointments like a man worthy of being called a man.

PULLING MY HAIR BACK WITHOUT ANY HANDS

erika lopez

even though I fell asleep on Arnold T. Smithers's sofa bed thinking about how it would suck once you were old and no one cared about impressing you anymore, I woke up emotionally farting and feeling financially cheap. Before I even opened my eyes, I was adding up all the times I covered things preparing for this trip with Magdalena and told her not to worry about it. *That wrench she needed, all the oil she got on my secured credit card, the loaf of bread . . .*

I took over two hours to pack up my bike and I took about eighty-five last good looks around before I set off to leave. I didn't wanna go because I had no idea how I was gonna pull this whole thing off: I'd forgotten how to ride. I went down to Arnold T. Smithers's store and took forty-five minutes to say good-bye. Finally around two or three in the afternoon I shoved off.

On my way into Nashville with six lanes of traffic merging and the slow lane torn up with grooves and craters in the road, it started to rain. Oh, not like a gentle cute rain, but a horizontal, crazy garden-hose rain.

It stung like a thousand tiny spankings, and my lips were peeled back from my gums and I hummed crazy things through my teeth. I'd actually bought a rain suit to wear, but I was already soaked and my toes were squishy in my boots. The only thing good about this rain suit was the plastic pouch it came in. I was using the pouch for my map, which I strapped to the gas tank.

Cars were weaving in and out of lanes and I stayed in the slow lane which just happened to be under construction. I kept close to the shoulder and watched for the potholes and grooves through what felt like seventy layers of Saran Wrap over my eyes. Cars were so sweet. I thought they'd pass me by in my own lane, but they gave me a wide berth as if they sensed my invisible masking tape boundary. I loved them and wanted to give them hugs without crashing into their windshields.

I lived, and just past Nashville the rain let up and I pulled over to a rest stop with truckers hanging out like big metal pigeons. A self-centered minivan family was parked under the only tree available and I practically rested my bike against the van to make a point. I lit a cigarette, and it was the first I inhaled all day. I felt my arm and leg muscles relax. I couldn't fucking believe I'd made it. The sky was clearer up ahead and I envied no one.

Not long after that, I was back on the highway going toward Memphis, and there were two lanes—I was in the right and a truck was directly to my left. To my right a truck was trying to merge real fast as if it didn't see me, but with a truck to my left and a car right behind me, there was nowhere to go so I had to ride screaming on the yellow line in the middle of the two trucks so I wouldn't get squashed.

So after Nashville and Memphis, I actually started to have fun even though my throat felt like a wet nylon stocking from screaming so much, and my ass hurt because my pelvic bone was trying to cut its way through my ass to the bike seat. I'd made it through a couple of my worst cold-sweat nightmares and I was alive with a rash on my ass.

When I stopped to get gas I actually think I swaggered, although not on purpose. After sitting with your legs open against a two-hundred-mile-per-hour wind, you don't stand real tall.

I felt alive and alone in the best way. No one could intimidate me or give me shit because I had bug guts all over me and could keep a bike upright and pass a truck in the crosswinds with a war cry. I'd just been through traffic hell and now I was actually a biker who'd earned the right to spit on any road, even though I never did because I never practiced, because I knew it'd just drool down my chin inside the helmet.

The counter girls kind of smiled at me like I had gotten a doctorate. I imagined this is how guys must feel a lot of the time, but often they never did anything except stand there.

Once some RV lady said, "Wow, it must be pretty exhausting riding on the back of that thing." I just smiled and said "Yeah. I guess so," slipped my leather gloves back on and took off.

FINALLY . . . HERE WAS the actual living in *the here and now* that took the edge off my existential fear of time going on forever.

I started taking photographs of my bike like it was a new lover. Still, I never gave her a name because I just don't get into naming dependable toasters and stuff. I took pictures of the bike in front of a couple of disappointing-looking post offices, and I also took pictures of it in a herd of cattle with the sun setting in the background. The cows looked at my bike like it was a cow they wanted to understand and I felt peace. I took three rolls of film that would later come out blank because my camera was broken.

That's okay. I enjoy the act of taking pictures more than looking at pictures because it really gets me to slow down and really take note of what's around me, without counting on some wimpy photo later.

YEAH, NO WIMPY photos for me when I'm old and cranky. When all my retirement community neighbors have their lives entirely recorded on videotape, and laugh and laugh at the memories. I'll just rock back and forth wondering where I last set down my teeth, dammit. I'll be thinking that if I'd only had a photo album, I wouldn't always be in my slippers yelling at somebody's grandkids across the street.

Here and now. Now that I was actually enjoying myself. I started seeing other bikes. And that meant I could start checking out the social structure of other bikers on the road. Here's how it goes:

If you have a Harley, there ain't a damn thing wrong with you unless you're a blatant asshole. But even if you are an asshole, a Harley can be personality spackle in that it'll cover over any deficiencies. That's why balding midlife-crisis boys get them.

Sadly enough, Harleys are usually the bikes you see broken down on the side of the road. I think they're better for riding around your block and showing off like a mating bird, but I don't know how far I'd wanna go. A whole lotta myth, and not known for being reliable. But you won't have to tap on people's shoulders and tell them how cool you are, because a Harley will do it for you. Once you get a Harley, you don't even need a relationship.

I want one so bad, my nipples sting just thinking about it.

If you get a Japanese bike, you'd better have one hell of a sense of humor or just stay at home. If you're a girl, they say you can ride just about anything and it's okay. But they're dependable and you can go far if you've got to get out of town fast because you've bought foreign.

I'm not much for breaking in with the crotch-rocket set. These are mostly hyper white suburban guys who like shiny red plastic things. In their teens and twenties, they still go around with Oxy wash in their pockets to look like they're glad to see you, pretending they're in a super-hero comic book world. But stereotypes often ring hollow and when you come face to face with one of these guys they end up being okay, so never mind.

I want acceptance from the slow-riding Harley set because they have a certain kind of panache. The men get big and hairy, and even the faded rose tattoo Harley chicks with their flat tits don't fear getting leather faces in the sun.

In Arkansas, I was trying to catch up to these two guys on Harleys way up ahead in the distance. I caught up to them, and they had their beat-up old leathers on and bandannas on their heads. I'm telling you, I felt cool just riding behind them on the cracked yellow highway. But they ignored me and now that I was a real live biker, *I demanded notice.*

Like a good dog introducing herself in the park, I sped up, passed them, and pulled in front of the first guy to show him my American-girl thighs and New Jersey tags. I let them sniff my ass in the park for a minute, then they pulled back out to pass me, and when they did they waved and nodded as they took their places back in front of me. I knew the Kawasaki thing was forgiven because I was a girl and they'd let me ride with them. Six paces behind, but that's okay: They were my high-way emissaries.

GIRL ON A MOTORCYCLE

rachel kushner

I often hid out in our garage as a little girl, when shooed outside to play on summer days. Of whatever was in that dark, hot and dusty place, I mostly remember three things: a wooden-wheeled scooter I could tool around on the smooth concrete floor, stacks of ripe and crated peaches, there for pilfering until my mother got around to the canning, and a 1955 Vincent Black Shadow. It was my father's motorcycle, bought in England and toured around the countryside with my mother and older brother, then just two, riding in a bullet-front sidecar, and lined up in front of the Ace Café with other luminary British cycles, BSAs and Brough Superiors, makes of which the Vincent was king. Eventually, it was shipped back to the U.S. on a Greek freighter. There's a dent in its oxidized black gas tank from where an unsympathetic stevedore launched it off a ten-foot drop to a loading dock below. When I was a child I would lift up its green canvas cover and listen for the tick and ting of it's cast aluminum engine shifting in the summer heat of the garage. It was coated in grime, leaking murky black oil into a pan beneath its enormous 1,000-cc motor, but even lodged on its center-stand, both wheels off the ground and only started as an annual event, to me it seemed an animate thing. My brother could've cared less about the difference between monkey and Allen wrenches; it was me who was willing to stand in the rain as the riders in the Vincent rally passed, my mother and I sinking into the mud on the side of the road, and me, at seven, computing in a flash of understanding that engine oil under the nails, the ability to kick-start a four-stroke or handle a suicide clutch—these were not just skills, but cause for a strange and unforgettable flutter.

Alain Delon gives Marianne Faithful, his young and inexperienced mistress, a Harley Davidson in the 1968 Anglo-French film *Girl on a Motorcycle*. For much of the film she is on the bike, blissful and wind-blown as she sails through the European countryside, musing in a sort of stream-of-consciousness voice-over. The motorcycle is a wedding gift: wheels to take her from Alsace, where she lives with her unwitting schoolteacher husband, to Heildelberg, where she surrenders herself to corrupting and neglectful Delon for sexual attention and an all-around sort of debasement (in one scene, meant to be heightened by its late sixties-style psychedelic effects, Delon spanks her with a bouquet of bri-ared red roses).

Although we see Faithful alone on the Harley, ultrasexy and inde-pendent and cool, in a sense it's Delon who's driving her destiny. He gave her the bike, after all, for the purpose of ferrying her away from her hus-band and into his control. Yet there's no getting around the machine's intrinsic nature. It has two wheels, is propelled by tremendous forward motion and steered by the rider. And when she's on it, she's alone and moving fast. She passes through the French/German border at sunrise, wearing a tight, black zip-up leather jumpsuit over nothing at all (the film's original title was *Naked Under Leather*). The surly border patrol are unnerved by her cycle-girl panache (she has no goods to declare under the catsuit). Although she goes to see Delon, theoretically she could go anywhere—tour Bavaria or shoot off to Poland, leave him waiting as the bed gets cold, cigarettes burn down, the next bouquet of roses wilts.

I think it's this idea, of a woman seduced by the freedom of a motor-cycle, yet not entirely in control of her life that I identify with so strongly in the film. In my early twenties I was attracted to men who lived and breathed motorcycles. That characteristic trumped some other, possibly more provident boyfriend traits. And I was into motorcycles as well. In fact it was the bikes that came first, the Motoguzzi and then the Motoguzzi mechanic. The mechanic turned out to be controlling and rather cruel, a bit like Alain Delon is toward Marianne Faithful (although he didn't look like Delon—no one ever does). And unfortunately, like Faithful's character in the film, I was halfway addicted. He didn't give me a Harley, but he did want me to compete in a race that he himself was going to do, and helped me put together a race-ready motorcycle. Participating in the race meant both pleasing him and, in a sense, individuating. A man setting a woman on a journey, and even if the purpose is to win his heart, or respect, or just to go back for more punishment, on the journey itself, she's a gliding particle—unfettered, unattached, kinetic. Meaning anything can happen.

ON A MAP, a thick black line indicates the Transpeninsular Highway, or Highway One, which spans the length of Baja—a long, variegated peninsula separated from mainland Mexico by the tepid, life-rich waters of the Gulf of California. Highway One is Baja's main highway, and beyond a few shorter routes from border towns to northern tourists destinations, it's the only highway; it was completed in 1973, a hallmark of modernization, an inaugural conjoining of north and south on a tract of land where people, separated by vast stretches of harsh, untenable desert and high mountains, once had little communication beyond their own regions.

But a thick black line on a map can be misleading for the uninitiated. Highway One is only regularly maintained (although without such luxuries as guardrails, or painted lane dividers) on the series of toll roads from Tijuana to Ensenada—a tiny portion of the 1,100-mile long road. Beyond Ensenada, the paved roads are macadam poured directly on dirt, meaning there as many dips and curves in the road as there are in the land beneath. Such road construction doesn't hold up well (but does create jobs), and there are huge potholes scattering the highway all the way down to the end of the peninsula, some of them gaping expanses of crumbled pavement that last 20 or 30 feet. The frequent and dramatic dips, called *vados*, are often filled with sand, or water, or, on a cold desert night, a sleeping cow seeking lingering daytime warmth from the highway's blacktop. Baja is mountainous, and with a few exceptional straight-aways, the road is a winding series of blind corners and hairpin turns. Many of the curves are not marked with warning signs, and the road is often coated with a slick sheen of diesel fuel that sloshes from Pemex trucks. The road can suddenly become one lane serving both directions, or turn from smooth pavement to grated dirt, a violent switch of terrain that can cause a broken axle for the unprepared car, and total disaster for a girl on a motorcycle, especially one foolish enough to race down the Baja Peninsula in a single day, a trip that

Marianne Faithful in *Girl On A Motorcycle*, 1970.

requires an average speed—hairpin turns, sleeping cows and all—of over a hundred miles an hour.

This race, called the Cabo 1000, was an annual event (it no longer occurs, but I'll get to that later) from San Ysidro, the last American town before the border into Mexico, to Cabo San Lucas at the tip of the Baja Peninsula, approximately 1,080 miles south. In a car, this trip is a full week of difficult driving, of extreme weather and road conditions. The required average I mentioned includes slowing down through Baja's towns (an honor code that a few bad apples always disobeyed), and stopping for water breaks, gas and repairs. Meaning to make the 100-mile mph average, on the straights a rider needs to push it over the top, go as fast as her bike will do.

I had been working on my Kawasaki 600 Ninja for months in preparation for the Cabo ride; I figured it would have enough power to go fast but be small and lithe enough to handle well on mountain curves. With new stainless steel after-market valves, a resurfaced cylinder head, a high-performance carburetor jet kit and a four-into-one exhaust with an unbaffled canister, I was ready. I had long discussions with friends over what kind of tires to choose, weighing the pros and cons of performance and durability. I would need a reasonably soft tire for traction and tight cornering, but something too soft would be shredded halfway down the peninsula. Little details like choosing the proper tint of helmet face shield and having some sort of system for cleaning it on the ride were important. Some people went with tear-offs, plastic adhesives that a rider could pull off as each one gunked up with bugs and dirt. Dale Shoal, an Isle of Man veteran who had won the Cabo ride many times (one year infamously finishing on an almost toy-sized race bike—a two-stroke 350), had an old tennis ball cut open and mounted on his handlebars, which kept moist a little sponge he could retrieve and use to clean his face shield. Dale is a fabricator by profession, and his Cabo bike was loaded with custom amenities to help him win. He designed his own automatic chain-luber, as well as a fiberglass double-decker gas tank that held an unbelievable eleven gallons of fuel (a typical motorcycle holds between four and six). His bike looked like a pregnant spider.

In the weeks before the race, I put up a map of Baja in our kitchen, with pushpins marking the towns with Pemex stations. I'd heard that some stations could be closed without warning, due to shortages or the proprietor's mood. It would be necessary to carry extra fuel. I bought an auxiliary gas tank from a boating supply company, and with the help of my then-boyfriend, the Motoguzzi mechanic, mounted it securely on the passenger seat of my bike and plumbed a line from it to my gas tank, complete with an electric pump and lighted toggle switch on my handlebar.

The last few days of preparing the bike got hectic, and by the time my then-boyfriend (who, for economy's sake, I'll henceforth refer to as T.B., an abbreviation with a bad reputation, deserved by both terminal illnesses and this particular ex) and our housemate, known as Stack (short for Stackmaster, meaning he crashed a lot) and I were ready to go, we'd been up one whole night, each frantically tightening and testing everything on our bikes, and in Stack's case, putting his motor together—needless to say, he was a procrastinator.

We rolled out of San Francisco at 6 am, planning to get to the border in plenty of time to get some sleep before the predawn race the next morning. Most people doing the Cabo ride were S.F. locals, and since Tijuana is twelve hours south, folks were towing their bikes down on trailers or in the back of flatbed trucks, in order to spare both tire and tread and rider energy. None of us owned a truck, but my T.B. had somehow arranged to sell a Tohatsu, a rare Japanese 1960s motorcycle to a guy in Los Angeles who agreed to pay for a Ryder truck to transport it—for him, it was cheaper than paying for shipping and for us, a free ride halfway to the border. The warehouse where we lived in San Francisco was the former storage facility for a famous after-market motorcycle accessory company and was full of old collectable Japanese stuff, as well as the ugly after-market Harley Davidson accessories for which this particular company is better known. The company founder's son inherited the warehouse when his father died, and being a flaky Zen-Buddhist/former-and-sometimes-drug-addict type, he rented us the place cheaply and made no effort to claim any of the leftover stock from his father's empire. Thus, my T.B. was always trying to unload old motorcycles and accessories to the right buyer (*trans.: sucker*) by advertising in *Buzz Walneck's Classic Cycle Trader*, the trade bible for bike collectors. It became such a regular thing that the T.B. was on a first-name basis with the woman who answered the Walneck's phone number out there in Illinois (he swore she wanted to sleep with him, sight unseen—a classic proclamation on his part).

The Tohatsu buyer lived in a chic part of West Hollywood. He was standing on the curb as we pulled up in a yellow Ryder truck on a sweltering fall afternoon. He had a meticulous *Wild One* sort of image, with perfectly rolled, double-height jean cuffs and a Brylcreemed pompadour. The T.B. and Stack exchanged looks as if to say *yeah, poseur*, as the guy handed over several hundred dollars for what they considered a silly little bike. It was a funny moment: there we were, on our way to participate in a completely dangerous, all-motorcycles-all-the-time sort of event, dressed in duct-taped race leathers and Kevlar gloves, and here was this other sort, but also an enthusiast. He'd gone to extravagant lengths to buy an obscure machine, and with his clothes, that hair—he reeked of a life tailored to fit the image, *I'm a retro bike guy*. He had his thing; it was an entirely different thing than our thing. Diametrically opposed sects referring to God by the same moniker, enacting the same liturgy, uttering the same prayers. Hinged by one fulcrum, yet separate.

Stack had grown up in Hollywood, and on his recommendation we went to a Middle Eastern joint on Hollywood Boulevard, none of us having eaten since early that morning back in San Francisco. It was a grease-redolent hole in the wall with no tables, and we ate our falafels sitting on the sidewalk where we could watch our bikes. LA was in a heat wave, and the temperature had risen that afternoon to over 100 degrees. I was wilting in my heavy race leathers and exhausted from not sleeping the night before. When we got on the freeway heading south toward the border, we were in the thick of rush hour traffic with 125 miles to go. Stack had been an LA motorcycle messenger, and with his seat-of-the-pants riding skills and LA freeway experience he led us on a 50-mph adventure riding between car lanes. I thought I was going to have a heart attack the entire time, just waiting for someone to switch lanes. But asking the T.B., who was following Stack, to please slow down would have been out of the question—and the sort of situation he relished. He would have yelled at me to "ride aggressively or die in the saddle," and then gone even faster, to show me that life was difficult.

At sundown, when we finally hit San Ysidro, a town that is nothing more than a Motel Six, a Denny's and a few currency exchange shacks, I was wiped out from the heat and beginning to sour on the T.B. My nerves were so shot from the lane-splitting adventure I felt like I'd been sweating carbolic acid, and the ride hadn't even started yet. But I began to feel better when I spotted my friend Michelle, who was riding her Honda CBR around the motel parking lot in shorts, a bathing suit top, and sturdy motorcross boots she'd enhanced with a purple felt-tipped pen. Michelle was one of three women, including me, of the 29 riders participating in the race, and a great motorcyclist. She came along to eat with us at the Denny's, as the T.B. talked about having outrun the police a few nights before on his dual-purpose bike, about how the Denny's waitress had a given him a "longing" look when he'd taken off his helmet, and how he could've been a prodigy computer scientist if he'd felt like it (he was a dropout pothead). When he got up to use the john, Michelle burst out laughing. She'd had her own romantic run-in with the T.B. and considered him a blustery pest.

There was a rider's meeting after dinner, and everyone congregated around the motel pool to hear Lee Jones, who organized the Cabo race, speak. Lee is sort of like nobility in the San Francisco motorcycle scene. When I signed up to go to Cabo I wrote a check to Lee Jones (it was $100 the year I participated). The money supposedly goes to the elementary schools of Baja, and no one ever questions the legitimacy of Lee's philanthropic dealings. He is a stoic man with steel-gray hair and eyes to match, and he owns White Thunder, a motorcycle messenger service in San Francisco with a notorious reputation and delivery boys who all look like Glenn Danzig. People enjoy saying that Lee Jones was "raised by Hell's Angels," and they say it with awe and reverence, as if he were raised by wolves.

Lee gave us each a letter written in Spanish to carry with us on the ride. It was apparently from the chamber of commerce, explaining that we were on a charity ride raising money for the children of Baja. The next morning I passed many children on the side of the road, but I was going 120, and they were just a blur of black hair and pastel clothing. And I get the feeling that all the children of Baja saw of Lee was a black-clad figure, money in pocket, hunched behind the windscreen of a screaming, dust-kicking motorcycle.

There were two girls at the meeting who were there to drive the crash truck, which would carry everyone's belongings and pick up bikes that broke down or wrecked. A guy who's name I can't recall accompanied the crash truck girls. I forget his name because we immediately started calling him Reggae on the River, after a hippie-dippie summer music festival on the Eel River that attracts laid-back, long-haired guys like this one. Reggae on the River had originally planned on riding in the race, but his front brake assembly had fallen apart as he came off the San Ysidro freeway exit, and he'd destroyed his gearbox downshifting through an intersection (and completely melted the soles of his boots) trying to bring the bike to a stop.

When the alarm went off at 3:30 am, I felt as if I'd just fallen asleep. I was alone in the room, as the T.B. had stayed up to make some last-minute adjustments on his bike, convinced that he was going to dust infamous and favored Lee Jones and Dale Shoal. I was awoken periodically by voices outside the motel window; it was a former roommate named Bill and another guy, talking about the pros and cons of synthetic engine oil and other inane topics that seemed unworthy substitutes for sleep. Bill rides on the street as if he's on the racetrack. He's a gifted but amoral rider, and he takes enormous risks. On the Cabo ride the previous year, he had been dicing with another rider, a guy from Los Angeles who, as it turned out, no one else really knew. Bill had out-braked the other guy on a blind curve overlooking a steep cliff, and other rider crashed, toppled over the cliff, and had to be airlifted up to San Diego. He ended up losing his leg. Bill kept going.

At 4:30 am we were lined up, all 29 of us revving our engines like a swarm of loud and angry bees. It was much darker than I had imagined it would be, and so foggy that the full moon, with which the ride had been scheduled to coincide, was completely obscured. I hadn't said any good lucks, or much at all for that matter, as from the moment the alarm went off the focus had been suiting up, warming up the bike, taking care of last-minute preparations, such as ensuring that my Ziploc-protected map would stay secured on the top of my gas tank, and then getting into position. People I knew had become dark, unfamiliar silhouettes in race leathers and full-face helmets, their shields down. The T.B. pulled up next to me and gave me the thumbs up, but I was already in my own world, overtaken by fear and some other more positive emotions—excitement, I guess—and then we were pulling out of the parking lot. He swerved around me and was gone. I was on my own and thinking, This is where entropy and rider skill set in; this is it, I'm alone in this thing. Those up front, doing up to 160 mph, would probably reach

Cabo by sundown, as others rolled in all through the night, 15 or 20 hours from now. I passed through the border and hit the first long incline up a dark mountain, my headlight slicing through the wet, briny fog. I was somewhere mid-pack, and trying to stay focused on not screwing up, going over and over what I knew, what I'd been told, what to expect next and how to be ready.

The mountains between Tijuana and Ensenada were harrowing. The fog was dense and wet, and the roads were slick and full of hairpin turns. By the time I reached Ensenada I was through the worst of the fog, but the dark, sleeping city had its own set of hazards. Speed bumps were not painted as they are in the States, and I flew over a set of them going 80, which meant sailing through the air and then—because the suspension on the bike was dialed down for stiff and precise cornering— a very hard landing.

Fuel gets burned at an exponential rate at speeds of over 80, and gas virtually disappears when you're flying at 130. The first time I flipped my auxiliary fuel switch—a comforting blue glow among my orange-lit instruments—it was a wonderful feeling to watch the needle on my gas gauge slowly rise instead of fall, as an extra four gallons filled the Ninja's tank.

After El Rosario, the land stretched out into a lowland farming valley. The sky was growing brighter, and the fog began to dissipate into big, translucent puffs that drifted across the road. At six am, with the sun not yet up but the light strong enough to see the irrigated green fields on either side, a farmer pulled out onto the road right in front of me. He must not have seen me, in his battered pickup, a single headlight mounted and glowing dimly on the truck's roof. I had to brake hard to avoid hitting him. Unfortunately, I braked on a patch of gravel. The bike got into what is known as a tank-slapper, when the front wheel loses control and wobbles violently back and forth, the handle bars hitting the tank alternately. It's a situation that's impossible to control, and best just ridden out. I somehow managed to regain control of the bike and kept going, adrenaline now pumping through me and the light getting stronger, as if I was waking up not only to the day but to the dangers at hand.

By the time I needed to make my first fuel stop, the sun was up and burning brightly. I'd been passing slow and lumbering recreational vehicles for a couple hundred miles through the Vizcaino desert, a place filled with Volkswagen-sized boulders, many of them decorated with makeshift grave markers, candles, religious deities and plastic flowers. I had made it to Cataviña, a barren and wind-blown rest stop more than a third of the way down the Baja Peninsula. When I pulled into the Pemex station, I was worried the attendant would insist on pumping my gas for me. They always do if you're driving a car, and I didn't want him spilling gas over the lip of the auxiliary tank. But after watching me take off my helmet, adjust and lube my chain and add a half-quart of oil to the motor, he knew I had some sort of agenda of my own, and he smiled and handed me the gas nozzle. I felt good, strong and in a rhythm, and completely on my own.

By noon I was approaching the halfway mark. I'd been passed, and passed a few riders, and knew I was somewhere in the middle of the pack. Five hundred miles down the peninsula, just before Guerrero Negro, the town that spans the North/South border, is the longest uninterrupted straight on the Transpeninsular Highway. I went into it going 120, tucked down into my fairing and rolled the throttle to its pegged position. I hit 142 miles an hour, the fastest I've ever gone.

I could see the giant metal sculpture that marks the North/South border, a 50-foot tall iron structure that I've heard is meant to be a bird, but looks more like a grounded oil dredge. I rolled off the throttle just a touch. Out of the corner of my eye I noticed two parked motorcycles and recognized Dale Shoal, who should have been miles and miles ahead of me, and another guy we called Doc. A third motorcyclist suddenly pulled onto the road right in front of me, a guy I knew who had the name of a popular biker bar stitched into the back of his red and black race leathers. After many hours of solitary and intense concentration, I was pleased to see those familiar and ridiculous leathers. But then reality set in—that he was only going 30 miles an hour and I was going 130—and I was approaching in no time. I swerved out to avoid hitting him. Just as I got around, I saw that the road took an unannounced and extremely sharp right-hand turn. There was a truck coming in the other direction, so I wouldn't be able to use up both lanes to try to make the turn. I was going way, way, way too fast to lean the motorcycle hard enough to cut the turn, and I didn't want to get smeared underneath trying. I opted to ride off the road.

The area around beyond the macadam was a shallow, sandy ditch, which in hindsight seems unbelievably lucky—most of the way down, the road is jagged rock on one side, ocean cliff on the other, or rocks on both sides. But hitting such a radical surface change at 130 mph, even if it is sand, will have serious consequences, and just as I left the pavement, the bike threw me. My recall of this event is pixilated into precise, visceral moments: I see the tire leave the macadam, and then I am up, frozen mid-air over the bike, above the instruments and handlebars, and then there's a quickfire, violent descent to a brutal, thudding impact, which must have been my head, as I later determined from the massive crater in the back of my expensive race helmet. And then I'm bounced up, my body whomped again to the ground, hipbone first, and that jutting, delicate bone feels likes it's become a bag of dust, it hurts so badly. And then skipping back up, finally rolling to a stop, face down and disoriented. I was screaming muffled screams inside of my helmet as pain rushed around inside of me. You always hear that this is when the endorphins kick in, but I felt vivid, terrible pain, as if I'd been ground under a truck.

The rider who'd pulled out in front of me came running up. I tasted blood and gravel in my mouth and tried to sit up. The bike had turned end over end twice, miraculously not hitting me in the process, and bits of plastic fairing, foot pegs, a brake lever, and other Ninja shrapnel littered the sandy ditch. There was gas and oil everywhere. I was so disappointed and angry, I couldn't believe I'd crashed after all that work. I kept thinking, My bike, my bike. But then I felt like I was going to vomit and said, "Could you take my helmet off of me?" The other rider seemed worried and was convinced that I should stay still and leave the helmet on. I think he felt slightly responsible, after pulling out right in front of me on the road. At this point, I tried to take the helmet off myself, but the desire to faint was overriding the desire to puke. I woke up with Doc holding me up, my helmet off.

Doc is actually a doctor. At that time he had a family practice, but I hear he is now a prison doctor at Folsom. Doc carries a medical bag stuffed with pills and exudes two oddly opposing, but equally creepy qualities: he's always suspiciously sedate, with heavy eyelids and a gentle, almost half-conscious giggle, and he rides motorcycles with imprudent aggression. Despite these quirks, I was comforted that a real doctor was there. Baja is no place to be in need of medical assistance—if you've got a real problem, they airlift you to the States. I told Doc my ankle hurt and he pulled my boot off and held it up. It was ballooning. Doc yelled to Dale to throw him a roll of duct tape, and he then began wrapping tape around my foot, right over the sock, tightly. He shoved my foot back into my boot, and as I groaned in pain he said, "Don't take that boot off. You won't get it back on."

Just then a Mexican ambulance came wailing toward us and launched off the road into the ditch, running over and pulverizing all the expensive fiberglass bodywork that had come off the bike. Doc and Dale lifted me under the armpits, and Doc called out to the men getting out of the ambulance, which looked like a 1960s boy scout van with a red cross painted on it's side, "She's fine. Everything's just fine." Baja medical clinics were rumored to be an expensive scam. I don't know whether this is or was ever true, but Doc and Dale believed it. They carried me across the road and laid me down on the steps of a hotel.

When I reached a more conscious state I heard Doc, in his half-sedated voice, mumble, "Oh gee, that's just a shame." I looked across the road and saw my bent-up Ninja strapped into the back of a pickup truck. The truck turned onto the road and headed north. My motorcycle had been stolen, and there was nothing I could do.

As it turned out, Dale's motor had blown up, and Doc, seeing him on the side of the road, had pulled over with mechanical trouble, hoping Dale could help him. The third motorcyclist, who'd pulled out in front of me, had stopped to say hello and get the three of them stoned. Doc had a leaky exhaust gasket, nothing Dale could fix without a new gasket. After surmising that I was basically okay, Doc started his bike, which sounded terrible. Dale laughed and said, "You're going to ride that thing all the way to Cabo?" Doc nodded, "That's right. I'm not waiting for the crash truck, you guys will be here all day." He double-checked my decline of any painkillers and took off, his motorcycle wheezing down the road like a sick animal.

Doc was right. We waited all day. When the crash truck finally showed up, it was after midnight. There were empty beer cans rolling around in the back with everyone's travel bags and tools, and Reggae on the River and the girls seemed to be having a jolly old time. I told them the story about my bike and got a consoling "Dude, no fucking way!" from Reggae on the River, who despite his inebriated state and flaky demeanor recognized the heartache of losing a bike. After Dale's bike was loaded onto the trailer, Reggae and the crash truck girls decided to eat in the hotel restaurant before heading south. It was one a. m., but I was too exhausted and out of it, after crashing and then waiting all day, to even protest.

When we finally got on the road I fell asleep under a blanket in the back of the truck. I woke up at a gas station near Loreto some time around four am, to the voice of Reggae on the River. "Oh fuck. Dude, no way!" He held up an empty duffel bag, the entire bottom of it burned away from road friction. Reggae and the two girls had repacked everybody's stuff after loading Dale's bike, and they had not bothered to secure many of the bags. The bag he held up had been carelessly looped to the tailgate, and as things shifted it dragged, while many of the other bags rolled out and scattered along the highway. My own bag, which contained all of my clothes, my camera, my house keys, all of my identification, and the majority of my money, was gone.

We pulled into Cabo San Lucas just before noon the next day. The bikes were lined up outside of the touristy victory restaurant, a place called the Marlin. Everybody ran out to greet us in their shorts and Cabo 1000 T-shirts. Dale's girlfriend had flown down to meet him, and she shoved cold and salted margaritas into our hands. With Dale broken down and out of the running, tall and blond Randy Bradescu, who owned a Marin County motorcycle shop, had won the race. Lee had come in second. My T.B. had eaten a bad omelette at Denny's the night before, and although—according to him—in the morning he'd been in first place, way ahead of everyone else, he'd had to pull over and puke every few miles all the way down to Cabo, meaning of course it wasn't his fault he'd come in near the tail end of the pack. As I later saw, this was a pattern: there were always rancid meals, needy women, nonsensical rules and jealous, less capable men thwarting his chances to take the spotlight, or even enjoy life. In light of my own crash, the T.B.'s problems began to seem farcical.

Stories were told as the pitchers of margaritas went around. My friend Michelle, to the surprise and irritation of many of the guys, had come in a more than respectable sixth. Stackmaster came in right after Michelle, although his head gasket had leaked all the way down, and he had to keep stopping and applying more sealant, and by the time he got to Cabo his engine was completely covered in orange sealant goop. Bill, in predictable form, had wheelied through the toll plazas between Tijuana and Ensenada, in a flagrant refusal to pay what amounted to something like $3.50. He'd set off a whole convoy of Federales, who had mistakenly detained my friend James. They had demanded that James hand over his California driver's license (which he could easily replace at the DMV back home), and then let him go. I finished half of my margarita and then hobbled to the hotel next door to pass out. It was three in the afternoon, and I'd been up for 48 hours. When I unzipped my leathers, I saw that the insides of my legs were dark as a blackboard, my entire side around the impacted hip bone a deep pomegranate-red, and I had road rash all over my arms from where my leathers, which were a size too large, had abraded when I hit the ground. I took off my boots but left Doc's duct-tape wrap over my sock.

For the next two days I could barely walk on my ankle, the bruises darkened and spread, and I would wake up periodically with my lake-sized scabs attached to the sheets. I had my ankle X-rayed in Cabo, and it turned out to be only a severe sprain. My T.B. paid for the room, since all my money was gone, and helped me get around, since I wasn't exactly mobile. In a way, I think he was proud, as the lore was starting to spread that I'd crashed at 130 mph, with Doc and Dale watching on the roadside. A spectacular bang-up, and it hadn't really been my fault.

But ironically, something about crashing made me feel no longer in need of the T.B.—I'd suffered without him, and endured. So many bad things had happened—the crash, then the bike stolen, all my things gone—but amazingly, I felt okay; in fact, I felt good. I hadn't been seriously hurt, which was most important, and my attitude was intact. I was laughing things off.

The well-maintained girlfriends who had flown down to meet their boyfriends lent me clean clothes, a bathing suit, shampoo and sandals, since all of my own had been donated to the desert as Reggae and the girls partied in the truck cab. On Lee Jones's advice I went to the American Embassy to try and track down my bike. Apparently, it's common that when foreigners have accidents their vehicles are taken to a junkyard north of Guerrero Negro, and then become the private property of the family that runs the yard. I get the feeling they comb the highway like vultures looking for wrecks, because my bike was taken no more than 30 minutes after the crash, calmly wheeled up in a flatbed and strapped down, business as usual. Through a series of lengthy phone calls in Spanish, a woman at the embassy located my bike. She said "It's there, but its up to you to get it back. They are going to want cash."

Cabo San Lucas is a beachfront town of Day-Glo swimwear and jet skis, a place people go to get tan and intoxicated, in equal measure (Sammy Hagar owns a drinking establishment there, if that gives any sense of the spirit). After two days of Cabo we'd all had enough. Randy, who'd won the race, flew to another race in Florida and left me his motorcycle to ride up to where mine was supposedly stored. His bike was a BMW K-100, sometimes referred to as a "flying brick" for its hefty and square engine. It was huge and top-heavy and difficult to steer, but I managed. We stopped in Mulegé on the way north, a beautiful place for luxuriating, with its blue-green bay, white sand beach, and the slow-moving Mulegé River, along which thick groves of shady date palms flourish. I swam in the ocean there, and my road rash loosened into oozing green streamers that sloughed off and trailed around me like seaweed.

Leaving the hotel room the next morning, I noticed a giant tarantula on the door. There were also scorpions in Mulegé, and at breakfast a guy on the ride who'd been a Green Tortoise driver and had taken busloads of people up and down the Baja peninsula for 20 years, let a scorpion crawl up his arm, claiming he knew how to avoid getting stung. We all waited breathlessly, until he flicked it from his wrist to the floor, crushed it with a boot and got back to his pancakes. We headed north to the junkyard, everyone anxious to see if my bike was retrievable. We got to the place just before dark. I knocked on the door of the house, while the

T.B. and Stack sneaked into the yard to make sure my bike was there. Dale came in with me for support, while Stack and the T.B. were busy wheeling the bike out. In my broken Spanish, I managed to buy my own motorcycle back for $150. Every possible thing that could be broken off of it in the wreck had been. In the darkening twilight, Stack poached a car headlight out of the lot and affixed it where mine had been, duct-taping it in place. The T.B. hot-wired it (the key was broken off in the starter), and re-bent, kicked and straightened until the bike was almost rideable. Stack even jammed flathead screwdrivers into the engine scuff plate to serve as foot pegs.

Secretly, I didn't want to ride that motorcycle. It was a mess—the frame bent, the steering out of whack, the tank pummeled and cratered, the exhaust canister ripped wide open (which I tried to fix the next morning by wrapping a cut open Coke can around it with safety wire). But the T.B. was pushing for me to ride the crashed bike; and the alternative was Randy's BMW, which was too tall for me and difficult to handle. So I left it for the crash truck to pick up and got on my Ninja—the thing that had hurled me onto the ground at 130 and then flipped end over end over end.

The road to Bahia de Los Angeles, where we were planning to spend the night, was in horrible shape. There were grooves worn in the pavement that were exactly the width of my front tire, and when the tire fell into one it become stuck like a gutter ball, making the bike impossible to control. In many places the road washed out completely and was all sand. Or water. My new nonadjustable, duct-taped car headlight petered out uselessly into the dark and off to the left, rather than illuminating the road down in front of me. I could barely see where I was going, and the bike, with its exhaust pipe ripped open, was loud as a funny car at the drag strip. I was terrified and miserable.

The water in Bahia de Los Angeles is a breathtaking chalk-blue, truly artificial looking in its perfection. Upon waking the next morning, I went for a brisk early morning swim. When I got out of the water, I noticed the pooled blood in the bruises on my legs were starting to drain toward my ankles, leaving long sickly purple streaks running down my legs under the skin. That's when the itching began, and didn't cease until two weeks later.

Just above Bahia de Los Angeles was a dry lakebed that everyone had been excited to visit. Leaving Bahia, we rode off the road onto a sand trail leading to the lake, which meant tricky off-roading on a street bike. The lake was a vast, cracked skin of powdery red dust that went for miles in every direction. Everyone was zooming around as fast as they could go, getting sideways on that strange surface. There was no traction, but the lakebed was forgivingly soft, so people were taking chances. I'd had enough adventures and sat and watched with the girlfriends who were riding up as passengers. Stack raced in a circle until he crashed and then stood up laughing, he and his greasy bike tarred and feathered with oil and red lake dirt.

From there, the trip north was long and exhausting. I couldn't keep up with the T.B., who refused to wait for me, so I ended up riding with Dale, his girlfriend, and a couple of other friends. At San Quintin, about 200 miles from the border, we all stopped to get gas, and my companions decided to eat dinner. I kept going by myself. It was getting dark, and I was worried about riding with such a sketchy headlight set-up. Night had fallen when I hit the windy mountains near Ensenada, and I had to keep stopping and re-taping the headlight to try and get it to aim at the road. I wasn't successful. My wind fairing was gone, and as cars passed they kicked up gravel which sprayed my tender bruises and pitted my face shield. I was stiff with pain and freezing cold, and like the night before on the grooved road to Bahia, I couldn't see the road, except now I was going much faster, with traffic — mostly huge trucks — oncoming and behind me, as I tried to control a bent and wrecked motorcycle.

I stopped at Rosarito to warm up. I went into an American-style diner and ordered hot coffee. My hands were shaking terribly. I was the only person in the place, and the old guy behind the counter set a huge plate of french fries in front of me and said, "Eat!" as if he understood what I'd gone through. A couple of hours after that I reached the Motel Six parking lot in San Ysidro, killed the engine, removed my helmet and gloves, and started to cry. It was over. I'd made it back in one piece.

What a strange and ridiculous idea, to span the length of Baja in a day. It's like spanning the length of California in a day, or driving from San Francisco to Denver, Colorado in a day. There is that much distance and that much geographical change. Why would someone want to blast through mountain and desert, and desert oasis, volcanoes and underground rivers, highland and lowland, in *one single day*? I'm not sure who thought of that race — I think it may have been Lee and Dale who started it. I picture a few guys sitting around a bar, or at someone's house, the requisite drinking of beer and firing of joints, and somebody mentions the concept as a sort of outlandish dare. They've all ridden motorcycles around Baja, but the one-day thing is novel. The first race is a success for some, like Dale, who are experienced racers and street riders. It's a disaster for others, who are not, and who either break down, as the stress on the motor and the overall bike is, to say the least, extreme, or they crash early on, with no sense of what the dangers are and how to pace themselves on the turny, treacherous roads. This disparity of success and failure is a main point of the event, like the disparity of potential outcomes when a person decides to cradle a scorpion: nothing can happen, or he can be fatally stung, which is why he chooses to pick up that particular arachnid in the first place.

The next year, more people have heard about Cabo, and want to try to complete the race. It's a test of will, and guts, and endurance, and some other things, why do men climb mountains, and all of that. When Bill's dicing incident with another rider, as I described earlier, results in a guy losing his leg, the ride takes on more mythical proportions. The lost leg isn't just a lost leg, it's a cautionary tale: *It happened to him, don't let it happen to you*, and a sacrifice of sorts: *It happened to him, not to you*. And it's true that there aren't any more lost legs. But a detail of that story lingers, an invisible gas that colors the group of riders who engage in this terrifically dangerous event. Bill deserted, left the other rider alone with his broken body on the side of the road, wan with shock and anemia, and waiting for the hope of help, for a car carrying empathetic people who will see him and stop.

After my own Cabo adventure, I went back to Baja several times, in cars, driving the speed limit, and camping in one place or another for weeks at a time. I think I felt I owed a certain debt after racing down that peninsula so carelessly, and I wanted to keep going back, to try to take in what I'd missed. Baja is an incredible place, full of rugged mystery and tender beauty. There's also a sadness to that place. Randy Bradescu, who won the year I rode, died in Baja, racing again two years later. He was winning, way out in front before the fatal spill. And although a few people, including Lee Jones, stopped for him, once they ascertained that he was dead, they got on their bikes and continued down the peninsula to Cabo, and the after party at the Marlin, and then the tour home, Mulegé and dry lakebed included. Randy died alone, on the side of the road. His wife had to send her brother down to get the body, go through skeins of red tape to have it released and sent home. His wallet had been stolen off his corpse, and with it went his traceable identity, since no one had been there to tell the Mexican authorities who Randy was. In the aftermath, someone offered the *DSM* term *Peer Apathy*. Needles to say, the Cabo 1000 is no more. It ended, as it should have, with Randy's death.

When I got back to San Francisco after the Cabo race, Michelle, Randy and I met on a Sunday night at Nightbreak, a bar on Haight Street. Randy had just returned from the race he'd left Cabo to attend in Florida, and the three of us were having something of a Cabo reunion. It was "Sushi Sunday" at Nightbreak, an event hosted by a chef named Nori, a surfer and S. F. local who was friendly with Randy. We ate sushi and drank beer and acted silly. The DJ played AC/DC and T-Rex, and Randy amused us with dance floor antics that seemed especially funny for a square-looking and extremely tall blond guy in a rugby shirt (Nightbreak was an all-black-leather-all-the-time sort of biker bar).

A year later, a friend named Lawrence Gill, who had originally introduced me to the T.B., died on his motorcycle. Nori the friendly sushi chef died on his motorcycle four years later, after opening his own successful restaurant. Michelle's roommate Julian died, just a couple of months after the Cabo race, riding twisty roads up in Marin County. And Randy, as you now know, died on a desert roadside, his friends kicking up dust as they passed, not beholden to any fundamental human decorum, just winning. But on that Sunday, we were all having a great time. Back in our hometown, not risking our lives, just having a couple of beers.

There are two important things about *Girl on a Motorcycle* that I failed to mention earlier. One is that Marianne Faithful's actual riding scenes, those that aren't her gleefully tossing her head back and clutching the handlebars against an artificial-looking screen, are taken with a double—a huge, hulking man dressed, like her, in tight black leather, a blonde wig flapping stiffly against his broad shoulders and plastered over his Teutonic forehead, as I discovered by watching the film with the remote on "slow." The other is that, after a protracted musing on her broken heart that involves a desperate visit to a rustic tavern where she drinks alone, kirsch after kirsch, Marianne Faithful's character gets on her motorcycle and proceeds to writhe in the seat suggestively, as if making love to the bike, and rides more and more recklessly, splitting lanes and swerving in and out between cars on the Autobahn. It's a peculiar and harrowing scene. She loses control and slams broadside into a truck, is launched up over the cab and plowed forcefully through the windshield of a four-door sedan. She dies, for the love of both Delon and the Harley, with the lower half of her leather-clad body jutting stiffly from the front of the car. That's the end of the film.

I sold the Ninja shortly after returning from Cabo. The T.B., who knew he was on the way out of my life, and suddenly, with his lost power, was giving and attentive, had completely fixed up the bike. But I was through, not only for having crashed but because I'd discovered that the engine was stolen. Originally, I'd given the T.B. $600 with which to purchase a motor, and he'd pocketed the money and procured a stolen one from a guy named Junior, an enormous teenager who, as legend had it, lifted motorcycles single-handedly up into his flatbed truck, high on crystal methedrine and PCP. I figured out that the T.B. had not only given me a hot engine but had enlisted Dale's services to restamp the serial numbers, involving a skillful fracturing of the crystal structure under the letters, which can be traced by X-ray.

I bought another bike after that, a Cagiva with a Ducati motor, but I didn't ride it much, and eventually sold that too. Now, my motorcycle hobby consists of me and my father tinkering with the Vincent Black Shadow, which still sits in the garage. We get it running about once a year, and I've taken it to British bike shows and spent hours tracking down parts in a patient quest to bring it back to original condition, which will probably take forever.

BIKERS FOR JESUS

denis johnson

on Thursday night Mark puts his Ford Econoline van on a small bluff overlooking the grounds of the Eagle Mountain retreat of the Reverend Kenneth Copeland and camps too close to a family who seem unable to keep their small children in line. The children's playing is an irritation of some magnitude to a man who's driven x-hundred miles from Missouri pierced in his spine with the very spear that killed Christ crucified. It's hard enough anyway to sleep with his marriage in flames back home, his wife turned against him and their six children baffled, and their pastor and the pastor's wife trying to convince him he's a disturbance to the congregation.

But as far back as he can remember Mark has felt the spirit of God in him, and he's not convinced that others feel it quite so strongly, study scripture quite so thoroughly, or find themselves quite so liberally gifted with discernment. He's suffering for it now, suffering the isolation of his gift, camped under a dome of stars on the grounds of this former Texas Air National Guard base, watching the sparks of scattered campfires and hearing the whacked guitar and lone hymnal wail of some cowboy believer. "Of those to whom much is given, much is asked." Last summer at the revival in Montreal, spiritual readers, several of them, and separately, approached to tell Mark they could see the spear of Christ embedded in his back. It represents his sorrows.

Friday morning he turns out and surveys the campground below him, where still only a few dozen parties have found their places. In his inward self he greets his Maker and his Savior, and his Savior tells him to move his van down the hill and park it near another Ford van, a brand new shiny blue one, an airport rental, beside which a freelance writer from Idaho has set a ragged nylon tent and filled it with an air mattress and sleeping bag and then discovered he's locked the keys in the rental with the motor on.

As he usually seems to do when acting on the direct instructions of Jesus Christ, Mark starts presenting his message before the other has had much of a chance to study the messenger—a tiny intellectual-looking messenger with spectacles and a goatee and a careful and very earnest way of speaking that makes him sound doctorly, or scientific. He does, in fact, identify himself as a scientist by trade, but gets no more specific than that, and it's clear from two minutes' conversation that Mark's a Bible wonk, the spiritual parallel to a computer whiz, and might understandably impress his fellow churchmen as something of an exegetical hacker, less a saint than a shit-disturber, who surfs scripture and verse mainly with an eye to running his own program. Anyway his pastor thinks so, and Mark's wife refuses to submit anymore to the head of the household, and the pastor's wife supports her in her challenge, which has come to consist mainly of a general ugliness and a lot of hateful put-downs, and Mark has taken himself to various three-day spiritual revivals like this one here in the flat middle of Texas, seeking . . . he doesn't say, exactly. Solace. Confirmation. Healing.

And in the case of this, the Eagle Mountain Motorcycle Rally near Newark, forty miles from Dallas, it's important to Mark that he's seeking it, whatever it is, among men. He expects to find men in abundance here because this is, after all, a *motorcycle* rally, and plenty of both men and motorcycles have arrived already. The country air is full of exhaust and the sawing fuzztone of throttles twisted back and forth. Mark has brought along his Honda dirt bike, a 90cc job with one-fourth the mass of a highway hog, the kind of bike children can be seen piloting around the grounds right now slowly with their feet stuck out for balance, cutting brodies in the dirt around the trash barrels.

Not that anybody would kid him about his ride. Most of the arrivals aren't bikies, but even if some look like the roughest sort of chargers in every other way, still they wouldn't be the type to compare and criticize. These are serious Christians—like Mark's other neighbor, for instance, Beauford (pronounced Bewford) Knabe, formerly a dealer in bulk amphetamine for a bikie gang in southern Illinois and now a Harley mechanic several years clean, sober, and celibate, who tries, displaying absolutely no symptoms of derision, to help the Idaho man break into his vehicle with a coat hanger, but unsuccessfully. "Don't sweat it," Beauford says. He looks like an extra in a sixties Roger Corman drive-in film. "For certain we'll find us a reformed car thief in this bunch."

They can see, on a rise a half-mile distant, Kenneth Copeland's Eagle Mountain Church, which they won't be attending. Kenneth Copeland Ministries, a televangelical enterprise dedicated to saving souls on a massive scale, expects as many as ten thousand people this weekend, and the preaching will be done from an outdoor stage of the type whose development was perfected in the seventies, for rock festivals: this arrangement facing a paved runway turnaround set out with three hundred rows of folding chairs, the stage flanked on either side by two cinema-size video screens and two eighty-foot-long U.S. flags hanging down like tapestries from the PA system's uprights, the stage itself mounted with several sharply gleaming Harley-Davidson motorcycles. Along the pavement's western edge, some two dozen food vendors have set up kiosks, and behind the stage is an airy hangar large enough to accommodate cargo jets, now accommodating stalls and tables and vendors of such paraphernalia as T-shirts and crafts and books and tapes and sew-on insignia, both the religious kind and the motorcycle kind. Behind the food-vendors' stalls a plump, moustachioed, affable man offers hand-lettered scrolls inscribed with more than a hundred verses from the Old and New Testaments depicting God's relation to man and twice as many verses depicting man's relation to God. "They're free," he says, standing beside his easel, handing away rolled-up copies right and left from two plastic buckets. "God told me to do this," he explains. There's no charge for the event itself either—you just turn up and find a spot. The firewood is there for the taking.

A Saginaw County sheriff's deputy cruises the lanes of this tent city for an hour or so. He finds nothing to stop for other than the Idaho man, who flags him down to beg for help with his locked vehicle.

All morning the attendees roll in steadily and arrange themselves in about thirty acres of trodden pasture sectioned off by chalk-line vehicular pathways. Knee-high signs along the paved drive into the grounds say CAMPING and point the way—otherwise no signs direct them. Although there's nobody around to prevent it, and in fact there's nothing to discourage it—no posted rules, no printed exhortations or prohibitions whatever—beer seems entirely absent. And hardly any of these people, from the Middle-American retired-NCO-looking motorhomers in their khakis, stretchpants, and baseball caps, to the slow hairy Bigfoot-type bikies in their gang colors and leather chaps, appears to smoke cigarettes. There's no psycho menace now in these riders, so many of whom have spent years in prison, and belonged there. Who murdered for pride, raped for amusement, stole and dealt and extorted and whored for money. Dope demons walk around the place clean, setting their tents and ballooning open their camper-trailers, lighting campfires and charcoal grills, letting down the tailgates of pickups with custom Harleys guyed down in the back.

Not too many of the ten thousand chairs have been filled on Friday afternoon when Gloria Copeland, a vaguely Dolly-Partonesque woman in white jeans and a black blouse, opens the weekend with a hymn and a prayer. In a friendly, no-nonsense manner, she states that this weekend's gathering has a special purpose, to minister to convicts. The evening sermons will be beamed by satellite into every prison in Texas. "It doesn't matter where you are, where you've been, or what you've done . . . God *loves* you." She's finished and off the stage before much of an audience has gathered. Then a number of singers follow, all backed by recorded music. Some of these seem to be ministry staff, young women, mainly, the imperfections of whose voices in praise and song go away forever out of the giant amplifiers—no mountains, no hills to echo off of—a kind of vast sweeping magnificent karaoke . . . But after a desultory start before the scattered audience, Isaac Petrie, a young black singer with the same phony taped orchestra and chorus behind him, breaks loose and lifts them out of their seats, the skins of their arms and necks dimpled with gooseflesh and the tears flowing down . . . Mark can't help himself, doesn't want to, he's sobbing, sobbing, sobbing. The young MC comes onto the stage clapping and shouting out verses from Isaiah, the uplifting, reassuring Isaiah, prophet of God's sweetest promises in an Israel gone to hell. "C'mon, put yourself there!" he cries, and they stand swaying with their hands upraised.

They've come home to God, and to America, their country—57-channel America, Airport Terminal America, Visa-MasterCard America, America with cameras at your tragedy, at your triumph. Even the bikies have come home to America, the one where you can ride flatout a long ways, run your own shop, mind your own business, be who you are. Like spears of wheat they sway with their hands up, only they're not being arrested, they're sanctified, members of a whole different gang—

SONS OF GOD MOTORCYCLE CLUB, their colors read, TRIBE OF JUDAH; THE UN-CHAINED GANG/SWORDS OF JESUS CHRIST.

IT'S THE COOL, sunny second weekend in October, weekend of the full moon. The USA Today weather map shows a big blue high front girding the state of Texas and steering Hurricane Opal well away to the east. Not that anybody here was ever worried about a little thing like a hurricane.

There's no telling where it comes from, this impression of an emphatic okayness about the psyches of the regular-looking Middle Americans here, unless they were actually utterly lost somewhere and now they've come home. In the heart of someone who might have just stumbled onto this rally, the man from Idaho, let's say, fifteen years a Christian convert, but one of the airy, sophisticated kind, the whole business is a millstone—if he's going to Heaven, shouldn't he be more excited? Is he going to Heaven? In his questions, his doubts, his failure to submit unconditionally, hasn't he been nothing but a cruiser, a shopper? Impressed with the drama of his own conversion—but as drama, rather than conversion—was he ever really broken? And more important, was he ever really healed?

Out on Highway 287, which cuts northwest out of Fort Worth and through the town of Saginaw and then abruptly, almost immediately, into a world half grass and half sky, a Kenneth Copeland Ministries billboard stands over the low empty prairie, the only thing higher than the horizon, looking like the remnant structure of some exalted race and visible from such a distance that its message is for a long time illegible to the approaching traveler; and then only the last and largest word resolves, and then it swings past: ONE WORD FROM GOD CAN CHANGE YOUR LIFE . . . FOREVER.

They don't mind being clear about the stakes. With rock-bottom Christians, it has ever been so. Large outdoor camp-revivals have been part of the American scene since late in the eighteenth century. Then, and also later, in the 1840s, it wasn't unheard of for twenty thousand frontier people to convene in tent cities in the middle of the wilderness to be saved from sin as the "earner" of death—to be saved, in other words, from dying. Despair, though it weighed on many souls, was at bottom a fear of Hell. Existential nausea was the plague of a mind ensnared by the Devil. Life was hard all over, life hardest in the American wilderness, but life wasn't the problem. Eternity was. At Eagle Mountain the stakes are the same as ever, but it's easy to sense that even beyond the technological differences—the vast distances easily covered to get to places like this, the tricked-out trailers, the showers, the toilets, the telecommunications—there now can be felt an altered emphasis on the Christian idea of spiritual rebirth itself. It's not just about Forever any more. Jesus has saved these souls from misery and meaninglessness, too, from the dope, the booze, the ripping and running, the chasing after. Saved them not just to be born again as the children of God and resurrected after death, but to be born again as America's sons and daughters—to be made brand-new right now, to start all over, to be reinvented, as is the right of every American.

When they were sinners they not only ignored the teachings of the Bible, but misinterpreted the rules of American striving. Rather than seek the bedrock values on which America's success is built, Bible-based values, they lusted after flesh and money and things that ran down empty. Some of these things they can still have—they are not anti-Bible, un-American things—but have them only by building on entirely new ground, and then have them extravagantly, burning gas and turning wheels and throwing away the mufflers and jacking up the amps. Kenneth Copeland teaches that poverty is a curse, and the testimonies in *Victory*, the Kenneth Copeland Ministries' monthly magazine, frequently concern themselves with the believers' glorious transit from rags to riches ("From Pennies to Prosperity"; "The ABCs of Abundance")—a transit Copeland himself has made, and not at all apologetically.

. . . Born again not only to Heaven, but also to this—a glittering stage hung with eighty-foot-tall American flags, decorated with Harleys. And Kenneth Copeland's son John Copeland, his baby in front of him and his wife in a U.S. flag vest behind him, on a Harley.

This is a biker rally, but Copeland attracts all types. As well as a tent set up by the Motorcycle Church of Christ, there's one sheltering folks from the Cowboy Church. Men and women seem to be equally represented. A scattering of blacks—a family here, a couple there, young couple, old couple. A Christian black rap group performs, trucked in from L.A.

African Americans were better represented at the frontier camp meetings of the early nineteenth century, but their campsites and services were segregated from the white ones. Outdoor meetings had long since become the form of worship most inviting to the outcast and the spiritually reluctant. In England as early as 1739, John Wesley held outdoor meetings at which, according to one diarist, "thieves, prostitutes, fools, people of every class and numbers of poor who had never entered a place of worship assembled and became godly." It wasn't a lucrative business. In the United States, Methodist circuit riders were salaried from $80 a year in 1816 to $100 in 1840. A populist religious movement characterized by emotional fervor, rejection of abstract creeds and formal ritual, lay leadership, a message emphasizing simple virtues and pinned firmly to cited scriptural verses—this was what swept the crowds together in young America.

The thread of this history leads straight to glitter-and-glory televangelism, a development in modern communications regarded by most of the viewing public, it's safe to say, as a hideous sham. It's not evangelism that's suspect, it's TV. In its mass appeal, its broad focus, TV softens and dilutes and equivocates: Any face on that screen has got to be a liar's, and for viewers by and large the TV preacher is a figure bobbing up sometimes above the broadcast surf, outfitted in really bad taste, striking at the hearts of little old ladies and the confused parents of sexually awakening teens and dealing extensively, it would appear, in printed timetables for the death of Earth.

Kenneth Copeland Ministries, for all their willingness to engage the medium, keep firmly rooted in the two-centuries-old revival traditions, particularly in their focus on the wretch, the prodigal, the outcast. On Friday night Hal Barnes, a young black lay preacher, stands in the disorienting glare of floodlights, his voice booming out into a great darkness and speaking the language of the disinherited: "Whoever you are, whatever you've done, it doesn't matter." He himself was a zealous doper for many years but shouts now that the Lord "*pulled* me outa that bag, *rolled* me up in a robe of righteousness, *fired* me up with the Holy Spirit, and *smoked—me—up* . . . *Hit* me in the *main*line with holiness . . ." The Texas night around him roars and shouts "Praise the Lord!"—"Praise God!"—"Praise Him!" Those in the back are fully a quarter-mile from the stage, but can watch the action on the massive video screens.

Then a regular storm of welcome breaks and nearly flattens Kenneth Copeland as he strides aboard the stage—in casual dress, jeans and sportshirt and motorcycle boots. Not the big-haired sequinned mannequin of TV evangelism, but an earnest, gleeful, boyish guy, almost giddy—very much informed by his own humble beginnings. He does this a lot, this is his fifth rally in six months, he has two more scheduled in the next ten weeks, but he still looks stunned by all the surrounding show, which he himself has produced through decades of ceaseless striving—starting with rallies in shopping malls, attended sparsely by folks gathered up from house-to-house calls and mimeographed fliers pinned by wipers to the the windshields of cars baking in the Southern summer—but not solitary striving, he would insist; he never walked alone. His first word: "Ha-lay-*looo*-yah! *Praise* the Lord!"

He welcomes everyone and reminds them of the prison mission, and he and the audience count down the last twenty seconds until the broadcast begins, four!—three!—two!—*one!* And as the screams subside Copeland begs the prisoners watching now "in every corrections institution in the *state*" to cast away their pride and listen to the sermons and come to Jesus Christ. "We don't want anything from you," he tells them. "You give nothing. *These* people"—with a sweep of his arm out toward the dark vital mass of souls—"give of their substance: money. Money they worked hard for." Will an amount be named? Actual numbers spoken? "It doesn't matter where you are, where you've been, or what you've done. Jesus can heal you, Jesus can release you not just from sin, but from anything." And with an immense, imperial confidence he commands—"You're coming *outa* there!" And there can be no doubt of it. He's seen the dead rise up, the crippled man walk, he's seen captive after captive forgiven and freed. This guy isn't lying.

This is Kenneth Copeland's moment, but it is not his hour. He embraces and introduces an old friend and preaching buddy, Jerry Sevelle from Louisiana, a suave gray man who delivers a lecture on the dangers of tradition, of following Doctrine but ignoring Scripture, and also recalls the days when he and Ken Copeland preached in rags, traveling in wired-together vehicles that ran on prayer as much as gasoline, standing on boxes in malls and theater parking lots. Before that Sevelle had been a countrified hippie, a pothead Cajun, but the Lord had called him, and he'd outgrown his youthful wildness.

From these reveries Jerry Sevelle segues gracefully, but frankly, into talk of tithing. "God gives to me; I give to others—to my church, to various ministries and mission programs—and then God gives me tenfold, a hundredfold, a *thousand*fold what I've sown. The money I give is *seed* I'm planting. And I expect a harvest when the season is ripe." He backs this up with biblical verses—"You reap what you sow,"—"Seed time and harvest"—perhaps, again, the original emphasis has shifted, but this isn't just a fresh, larcenous reinterpretation of worn phrases: the Apostle Paul, too, aimed an appeal to the Corinthians for donations to the poor at exactly this hope of returns: "Now he that ministereth seed to the sower both minister bread for your food, and multiply your seed sown." "If I give you seed and you don't plant it," Sevelle points out, "it doesn't grow."

Like most lay preachers laboring without benefit of the endorsement, the authority, of an established denomination, Sevelle seeks both to entertain and edify, focusing steadily on twin points: the Bible and his own experience. Copeland, too, in his occasional chats with the audience, refers constantly to the Word and quotes the verse, never straying from it except into the realm of what he's personally done, personally witnessed. It's Copeland's show, but for the most part all weekend he acts as a kind of MC for speakers with wild and enviable memories of slam-bang conversion, ecstatic worship, sudden visions. The mature Christian, Copeland insists, can expect direct access to guidance. "So then God says to me," Copeland remarks in the midst of a little story, and stops. "Listen here. Don't you think I know when God's saying something to me? If I had a friend and I'd been talking to him ever *day*, for twenty-five *years*—wouldn't I know his voice if he called me on the phone?" "God sent me." "God told me." "Jesus said I should." The Holy Spirit directs minutely—moment by moment—down to left and right turns.

MARK'S NEWEST NEIGHBORS have built a campfire, and he sits with them in its warmth on this chilly night—an almost straight-looking couple from near the Gulf. Among the others who come and go in the firelight, warming their hands a minute and saying good evening and perhaps not much else, are two extensively tattooed volunteers who man the tent for the Motorcycle Church of Christ. One of them shows how he's had to have some details changed in his decorations: "This used to be a demonic thing," he says of a beautiful, complicated scene on his forearm. "I had it changed into this cross. This one, I had to have her breasts covered up. Otherwise of course I wouldn't've had any tats done, after I got saved, because it says in the Bible not to mark your body."

John, more or less the host of this gathering, still drinks beer in moderation, but Beauford, who has joined them in the firelight, hasn't touched a drop in over three years. "I was driving home from this guy's house one night and I saw this thing on the highway, just beside an overpass. Like a Christmas display. I kept going slower and slower, just looking at this thing—a cross about twenty-five feet tall with two angels kneeling down on either side of it. I stopped the car and I got out and I started walking toward this thing—it was Jesus on the cross. I couldn't believe how detailed it was, just perfectly lifelike, and when I got close enough I realized it wasn't a display. It was Jesus. It was two angels looking up at him. He was bloody and suffering and dying. And he raised his head . . . and he just looked at me. With such pain. With such suffering on his face. And I knew it was for me, all that pain.

"I don't know how many times before that he was watching over me, and I never realized it, driving around no-hands with my head on backwards, thinking, 'Man, I'm not high enough.' I was moving thirty pounds of meth at a time. I'd say, 'Man, I feel like splitting,' and an hour after I'm gone the narcotics squad busts in. I got a feeling to leave this clubhouse one night and just a while afterward a rival club came down and four people got killed in the firefight. It got so people would point me out and say, *I'm* leaving when *he* leaves.

"So after I saw the cross, I got down on my knees and prayed to get right, especially to quit drinking, because I'd gotten a DUI. And I quit. After about six months, I was cleaning up my yard one time, picking up sticks and trash, and I bent over and there's this old empty beer can. I tossed it in the bag and I thought, I'm really *proud* I don't have to drink no more, *proud* of what I've done. And man, this voice comes behind me, a real voice, louder than I'm talking now, not a mental voice. I didn't turn around to see who it was. I knew who it was. And he said, 'Beauford, you didn't do this. I *gave* you what you *asked* of me.'"

Beauford is moved by his own account; he wipes his eyes and draws a ragged breath. But he doesn't appear agitated, or drunk with religion—rather, genuinely gifted with inner peace. When he went in for evaluation after some months' probation on his DUI, he says, he told this story to the psychologist from beginning to end—"'and that's it,' I told her. 'That's what happened. I don't care what you think.'" She stared at him for some time, her hand on a stack of forms and tests she'd intended to administer. "Then after a while she said, 'You know what? I gotta get some coffee.' A few minutes later she came back in and said, 'Look. Just go home,' and tossed all that stuff in the trash."

"Praise the Lord," Marks says. "What was the evaluation?"

"She recommended me to get the probation lifted."

"I would, too," Mark says.

One Word From God Can Change Your Life. FOREVER. But God has apparently been willing to grant much more than a single word to the Tribe of Judah and the Church of the Highway and El Shaddai's Warriors. Accounts abound with messages, rescues, apparitions, unmistakable voices—and the bikes, the hurtling fever maniac drifter bikes, the bikes themselves, figure notably in the visionary moment and its beautiful story. "I went up to get healed one time," says Mike, a youthful, uncharacteristically frail biker, lifting up a malformed left thumb. "Right there. It don't bend right. The lady healing touched me on the neck and I turned around and was walking away and I didn't feel a thing. Then all of a sudden I felt this tingling rush from where she touched me, down through my big vein here right to my heart, and my heart was *glowing* inside. Well, that night I was riding home, and my headlamp went out. Poof. Just like that. So I tried this and I tried that—nothing. Got back on the bike, sitting there with my head hanging, and all of a sudden it's just bright as day out ahead of me—but the headlamp was still broken. I fired her up and rode along fine with this bright light ahead, no problem. And when I got to my home a voice spoke out just as clear as I'm speaking to you now. 'Mike, the reason I didn't heal your thumb is that I first had to heal your heart of its hardness. And the reason I gave you light was to let you know that no matter what, no matter what, I'll always show you the way in the darkness.' "

SATURDAY MORNING THE Idaho man attends a "Healing School" run by Gloria Copeland from the same big stage. She's apparently a serious person, not interested in oratory, in entertainment. She starts right in with a prayer—"Thank you for the Blood. There is healing in the Blood. Power in the Blood! Jesus Christ! There is power in the Blood!" She moves on to cite passages from Gospel pertinent to this subject—the story of the woman who only had to touch the hem of Christ's garment to be healed, the Centurion who expected him just to "say the word" to accomplish his daughter's healing. She asks the gathering to bow their heads, close their eyes, ask for whatever healing they want. Those who feel the need of a human touch form three lines and come forward—some on crutches, some on wheels, some just limping—to the waiting hands of various staff.

Ushers come to the head of each row with buckets for donations. Kenneth Copeland steps onto the stage and leads a prayer of thanks: "Lord, we're enjoying each other, enjoying our bikes, enjoying the praise of God . . ." As the white buckets go wobbling along the rows from hand to hand a woman up front pitches over unconscious, and a bunch around her begin fanning her with their Bibles and hankies. "Whatever it is, God's more than enough. Help her there," Copeland says. "God is greater than whatever is disturbing her comfort." In a couple of minutes a medical tech slides along the rows, and still later Copeland says, "That lady who—I found out from her grandson she's a retired preacher, been preaching many years—she got a little too hot, is what it was—and, praise God, she *deserves* a little extry attention."

Next come testimonies of healing. A man who'd wheeled himself forward is standing now, talking excitedly into a microphone below the lip of the stage. Another guy has had his sight restored, and pitches away his bulky mechanical glasses and says, "I can read those signs way over there!" He points at the signboards above the kiosks 150 yards away—the man from Idaho can't make them out himself, in fact. "Steak Subs!" the blind man shouts. "Ready Spaghetti! Indian Fried Bread! Mudslide! Sanctified Swine Memphis BBQ! Texas Taters! Thirst No More Lemonade! Root Beer Floats! Chopped Beef Sandwiches!"

The Idaho man introduces himself to the nearest person in his row, a middle-aged black woman who turns out to be Nancy, from Chicago. "God is saying something," she says intensely as they shake hands, and won't let him go, staring into his eyes . . . "He says you've been seeking, and just go ahead, you're doing fine. He says you got a cross in your back, but that's healed. And He says be sure and take a pen and a note-pad with you, so you can write things down."

The man turns away, but something about what she's said strikes him now—more than the coincidence of the pen and the pad and the seeking. "Excuse me," he says, returning to her. "Nancy, did you say something about my back?"

"You got a cross pinching your right back, down low. But it's gone now. He fixed it yesterday."

For four months the Idaho man has been undergoing weekly treatments for a pinched sciatic nerve in his lower right back. It hasn't occurred to him until this minute that it didn't bother him last night and hasn't bothered him all day. "I believe you're right," he tells Nancy.

"You didn't want to ask for healing," she says, "but He healed you anyway."

"Do these little incidents happen to you very often?"

"Every day."

SATURDAY NIGHT KENNETH Copeland chats informally on stage with Mike Barber, former National Football League pro and currently a lay minister evangelizing in Texas prisons. "I expect God enjoys football," Copeland says. "Probably not near as much as we do, 'cause He's playing in a much bigger game."

Barber tries to tell about his work in prisons. He isn't at all slick, but rather nervous and stumbling over his tongue. "And he who has the Son has the Spirit. And he who doesn't have the Son doesn't have the Spirit . . . doesn't say, 'I have the Spirit in my heart . . .'"

The night's principal speaker is Mac Gober, Texan, Vietnam veteran, former Navy Seal, former bouncer, still a biker; a big-bellied, bald-headed, really *piled-up*-looking man in jeans and gang colors. In his youth he ran with the Devil, ended up hiding in the mountains, wanted on attempted murder, his brothers bringing him supplies. Hit with the Light in a bathroom, in a bar. Though Hell is alluded to in these sermons, fierce images of it have given way to personal anecdotes of misdirection and misery: sin as its own punishment. Gober offers the weekend's only graphic of damnation: "I go scuba diving sometimes and when you get down past sixty feet the pressure is unbearable—right in your ears, right into your head—and when I read in here that if you lead one of these little ones astray it'll be for you just as if a stone were tied around your neck and you were cast into the depths of the sea—I know it's gonna be *bad.*"

The problem is sin. Any problem, every problem, all problems. "There ain't no crime problem in this country. There's a *sin* problem. If you empty your heart of sin and fill it up with Jesus, you ain't gonna hurt *no—body.*"

"Amen! Amen! Amen!"

"There ain't a racial problem around here—there's a *sin* problem. If sin is removed and you're filled up with Jesus—man, you'll *love—ever—body!*"

The audience goes crazy. The woman seated—now standing—in front of the Idaho man is speaking, he guesses, in tongues, uttering a stream of miscellaneous syllables while her husband, of whose presence she seems oblivious, embraces and comforts her. On either side of the stage the colossal image of the preacher's colossal head stares soberly forward and a caption beneath it reads: MAC GOBER.

Gober speaks not just to the convicts watching—and Copeland has reported thousands saved by last night's broadcast—but also to the wavering and tempted and troubled Christians among the audience in front of him—"the backsludden" he calls them. "You gotta stay away from the places where temptation hangs around. Guys I'm working with say, 'Mac, I just can't keep away from the prostitutes.' 'Well,' I tell them, *'stay offa Fourth Avenue.'* "

He asks them all to bow their heads, "and you fellas, you fellas, too"—looking into the cameras, into the eyes of the criminals he can't see—"don't mind about that guy next to you, never mind about what he thinks, this is *you,* your *life,* your *soul.* Now close your eyes and I'm gonna give you three categories to consider. Don't nobody look up. Just raise your hand if you're in this category: 'If I died tonight, I'd go to Heaven.' Now the next group, eyes closed, raise your hand: 'If I died tonight, I'm not sure where I'd go.' Now the ones who think, 'If I died tonight, I've done something so bad—and I'm so far away—I'm so lost—I know I'd go to Hell.' " People are sobbing now, just a few here and there in the vast audience. "Now put your hand down and lift up your head. If you were in the last two categories, come forward now. Come down here close as you can get to the stage, right here." Fully a third of these thousands get up. The audience is a scarcely visible ocean on the western shore of which the vendors' stalls are lit and selling Mudslides and Snocones to the teenage sons and daughters of these penitents flowing forward to confess as a general group, repeating the words in unison after Mac Gober.

SUNDAY MORNING, BEFORE the afternoon baptisms that will be the Eagle Mountain Motorcycle Rally's ultimate event, a young woman from the Kenneth Copeland Ministries staff stands on the stage giving out the prizes. There's one for the Oldest Biker: "Olin? Does this say Olin? I can't read this. Olin, the oldest biker at the rally." Olin doesn't come forward because, as somebody in the crowd who knows him reports, "He's resting." The Farthest Biker's prize goes to two men who straddled their hogs here all the way up from Guatemala. The Longest Woman gets a prize too—she came 1,800 miles. A man whose colors read JESUS IS LORD/CHURCH OF THE HIGHWAY lands the prize for Best-Looking Bike.

Kenneth Copeland comes out to honor the person with the Best Testimony. Entrants have turned in written stories the afternoon before. The staff have read and judged among them and been most impressed with Meg's. "Meg didn't know how she'd get here. Didn't have hardly two dimes to rub against each other. But she knew God was gonna get her here. She quit her job in August, in Alaska, and just started out. Whenever she got a little money, she'd stop and send a tithe, a good part of whatever little she had. And she ended up here with a *new* set of clothes, and a *thousand* dollars in her pocket—literally *gave her way* all the way down here!"

Copeland leads a prayer of thanks: according to the registration forms the attendees have been encouraged, but not required, to fill out, the population of this tent city is 10,700. "We thank You, Lord, for soul-winning Gospel preaching . . . bikes . . . boats, airplanes, whatever we can get our hands on, Lord, to witness to You.

"I know you might not know this about me, but my grandfather on my mother's side was a Cherokee Indian," Kenneth Copeland suddenly reveals. "So I think I can look on two sides of the experience of Native Americans, that's what I'm getting at. And I've had to reconcile those two sides, and *we* have got to reconcile those two sides—now I know we have some Natives here today. Come up here. Come up here." He brings the Natives forward, about eight of them, and calls now for some whites—"I mean *lily white* people, *you* know the kind I mean," and several men and women turn up at his feet below the stage, whether shame-faced or not at the purity of their heritage it's hard to tell, because their backs are turned to the audience. Copeland puts the two groups face-to-face and the whites repeat after Copeland: Forgive my forefathers for "the pain, the theft, the breaking of covenants." Then the Natives ask forgiveness from the white forefathers for "raiding their camps and bringing strife. The strife," Copeland now declares, "has ended!" Now speaking as a Cherokee, he tells the Natives, "The Old Ways got us in trouble. It wasn't the White Man—it was the witchcraft. But there's a New Way—not the Red Man's Way, not the White Man's Way—GOD'S WAY!"

The white buckets ride the rows. On the first day the Idaho man put ten dollars in, twenty dollars on the second day. This time it's a lilly.

These things accomplished, these truths preached, these prayers spoken, these testimonies heard, these prodigals welcomed, these tithes received, these prizes awarded, a thousand souls, more or less, hike in cutoff jeans, swimsuits, terrycloth robes down the runway, past Kenneth Copeland's small red jet airplane, and along a path for a mile to the east edge of Eagle Lake to be baptized. It's the weekend's most organized event: dozens of ushers, five lines of initiates divided by Day-Glo-orange traffic cones, repeated instructions of crowd control from a sound truck—belongings on the right, observers to the left—amplified music, announcements about lost children.

Mark and Beauford and their Idaho companion won't be getting wet today. Although Mac Gober, among other speakers, has assured everybody a little repetition can't damn you, they've each been baptized once already, and they sit about fifty meters from the action, beside a woman whose T-shirt says IF YOU CAN'T TAKE THE HEAT STAY OUTA HELL and two young cowboys both smoking away on cheroots, on a knoll where observers are repeatedly encouraged to take themselves. Many of those watching, almost all of them, hundreds of people, have crowded around the shore, both to get a closer view and to avoid the fire ants and pointy Texas devil-burrs in the vegetation. Just offshore fourteen men, most of them in gang colors, stand up to their waists in the steel-blue water beckoning, beckoning, as the lines of people break off on the watery ends and each person slogs forward into the embrace of two or three or four of the Tribe of Judah or the Swords of Christ and goes down backward and comes up joyful, redeemed, entirely new. On the lake's far side, which is not owned by Kenneth Copeland Ministries, some people are fishing from a small motorboat.

No estimate of this year's numbers has been offered, but last year nine hundred people received the sacrament of Baptism on the rally's final day. By midafternoon the men in the water must be chilled and exhausted, but they're having the time of their lives, and even Mac Gober stands in Eagle Lake with his arms open wide. "Now, just go to the first available person, please," the PA insists. "God is no respecter of persons, so don't hold things up by waiting to get baptized by one particular person or another particular person . . ." and when the last has washed forward, fallen backward in their arms and been immersed and come up clean and labored back ashore with glittering eyes, the bikies get into a water fight. Another Lost Child announcement—little boy about four in a T-shirt that says DAD'S BEST FISHING BUDDY on it. "Wait a minute!" the big voice cries out over the lake. "He's been found! He's been found! Praise the Lord!"

Karl Taro Greenfeld, excerpt from *Speed Tribes: Days and Nights with Japan's Next Generation*. Copyright © 1994 by Karl Taro Greenfeld. Reprinted with the permission of HarperCollins Publishers, Inc.

Ernesto "Che" Guevara, excerpt from *The Motorcycle Diaries: A Journey Around South America*, translated by Ann Wright. Copyright © 1995 by Ernesto "Che" Guevara. Reprinted with the permission of Verso.

John Hall, excerpt from *Outlaw*. © 2002 Reprinted with the permission of John Hall, courtesy of the Carol Mann Agency.

Chester Himes, excerpt from *All Shot Up*. Copyright © 1960 by Chester Himes. Reprinted with the permission of Thunder's Mouth Press.

S. E. Hinton, excerpt from *Tex*. Copyright © 1979 by S. E. Hinton. Reprinted with the permission of Delacorte Press, a division of Random House, Inc.

Denis Johnson, "Bikers for Jesus" from *Seek*. Copyright © 2001 by Denis Johnson. Reprinted with the permission of HarperCollins Publishers, Inc.

Rachel Kushner, "Girl On A Motorcycle" Copyright © 2002 Rachel Kushner. Reprinted with the permission of the author.

Erika Lopez, "Pulling My Hair Back Without Any Hands" from *Flaming Iguanas: An Illustrated All-Girl Road Novel Thing*. Copyright © 1997 by Erika Lopez. Reprinted with the permission of Simon & Schuster, Inc.

Horace McCoy, excerpt from "The Grandstand Complex" Copyright © 1962 by Horace McCoy. Reprinted with the permission of Harold Matson Co., Inc.

Thomas McGuane, "Me and My Bike and Why" from *An Outside Chance: Essays on Sport*. Copyright © 1980 by Thomas McGuane. Reprinted with the permission of Farrar, Straus & Giroux, LLC